1922: THE BIRTH OF IRISH DEMOCRACY

1922

THE BIRTH OF IRISH DEMOCRACY

TOM GARVIN

GILL & MACMILLAN

Gill & Macmillan Ltd
Goldenbridge
Dublin 8
with associated companies throughout the world

© Tom Garvin 1996
0 7171 2438 X hardback
0 7171 2439 8 paperback

Index compiled by Helen Litton
Print origination by
Carrigboy Typesetting Services, Co. Cork
Printed by ColourBooks Ltd, Dublin

A catalogue record for this book is
available from the British Library.

1   3   5   4   2

In memory of my parents, who lived through it.

I said to Ginger, 'Wicklow will never be any good until we burn the town and blame it on the Tans, then the bastards will fight through.'

—Seán McGrath, IRA leader, 1919–21

Let me remind you that we have not got Irish unity in exchange for this oath. The two great principles for which so many have died and for which they would still gladly die—no partition of Ireland and no subjugation of Ireland by any foreign power—have gone with this Treaty, and some good men are thinking of voting for it.

—Seán T. O'Kelly, Dáil Éireann, 20 December 1921

It is necessary to state that our National Policy is to maintain the established Republic. Since the attack on H. Q. Four Courts and the splendid rush to arms of I. R. A. in defence of the Republic against domestic enemies we are finished with compromise or negotiations unless based on recognition of the Republic. This policy is and will be carried through by all officers and men who have all definitely made up their minds to make all the sacrifice necessary. As you are aware, we have no notion of setting up a government, but await until such time as An Dáil will carry on as a Government of the Republic without any fear of compromise; in the meantime no other Government will be allowed to function.

—Liam Lynch, Chief of Staff, IRA, July/August 1922

Yes, there is a lot of peace talk going on which I nor anybody else cannot stop. I could never stop the people or the men of the column from holding their views.

—Munster IRA leader, September 1922

Ireland's recent story which in essence is that the fundamental and traditional character of the people stood fast and constructive in spite of the drama, the indiscipline that drama makes up, and the chancers who are nurtured in its atmosphere, and whose operations disintegrate the natural solid foundations of a people.

—Richard Mulcahy, 1963

After the first executions, the morale of the Irregulars cracked. The rank-and-file deserted from the columns, particularly the Trucileers . . . The Irregulars were boastful after arrest right up to the executions . . . Some Irregulars [were] convinced no Irishman would sign [an] execution order.

—Tom Ryan, South Tipperary IRA and Free State Army, mid-1960s

I'm teaching them Irish and paint their letter-boxes
All over with green, sure what more can I do?
For they tell me they want an Irish Republic,
Without any trimmings of red, white and blue.

—Popular song, 1922–23

An affable Irregular,
A heavily-built Falstaffian man
Comes cracking jokes of civil war
As though to die by gunshot were
The finest play under the sun.

A brown lieutenant and his men,
Half dressed in national uniform,
Stand at my door, and I complain
Of the foul weather, hail and rain,
A pear-tree broken by the storm.

—W. B. Yeats, 'Meditations in Time of Civil War', 1928

Move over, Mick, make room for Dick.

—Dublin graffito, 1923

Contents

Acknowledgments

The relatively recent decision by the Irish Government to release a seventy-year backlog of official records has caused an information revolution in the study of Irish politics. It will take many years for the small community of Irish historians, political scientists and journalists to absorb even a large fraction of this new information. The recent acquisition by academic archives of the private papers of individuals who were at the centre of crucial events in Irish political development has caused a similar revolution. This book is in part a very preliminary reconnaissance of some of that vast territory, focusing on the regime change of 1921–23 and putting it in a comparative context of such events elsewhere at that time.

As a result I have had to try to marry the macro and micro, the behaviour of collectivities and those of individuals. I believe that any rounded understanding of political life requires both styles of analysis. Early versions of some of the arguments in chapter 1 were published by me in John Coakley and Michael Gallagher (editors), *Politics in the Republic of Ireland*, Dublin: Folens/PSAI Press 1992, 250–61; an early version of chapter 2 appeared in Ronald J. Hill and Michael Marsh (editors), *Modern Irish Democracy*, Dublin: Irish Academic Press 1993, 9–23. The ideas in chapter 3 were the subject of a lively seminar at the Daniel O'Connell School, Caherdaniel, County Kerry, October–November 1993; a very preliminary and abbreviated report on those ideas appeared in Maurice O'Connell (editor), *Decentralisation of Government*, Dublin: Institute of Public Administration 1994, 20–31. The other chapters are new.

My debts to fellow-scholars, friends and the brave few of those who belong to both categories are many. Stuart Daultrey overrode my deep technical incompetence and rescued the entire typescript from an apparently impenetrable electronic prison, defying my best efforts to keep it there. Anna Garvin repeated the exercise. I have benefited greatly over the years from conversations with Just Augustijn, Tom Barrington, Francis John Byrne, John

Coakley, Tim Pat Coogan, Mary Daly, Richard English, Brian
Farrell, Dermot Foley, John Garvin, Peter Hart, Iseult Honahan,
Síghle Humphreys, Michael Laffan, Denis Lehane, Muiris Mac
Conghail, William MacCormack, Maurice Manning, Patrick
Maume, Brian Murphy, Conn Ó Cléirigh, Maurice O'Connell,
Eunan O'Halpin, Diarmaid Ó Muirithe, Desmond Roche, Richard
Sinnott, Jennifer Todd, Maureen Woods, and many others. On
democracy and local initiative I have been influenced greatly if
indirectly by conversations with Neil Collins, Richard Haslam,
and Joan McGinley. Commandant Peter Young of Army Archives
shared fascinating insights on the period, as did James Dukes,
unpaid archivist extraordinary. The staff of the National
Archives, Bishop Street, were of great assistance. Gerry Lyne of
the National Library went out of his way to help. Séamus
Helferdy, Jennifer O'Reilly and Bríd Reason of UCD's marvellous Archives Department (*semper floreat!*) were of enormous
assistance. Colonel Michael Gill (retired) cleared up an important empirical issue.

1

Democracy, Republicanism, and Nationalism

Studies of contemporary Irish society, history and politics have tended to suffer from a habit of viewing Irish affairs as unique and generally unlike such affairs elsewhere. There is also a tendency to underrate the influence of outside forces, based in America and continental Europe, in favour of seeing Ireland as blanketed by British culture only. This tendency was generated in part by the usual British Isles parochialism that overshadows social studies in both countries: England was unique in being the first true nation-state, and therefore Ireland had to be unique in being the first true colony. But this illogical though pervasive syndrome was also in part generated by an Irish habit of navel-gazing. The tendency has weakened somewhat recently but still stultifies much of Irish social studies; Northern Ireland, for example, is not a uniquely horrendous or incorrigible entity, as it has often been represented; similarly, the Republic of Ireland is, despite stereotypes that emanate from certain ideologues, arguably about as theocratic as the United Kingdom, the Republic of Italy, or the Federal Republic of Germany.

Actually, if one raises one's head from the usually reassuring, occasionally horrifying and often entertaining detail of Irish politics, it can readily be seen that Ireland, despite its undeniable oddities, is not unique. For example, Irish democracy emerged as part of a general wave of European democratisation in the second decade of the twentieth century; Irish political ideas are recognisably local versions of European and American political ideas; Irish constitutional traditions are heavily influenced not just by some British Isles parochialism but by American and continental European example as well. Furthermore, Ireland is not merely an ideological importer: Jonathan Swift, Edmund Burke,

Daniel O'Connell, James Connolly and Conor Cruise O'Brien all owe their political thought to the Irish experience and have certainly contributed, in utterly different ways, to the general human debate on how human beings should be governed. Similarly, Irish republicanism and nationalism have clear classical, mediaeval and Enlightenment roots, as has the undeniably original mix I will dub O'Connellism—a blend of Catholicism, democracy, nationalism and liberalism that characterises modern independent Ireland.[1]

Democratic government, in the sense of government by a group of people elected by the adult population of the community and subject to regular electoral testing, came to most of the island of Ireland for the first time in the crucial years of 1921–23, a period I will refer to as the 'Long 1922', running as it did from the Truce date of 11 July 1921 to the Dump Arms order of 24 May 1923. Democracy in Ireland came rather late by the standards of the white English-speaking world, early by the standards of much of continental Europe, and very early indeed by the standards of most of the rest of the world. This is so despite the perception of so many nationalists of the time that Irish independence and democracy arrived 'too late', typically seen as too late to rescue traditional Irish, and sometimes Gaelic, culture from near-oblivion.[2]

In this book I wish to look, admittedly implicitly, at certain Irish assumptions about national identity and its relationship to democratic political life. Equally implicitly, I will look at popular and even official perceptions of the process, one that mixed politics and violence, by which most of Ireland achieved independence, democracy and, eventually, formal sovereign and republican status after 1921. The events of 1919–23 have been so much written about as almost to detract from the sum of our knowledge of the time.[3]

This book does not constitute an attempt to set the record straight but rather tries to point out some crucial aspects of the political period that seem to have escaped the attention of some writers. In this I have been much aided by the extraordinary expansion in Irish historical archives that has occurred in the last ten years. On my intellectual travels I have been struck particularly by the control exercised by the Dáil over the twenty-six counties' local governmental structure long before the Anglo-Irish Truce of 11 July 1921; the stubbornness and stupidity of the British authorities in the face of independent and police advice; the extent to which partition was a *fait accompli* long before the Truce; the fear and contempt of democracy exhibited by the leaders of the guerrilla army of the Irish Republic in 1921–22; the ideological and terminological confusion exhibited by nationalist ideologues between the terms 'Gaelic', 'Catholic', 'Christian', and 'Irish'; the technical virtuosity displayed by the pro-Treaty leaders in putting together a new, democratic and generally law-bound state; the ease with which the Irish Free State both raised and demobilised an army in defending its nascent democracy, under attack by an authoritarian IRA rump; the thievishness, sectarianism and murderousness of some revolutionaries; the bravery and idealism of many other revolutionaries and democratic leaders of that time; the destructive activities of many revolutionaries in the period of construction of the state that they were eventually to preside over with such aplomb; the mendaciousness of so much of the political culture of the period; and in particular, the almost unselfconscious, occasionally murderous and certainly ruthless determination with which the new Irish Free State forcibly imposed democracy on the rebellious republicans and on a large minority section of the population.[4]

Irish political terminology, as I have just suggested, is sometimes idiosyncratic: the term 'republicanism', for example, has drifted from its classical significance and has come to mean a brand of revolutionary nationalism rather than a theory of government. In the rest of this chapter I look at the meanings of some central political terms in Irish political debate and offer a comparative perspective on the emergence of the Irish Free State. The three terms I will discuss are 'democracy', 'republicanism' and 'nationalism'.

DEMOCRACY

The system of government loosely termed 'democracy'—derived etymologically from the Greek words for 'people' (*démos*) and 'rule' (*kratía*)—has historically not been common, nor has it had too many determined intellectual defenders until very recently; the governments of humankind have generally been seen by political theorists as inevitably elitist. Elitist government has often been regarded as not only inevitable but desirable: the masses were commonly seen as less wise and therefore unfit to rule the state; elites must be given the power to act as guardians of the non-elite majority. This view of the masses has often been shared by the people themselves; the vote for authoritarian, anti-democratic parties in many twentieth-century European countries testifies to this.

Insofar as democracy has become established, it has commonly been in circumstances in which it has encountered great intellectual, ideological and practical political resistance. Democratic values have had to be internalised not only by the political elites but also by the general population if the system were to work and achieve a stable existence. The most famous case of the masses voting against democracy is, of course, that of Germany in 1932–33, but it is not the only such case.[5]

Furthermore, even when established, democracy has tended to be subject to various forces that have attempted directly or indirectly to weaken its central principle of 'people-rule'; in particular, representative democracy has, in the twentieth-century West, been subjected to a subtle subversion generated indirectly by its own success: the non-democratic power of money. The subversive effect of money on the spirit of democracy is rendered stronger by the fact that democracies tend, by and large, to be wealthier than non-democracies. It is rendered stronger still by the fact that there appears to be a benign causal relationship, possibly reciprocal, between economic progress and democratic government.[6]

Direct democracy, defined rather minimally as giving full citizen rights to all native, propertied and adult males of non-slave status, was invented by Cleisthenes and established at Athens at the end of the sixth century before the Christian era (507 BC by estimate). The cultural achievements of the tiny Athenian democracy are unparalleled; quite apart from anything else, the Greeks gave us political theory and our very vocabulary of politics, which is disproportionately of Greek etymology. The words 'democracy', 'aristocracy', 'monarchy', 'plutocrat', 'psephology' and 'politics' itself are all Greek in origin.

However, Greek and, later, Roman experiments in democracy or quasi-democracy, although of great philosophical consequence, were smothered within a few centuries by the great oligarchic empires of Macedonia and Rome, respectively, neither of which had much use for the idea; the Roman imperial attitude towards the multitude was, notoriously, *panem atque circenses* (bread and games), the pre-industrial version of Orwellian 'prolefeed'. Significantly, the Roman emperors carefully preserved the forms of the Roman Republic, including the formula *Senatus Populusque Romanus*, in an almost shamefaced fashion, up to the fall of the western empire. The memory of republicanism and democracy lingered in Western culture.

Later small-scale experiments in democracy and aristocratic republicanism, democracy's forebear, in northern Italy in the fifteenth century, suffered a similar fate at the hands of monarchical France in 1495. Democratic and quasi-democratic experiments occurred afterwards only in peripheral areas of a West increasingly dominated militarily and even intellectually by absolutist monarchies. By the eighteenth century, democracy of a sort survived only in Switzerland, immured in its mountains, in isolated Scandinavia, and in the disregarded and faraway American colonies of Great Britain. In Europe, representative parliaments went into eclipse during the age of absolutism. Local parliaments fell into disuse in France, Scotland, Ireland (belatedly), Spain, and many of the German states.[7]

Democracy, far from appearing to be the wave of the future, seemed increasingly a quaint echo of mediaeval representative systems. Imperialism, in the form of an invasion of the rest of the planet by a technologically sophisticated and ruthless set of highly organised European states, was generally seen in company with a rapacious political aristocratism or absolutism. The contrast with Plato's eloquently denounced democracy-driven Athenian imperialism is striking.

Clear moves towards large-scale democratic government occurred in America and Europe in the nineteenth century, but, as Arno Mayer has pointed out in his classic *Europe under the Old Regime*, few European powers, great or small, were democratised to any serious extent even on the eve of the First World War.[8] The old 'feudal' regimes hung on even in Britain (in particular in the form of the House of Lords), in Second Reich Germany (in the form of the Kaiser's effective executive monopoly), in Spain, and very certainly in Imperial Russia. In Russia, representative institutions (the Zemski Sobor) were only a vague memory from the seventeenth century, because Peter the Great had abolished all such institutions, and attempts in the middle of the nineteenth century to revive or create local representative institutions in the form of the *zemstvo* movement had only been partially successful. The Tsarist Duma, established with great reluctance after the 1905 revolution, was a weak and unrepresentative assembly.[9]

Only France among the larger countries had actually conceded manhood suffrage and effective local and national republican and democratic institutions, partly because of the reaction to Louis Napoléon's humiliating debacle over the Ems telegram and the defeat of France by Prussia/Germany at Sedan in 1870. The victory of electoral democracy in France was stiffly contested into the twentieth century by the aristocracy, the army, and the Catholic Church; the nascent French democracy of the period was paralysed by internal political deadlock, symbolised by the Dreyfus case of the 1890s. There, a combination of frustrated militarists and Catholics, sometimes terrified of an imagined Jewish-led movement of intellectual scepticism and socialism, confronted a front of democrats, socialists, secular intellectuals, and communists. Eventually this confrontation was to wreck democratic France in 1936–40. A clearly consensual and post-imperial democratic order only finally emerged in France under Charles de Gaulle between 1958 and 1968.

In Britain, a propertied voting minority presided over a disenfranchised majority, and the House of Lords was still a serious political force, literally lording it over even that enfranchised section of the male population; the officer class were heavily involved in anti-democratic conspiracy of an occasionally treasonable kind; by way of parallel, in Germany the Kaiser referred to the Reichstag contemptuously as the 'Chatterbox' and generally governed without too much reference to it, eventually to the total undoing of Germany. In Italy the Vatican's effective outlawing of democracy, because of Pius IX's resentment at the loss of the Papal States, permitted the emergent Italian democracy to be run by anti-Catholics—one of the greatest ecclesiastical own-goals of all time. Eventually the evident absurdity of the situation did result in the gradual emergence of Christian Democracy, influenced heavily by Daniel O'Connell's marriage of electoral democracy and Catholicism.[10]

It is only since the end of the Second World War that any really significant proportion of humanity has been governed according to principles that are generally democratic in form and, to a considerable extent, in substance. As I have noted already, historically most human beings have lived under one or other form of oligarchy or monarchy, and the political opinions of most human beings have been given no regard by their rulers; with little exaggeration, it can be said that most human beings in the putatively civilised world were treated by their rulers as suppliers of food, taxes, soldiers, and young women. In return, at best, the mass of the population were given some form of rule-guided order and some military protection from the outside world. The practical political theory of the average human being was summed up in the simple mediaeval proverb, 'Defend me and spend me.'[11]

Furthermore, it is only in the twentieth century that democracy has become an intellectually approved form of government. Throughout history, many highly influential political theorists have been hostile to it; much of what is known about its Athenian prototype is known only from the anti-democratic writings of Plato, democracy's most brilliant enemy, and from the more balanced scepticism of Aristotle, Plato's greatest pupil. Parenthetically, Plato was closely related to the murderous tyrant Kritias, whom the democrats, resisting the tyrants' coup d'état, deposed and killed in 411 BC.

Admittedly, Plato and Aristotle were criticising a system of direct democracy that worked very differently from (and arguably more 'democratically' than) modern representative democratic systems. Democracy was seen as, and described as, the rule of the unwise and self-serving poor—the people who lynched Socrates and who constructed an exploitative Athenian empire. Anti-democratic 'elitist' political thought has flourished in Europe and was perhaps particularly strong in the late nineteenth century and early twentieth century. The intellectual roots of the anti-democratic doctrines of fascism and communism lie in the centre of modern European political thought, in particular in the ideas of Darwin, Marx, and Gobineau. Marxist insistence on the primacy of economic democracy over institutional democracy and Gobineau's obsession with imagined racial contrasts barred the way to formal electoral democracy in many historical cases. 'Social Darwinism' supplied a pseudo-scientific argument in favour of political elitism. In mainstream political theory the works of Wilfredo Pareto, Robert Michels and Gaetano Mosca formed an intellectually powerful set of arguments for the proposition that mass electoral democracy was impractical, as organised elites, whether nominally of the left or of the right, would always get the better of majorities.[12]

The representative democracies that have evolved in western Europe, North America and Australasia since the time of the French and American Revolutions have been intellectually related to, but structurally quite different from, the small-scale direct democracies of the classical era. Most obviously, the decisive contrast has been one of size. Modern democracies typically have millions rather than thousands of citizens with voting and participation rights. In part because of their size, modern democracies have almost invariably resorted to the device of representation: citizens are not typically entitled to legislate or govern directly, other than in exceptional cases, but instead delegate that right to representatives chosen by secret ballot from time to time. This indirect structural character is commonly modified by the use of popular referendum in cases of entrenched or constitutional law or in cases of particularly crucial and controversial issues. However, modern democracies are, by Athenian, or even traditional Swiss, standards, very indirect in character. Greek political theory regarded government by elected persons as essentially plutocratic; true democracy consisted in having the governors chosen by lot rather than by counting heads.[13]

Irish electoral democracy, as recounted later in this book, was born in conditions of considerable violence. The birthmarks of that violent birth have persisted to the present day. Nineteenth-century Ireland, with all its local problems, was usually subject to a Britain-based majority tyranny in the form of the parliamentary supremacy of either the Conservative or the Liberal Party. Occasional exceptions to this generalisation occurred, most notoriously in the holding by Charles Stewart Parnell of the balance of power between the two British parties in the House of Commons in the late 1880s. Most of the time, however, the Irish members were in the humiliating position of mendicants, sitting in impotent, if noisy, opposition. Nineteenth-century Ireland's half-polity could almost be described as a debilitating mixture of aristocracy and rule by beggars' votes; it was part of a putative democracy but was not governed democratically.

This is not to say that the inhabitants of British Ireland had no civil rights: they had, but these rights were conceded by an external power, albeit often a benign power; rights were not enforced by the authority of a local democratic majority and by an entrenched constitution approved of by that majority. Furthermore, these rights could be, and often were, revoked arbitrarily; British rule in Ireland was a curious mixture of bossiness, obtuseness, and generosity. The United Kingdom had, and has, no written constitution that could be held to be superior to Parliament or the executive government. In Ireland this encouraged an often well-meant but arbitrary style of rule by the British. It also meant a non-democratic willingness to resort to armed police or military solutions to political problems.

At the time of the First World War, democracy was everywhere still a rare form of government, as already suggested. Of forty-eight independent states in the world during the first decade of this century, only eight, or 17 per cent, were substantially democratised (United States, Canada, France, Switzerland, Belgium, New Zealand, Australia, and Norway). Similarly, of sixty-four independent states in the world in the early 1920s, only twenty-one, or 33 per cent, were substantially democratised (the above states together with Austria, Denmark, Finland, Italy, Netherlands, Sweden, United Kingdom, Costa Rica, Czechoslovakia, Germany, Ireland, Poland, and Uruguay). Many of these precipitately abandoned democracy in the twenties and thirties. Even in the established democracies it was still uncommon for women to have the vote.[14]

As I have already argued, the Irish democratic political system founded in 1922—which, fairly unusually, included full suffrage for women—was part of a general European wave of democratisation that followed the First World War. Ireland's democratisation coincided almost exactly with the displacement of local oligarchies or external powers and the coming of democracy to Costa Rica, Czechoslovakia, Germany, Poland, Uruguay, and Finland. Of these, only Costa Rica, Finland and Ireland were to retain their democratic institutions uninterruptedly, unaided by outside forces, to the present day. Costa Rica and Ireland preserved their democracies because of isolation and because, in different ways, they managed to tame their armed forces. Finland had a different solution: instead of demilitarisation, it became a democratic but heavily armed camp, determined to defend Finland and its democracy against Russian and Soviet tyranny. These three curious contemporaries used different methods of maintaining electoral democracy. The Costa Ricans actually abolished their army in 1944, because of its appetite for political power; the Irish, by contrast, hired an army to destroy a large part of their own national liberation force and then subsequently virtually abolished that army; the Finns, faced by huge totalitarian armies, some of them internal, created a democratic people in arms, echoing the Swiss formula. Three small countries, superficially so similar, have had quite different transitions to electoral democracy and the rule of law.

Even today, and despite its growing fashionableness, electoral democracy of a stable kind is characteristic of only a large minority of sovereign states, mainly concentrated in the West. By and large, democracies with any claim to stability are in the West or in areas colonised or culturally blanketed by the West. They also tend, as noted above, to be richer countries. To put it in chronological perspective, in 1922, in an imperial world, of 64 independent states 33 per cent were democratic, and many of these were not to remain so for very long; by 1962, in a world where western empires were in full disintegration, of 111 independent states only 32 per cent were democratic; in 1990, in a world where the Soviet communist empire had by and large disintegrated, of 129 states 45 per cent were at least notionally democratised (this overall total omits all states with less than a million population). Furthermore, as was the case in 1920, many of these democratic systems were unstable and probably ephemeral.[15] Perhaps one-quarter of the world's states are stable democracies, amounting perhaps to one-fifth of the population of the earth. The near-universality of democratic and pseudo-democratic ideological assumptions in the last decade of the twentieth century blinds one to the fact that electoral democracy is new, unfamiliar, and often not too welcome as far as many peoples are concerned.

REPUBLICANISM AS INTELLECTUAL TRADITION

Modern Irish democracy is republican in form, an aspect that immediately marks the main Irish political tradition off from its putative English forebear and equally immediately points to American and French inspiration. The historical roots of the republican idea in Ireland are somewhat obscure, and also deeply ironic: Irish republican ideas have many of their origins in Scottish and American Presbyterian political thought in the eighteenth century.[16] This political tradition was deeply anti-Catholic and anti-authoritarian. Strangely, it was mainly Catholics, many of whom were enthusiastic about their traditional faith and rather fundamentalist in their religious beliefs and political attitudes, who were to adopt versions of republican ideas. This mongrel ideology, which came to be closely associated with Irish nationalist Catholicism, also had, paradoxically, anti-clerical French inspiration. It was not until well into the nineteenth century that republican ideas of a sort gained a firm hold in the minds of a proportion of the Catholic majority in the country.

Prior to then, most Irish Catholics were probably monarchist in their political thinking, such as it was. Many hearkened back wistfully to the lost Jacobite cause and sang ballads in both the country's languages in praise of the white-headed boy, Bonny Prince Charlie. Under the veneer of modern Irish republicanism it is sometimes possible to detect echoes of this older, almost dreamy but clearly monarchist style of thought; a well-known 'republican' ditty of the 1920s, for example, promised to 'crown de Valera King of Ireland.' The cult of the charismatic leader, repeatedly conspicuous in Irish nationalism over the last two centuries, may be connected with a subconscious hankering after a legitimate Irish kingship. Patrick Pearse, in the GPO in Dublin, making his gallant stand for an Irish republic in 1916, was quite happy to contemplate an independent Ireland under the reign of a Hohenzollern monarchy; his comrades seem to have listened with toleration, if not acceptance.[17] Kevin O'Higgins and other members of the first Free State government toyed with some seriousness with monarchist political ideas in the 1920s.[18]

Republicanism in Ireland, then, has developed a local significance as a shorthand term for insurrectionist anti-British nationalism, usually, but not invariably, combined with a rather vaguely expressed preference for political democracy, representative institutions, and human rights. Irish insurrectional republicanism is commonly pre-political in character, representing a somewhat unstructured wish for independence, 'freedom' and change from an uncongenial present to a hazily imagined future rather than a highly organised political blueprint. Once the Stuart cause was lost even in the eyes of its strongest devotees, 'republicanism', however misunderstood, was the only label that could conveniently be used to express in one word both hatred of the British monarchy as symbol of British power in Ireland and a rhetorical national populism. Irish republicanism commonly represented itself as coterminous with Irish democracy and self-determination but has been demonstrably more interested in the latter political goal than the former. Republicans believed that with the coming of independence, political problems would be easily solved. Eamon de Valera once said that Irish labour would have to wait until independence was fully achieved; republicans in Ireland commonly felt that politics would have to wait too.

Republicanism as a part of the Western intellectual tradition constitutes, of course, far more than an interest in national self-determination. The word itself comes from the Latin words *res publica*, which mean literally the 'concern of the people' or 'public concern'. The root idea is of a state that makes decisions in the open rather than secretly and that is in some sense the property of the people rather than they being its subjects or even its property. The inhabitant or, perhaps, joint possessor of a republic is seen as a participant citizen rather than as a compliant and loyal subject. Modern European and American republican political thought has been heavily influenced by the classical traditions of Greece and Rome, by the writings of the Italian Renaissance, and most proximately by the writings of both the English Enlightenment of the seventeenth century and its American offshoot. It was also influenced by the French Enlightenment of the eighteenth century. The eighteenth century was to prove particularly crucial in the evolution of republican thought, and not just in Ireland. Ulster Presbyterian thinking, in so many ways an overspill from the Scottish Enlightenment, did much to crystallise the republican dream in Ireland. Ian McBride, following the New Zealand oceanic historian J. G. A. Pocock, terms this complex of ideas 'civic humanism'.

Civic humanism is the name given by historians to certain ways of thinking and talking about politics and society which were derived from the city-states of ancient Greece and Rome. Its original sources included the political philosophy of Aristotle and Polybius, the historical writings of Tacitus and Sallust, and Ciceronian moralism. At the centre of this configuration of ideas lies the classical opposition of virtue and corruption. Man is viewed as an inherently political animal; it is only by participation in the public life of the polis or republic that he can be fulfilled. Virtue was accordingly bound up with the practice of citizenship. It demanded the sacrifice of private interest to the common good, it offered the individual a share in his own government through participation in civil and military affairs, and it was dependent upon the preservation of a state of equality among the citizenry.[19]

Republicanism was to be distinguished sharply from democracy: at one stage, for example, the names of the two American political parties, Democrats and Republicans, actually referred to different political philosophies, however tangentially. Sometimes it was argued by republicans that full membership of a true republic was to be confined to that proportion of the adult male population that was economically autonomous, or sufficiently well off to be able to express an independent political opinion; poor people could not afford to speak their minds, because of their inevitable dependence on powerful, richer people. Democrats, however, would argue for the essential equality of all people and advocate the political right of all citizens to the suffrage, regardless of economic condition. Republicans might argue that poor people are psychologically enslaved and should therefore not be permitted to vote, but would also argue that too much wealth could corrupt a citizenry and encourage it to stumble into a greedy slavishness and an acceptance of political tyranny in return for material plenty. Republicanism was, in some generic sense, essentially a middle-class and skilled working-class philosophy. It was commonly a puritan one as well. It could easily be seen as hostile to both beggars and millionaires, and in Ireland, as we shall see, certainly often was.[20]

Republics evidently did not need to be fully democratic in the conventional late twentieth-century sense. Furthermore, an aristocratic republic, where only the relatively well off had the vote and the rights and duties of citizens, was perfectly feasible and had often occurred historically. A democratic republic, where all adults are citizens and share the right to participate in political life, was only one of several possibilities and one that was ideologically somewhat doubtful; not all the adult citizenry could be trusted to vote for the moral cause: many would vote for self-interest and for demagoguery. A traditional republican would have had no problem with de Valera's remark to the effect that the people had no right to do wrong. In fact, as just suggested, a certain exclusiveness has often run through traditional republican political thought; it was commonly thought just to exclude from participation not only women and the poor but any other elements that were regarded as not being morally fitted for full national citizenship. Republicanism and outright majority rule did not always consort very happily.[21]

Exclusivist and inclusivist versions of ideological republicanism have therefore competed. These can usefully be labelled rightist and leftist republicanism, respectively. Leftist republicanism, with its acceptance of universal suffrage, its hankering after a single-chamber legislature and liking for frequent use of the popular referendum has tended to win out in Western countries in the last hundred years. The weakening, or even abolition, of exclusivist second chambers has been a central part of this process. In the smaller Western democracies of Denmark, New Zealand and Sweden, for example, second chambers have been dispensed with. In Ireland, the second chamber was soon reduced to a cipher. Federal polities have offered an intriguing and only partial set of exceptions to this generalisation. Rightist republicanism, with its preference for the virtuous middle-class or skilled artisan citizen, has gone into eclipse everywhere except perhaps in the United States, the world's oldest liberal democracy, and in Switzerland.

Thus a central, even defining, idea of republicanism has been the citizen as a moral actor in the polity, an idea that has classical roots and an enduring appeal. The IRA guerrillas of 1919–23 certainly had internalised a form of that ideal; commonly, for example, the IRA ordered the banishing of people from Ireland on the explicit grounds that they were unworthy to be citizens of the Irish Republic. The notorious hatred of some of the IRA at that time for upper-class people, particularly if they were Protestant, was matched by their occasionally murderous contempt for the lower orders; tramps, travellers and other itinerant outsiders sometimes received short shrift from the west Cork IRA between 1919 and 1921. People accused of informing the British authorities of IRA activities were commonly killed; significantly, a common explanation offered by the IRA for the killing was that the victims were immoral, drunkards, sexually deviant, or of low status, and therefore dispensable. In modern Ulster, similar justifications for murders and 'kneecappings' have been offered by the Provisional IRA. Admittedly, republican ideas took a perverted form under the stress of conflict in 1919–21; however, the social attitudes associated with republicanism persisted.[22]

The citizen as moral political actor with duties as well as rights is an idea that runs through the thought of Hannah Arendt, Robert Dahl, Leo Strauss, and many other influential modern political thinkers.[23] These writers also put forward a central theme of republican thought, which is the idea that political participation is itself ennobling and that the person who minds his own business and does not express his opinions on public affairs openly is a less moral person, perhaps a coward, and certainly an 'idiot' in its original Greek sense. Intriguingly, another modern scholar, Ellen Meiksius Wood, has put forward the proposition that the root ideas of republicanism, in particular the concept of the person who is free and owes no obligation to any other human being, are to be derived not from any aristocratic ideal of Plato's but rather from the direct personal experiences and aspirations of the free peasant-citizens of ancient Athens. Far from being in its origins an aristocratic ideology, as is so often claimed, Wood argues,

> there is no reason to suppose that peasants need instruction by aristocratic culture to generate a desire for freedom from servitude or an appreciation for the value of liberation. This appreciation may not be systematically expressed in judicial or philosophical concepts until it is articulated by members of dominant classes . . .[24]

Wood describes the Athenian peasant-citizen core value as possessing a strong sense of 'autonomy, masterlessness and freedom from servility,' which is to be associated with 'the assertion of the right to labour for oneself and serve no mortal man.'[25]

Ireland at the time of independence was overwhelmingly a peasant society, the dominant rural class being owner-occupier farmers possessing small to medium-sized farms. Such a complex of ideas had a natural resonance with such people, as it had in similar 'free-farmer' societies elsewhere in the West. Hatred of banks and of local gombeen-men or usurers derived from fear of debt-slavery and a wish for personal economic independence.

However, a full internalisation of republican values did not take place in Ireland, either on the side of those who made their peace on the terms of the Treaty or those who rejected those terms, as I will argue later. In effect, the concept of the free and 'masterless' citizen has been contemplated with some unease in Irish political culture, heir as it is to a long experience of political, social and spiritual subordination. Another reason for the still-born character of the concept of the republican free citizen has been the relentless domination of Irish society not just by the non-individualist bureaucracy of the Catholic Church, so often denounced by anti-clericals, but also by the weight of the public sector, inherently anti-individualist and non-republican, protected by the weight of its own votes and those of its dependants and by its close ally, the trade union movement.

In Ireland, republicanism, nationalism and democracy tended to be confounded in everyday political parlance, because of the peculiar character of the Irish political experience. In the terms of Robert Dahl, Irish public ideology was 'blended', the elements 'hanging together' in a logically anomalous but psychologically satisfying way.[26] The experience of a struggle for independence encouraged in particular a tendency to equate republicanism rather negatively with absence of monarchy, absence of a British connection, and achievement of full, unambiguous sovereignty. The positive connotations of republicanism tended to be forgotten or weakened; the right of free speech and the values of open government were not always held very high by many putative republicans. In the notorious words of Frank Ryan, the IRA firebrand of the 1930s, many republicans felt that 'traitors' should have no free speech as long as republicans had boots and fists. The terms 'republicanism' and 'democracy' tended to be equated, for similar reasons.

Even eminent scholars were liable to fall into this trap. Hans Kohn, in his classic *The Constitution of the Irish Free State*, pub-

lished in German in 1927 and in English in 1932, was one of the
first to point out authoritatively and in a detached fashion that
the Constitution of the Irish Free State, notionally the cause of a
civil war in 1922–23, was, despite its 'dominion' status and its
monarchical trappings, actually democratic and 'republican', having more in common with the constitutional experiments then in
progress in continental Europe than it had with the dominion
constitutions of Canada, South Africa, Australia, or New Zealand.
In this analysis he was apparently heavily influenced by Hugh
Kennedy, first Attorney-General of the Irish Free State, whose
major contribution to Irish political development will be looked
at later. Kohn accepted implicitly the Irish opposition between
monarchism and republicanism and observed that the constitution of 1922 bore 'the paradoxical impress of a dual inspiration.'

> Moulded in the frame of the Dominion Constitutions, and
> subject to their formal limitations, it yet derives its origin
> from the enactment—'in the exercise of undoubted right'—
> of an Irish Assembly which acknowledges 'that lawful author-
> ity comes from God to the people' and implicitly denies any
> other. Its structural origin is that of a limited monarchy, but
> its tenor is essentially republican. A King, invested with the
> attributes of a 'constitutional monarch', forms the apex of the
> governmental pyramid, but it is a King without divine right
> and without prerogative. As a *Deus ex machina* he appears in
> the centre of a constitutional framework which derives all
> authority in Ireland from the sovereign will of the people.[27]

Kohn evidently accepted the Irish conflation of the terms
'democracy' and 'republicanism', although, as I have suggested,
the two terms may overlap but are by no means coterminous.
Coming as he did from the disintegrating democratic republic of
Weimar Germany, such a conflation was eminently excusable. As I
will argue later, the Civil War was partly fuelled by the apparently
non-German idea that majoritarian democracy and national republicanism could be at odds with each other, and if that were the case,
the former would have to give way to the latter; majorities must give
way to the virtuous, even if the latter are in a minority.

The confusion between the terms 'democracy' and 'republicanism' was shared by many of those who supported the Treaty as

well as by those who opposed it. This confusion and conflation was in a sense a classic one: a true democracy was thought of by many Irish revolutionaries as a republic where everyone had virtue and, by the possession of citizenship, the duty to adhere to the moral code of the state. Ignoring this duty involved the forfeiting of citizenship in the minds of extreme republicans; to borrow the phrase of Thomas Drummond, citizenship, like property, had its duties as well as its rights. Thus Kohn's eloquent and well-informed argument for the essential republicanism of the Irish Free State constitution often fell on deaf republican ears. By way of contrast, advocates of the Free State argued in favour of the will of the people as expressed at election time. This will was held, almost frantically, to be sovereign by the supporters of the Anglo-Irish Treaty; the people had the right to do wrong, even if that involved voting for William Cosgrave rather than for Eamon de Valera. Furthermore, by demonstrating the sovereignty of the Irish people, the supporters of the Free State were denying the possession of sovereignty in Ireland to the British monarch, a point Kohn grasped fully. If de Valera wanted power he would have to win an election. The anti-Treaty response was that the will of the people was tainted, because the Irish had a collective slave mind and would have to be taught how to be spiritually free by the minority of true republicans.

Rousseau's famous distinction between the 'general will' and the 'will of all' was, then, the issue over which the Civil War was fought. The general will was the collective will as expressed by a people of republican virtue, whereas the will of all was merely the arithmetical result of the rather contemptible counting of heads of all inhabitants, regardless of virtue or dependence on others for their political opinion. Rousseau's problem is one of the central philosophical contradictions at the heart of modern democratic political thought and one to which there is no clear solution. It is strange, and perhaps fitting, that it was the Irish, one of the most politically adept of peoples, who should fight a civil war over such a profound political issue.

NATIONALISM

Democracy in the twentieth century has commonly, but not automatically, walked hand in hand with nationalism. Benedict

Anderson, in his already clichéd *Imagined Communities*, has argued that modern nationality is a cultural artefact of the rise of vernacular literacy; it is a child of Gutenberg. Nations exist because their members imagine them to exist and not because of some primordial identity that has been passed down to the present almost in a biological fashion, as nationalist ideologues claimed.[28] Anderson almost certainly overstates his case, although he is right to emphasise the newspaper as a central agent in the strengthening and elaboration of modern collective identities. Before universal literacy, however, there were other ways of creating and maintaining ethnic identies. In particular, ecclesiastical organisations have long been active in creating communities that are often quite recognisably the ancestors of modern nations. Ireland, England, Scotland, Sweden, Denmark, Spain, France, Russia and Israel are all, in their very different ways, national entities in whose creation, and subsequent maintenance, religious organisations played an important part.

Nationalism, according to several writers, in particular perhaps Ernest Gellner, is that creed that asserts that every significant nation should have its own state and that claims also that every nation can only be ruled legitimately by members of that nation, thereby denying the legitimacy of rule by non-nationals.[29] Thus, Gellner argues, political nationalism in the nineteenth century in Europe offered a direct and profound challenge to the political legitimacy of the old order, which consisted chiefly of multi-ethnic states ruled over by aristocratic castes. These castes were commonly of a different culture or even 'nation' than the common people, and sometimes they were even speakers of a foreign language or practitioners of a different religion. Russia, for example, had aristocrats who commonly spoke French; Ireland was ruled by Protestants, although four-fifths of the country was Catholic; in the eighteenth century the religious dichotomy was reinforced by a linguistic one. German-speaking Prussia had a French-speaking elite in the eighteenth century; as Frederick the Great allegedly put it, he spoke Latin to his confessor, French to his mistress, and High German to his horse.

Generally, the rulers of Europe were, almost literally, a race apart: related to each other, speaking the same languages, and inheriting, or marrying into, each others' kingdoms. Nationalism was a doctrine that was intensely subversive of such political sys-

tems yet, paradoxically, increasingly necessary to their maintenance. Nationalist doctrine commonly promised a reign of
harmony and peace once national claims were satisfied; their
prescription did, however, demand the dismantling, and perhaps the violent dismantling, of the established order. The true
spectre that haunted Europe was not that of socialism but that
of nationalism.

Nationalist ideas, like democratic ideas and republican ideas,
swept out of France in the late eighteenth century in one of the
greatest popular ideological and intellectual revolutions ever
known. These ideas, in popular form, hit Germany, Poland,
Russia, Britain and Ireland like a hurricane within five years of
the outbreak of the French Revolution. They seem to have hit
Ireland with particular immediacy very early; by the end of 1790
the notions of the French revolutionaries seem to have been
common parlance, however grotesquely misunderstood, in fairly remote areas. Irish political pamphlets abruptly ceased to consist of arguments concerning the political legitimacy of one or
other version of Christianity and started to be about the rights
of man, ideas of equality, and the events in France.[30] The ideal
of the 'nation-state', which has caused such bloodshed in the
last two centuries, took over many minds.

The core idea was that there are natural nations that have
natural rights to a state, which would, in turn, exert itself to
realise the particular cultural genius of that nation. The new
national state would be the servant of the nation, its tool, and
the scourge of its enemies, whether internal or external. In the
French tradition the symbol of this ideology was the Tree of
Liberty, whose flowers, some still in the bud and some opened
fully so as to display their full beauty, were the nations of
Europe, flourishing anew in the beneficent sunlight of the
French Revolution. In Ireland, of course, the idea of the Tree of
Liberty caught hold immediately. The three kingdoms of the
British Isles—England, Scotland, and Ireland—went into folk
song as the Bonny Bunch of Roses, lost by Napoleon in the flames
of Moscow. The theme of the Tree of Liberty recurs over a century later in the rhetoric of Patrick Pearse, who called for it to
be watered by the 'red wine of the battlefield'.[31]

As formulated by Rousseau, no-one was to be admitted to the
nation who did not have national virtue. Herder called for the

reorganisation of Europe around nation-states, to use the modern term, and Fichte, in his *Lectures to the German Nation* (1808), called for a 'national' school system that would keep all children of the nation together, cleanse their minds of corruption, teach them to love each other as national comrades, and infuse them with a fervent wish to further the destinies of the nation: they were to be the children of the dream.[32] All these ideas, circling around the notion of nationhood, recur, sometimes in distorted, 'baptised' but instantly recognisable form, in the nationalist thought of Ireland in the early twentieth century.

PRECONDITIONS OF DEMOCRACY

A generation ago, in an extremely influential set of papers and a book, Seymour Martin Lipset argued that stable representative democracy was closely associated with high living standards and was difficult to establish in poor countries. Democracy tended to prosper in countries that had an open class system, that is, one in which it was relatively easy to move from one class to another. Wealthier countries were relatively materially egalitarian and had less class conflict. On average, such countries tended to be more literate and to possess egalitarian cultures. Later writers have qualified this picture, but it remains clear that poor countries have great difficulty maintaining democracy, fundamentally because any wealth in the society is in the hands of a tiny and powerful minority, who resist sharing it and also resist any change in the property system that might endanger their political position. The maintenance of democracy in India, for example, a very poor country, is an extraordinary achievement; India is the exception that proves the rule. Costa Rica is another such anomaly. To some extent, it has been argued by some, so is Ireland.[33]

Ireland, it was claimed, has long been one of the senior Western democracies, but also one of the poorest. For a generation after independence, Ireland's standard of living contrasted with those of its geographical and cultural nearest neighbours, Britain and the United States. Not only was Ireland relatively poor but the Irish had in front of their eyes the demoralising demonstration, in Britain and America, that a far higher level of wealth was feasible. Emigration to these two countries became a

way of life, long before independence, and this situation persisted after independence. Arguably, it was in part this very emigration that permitted Ireland's democracy to put down deep roots.
Ireland exported its social problems rather than tackling them at
home. I will look again at the alleged relationship between democracy and economic well-being in chapter 7.

However, there was more to it. Irish commitment to democracy,
I argue, was somewhat equivocal. As Michael Gallagher has suggested, democracy, and a constitution modelled on the British
prototype, were accepted by the Irish simply because the Irish
were very conservative and found other systems not so much
repulsive as unimaginable.[34] Communism, vaunted by many
intellectuals of the 1920s as the progressive system of the future,
was repugnant to the Catholic majority and, of course, to property-
owners. Also, it was unfamiliar and exotic.

Fascism, attractive to a section of the Catholic middle class for a
time in the 1930s, never really caught on; Irish 'fascism', paradoxically, was to take the form of what was, in large part, an anti-'republican' free speech movement, the Blueshirts. One could argue that
the 1930s IRA, with its hatred for free speech and its willingness to
ally itself with Nazism and Italian fascism, was more truly fascist
than was the Blueshirt movement, shirted as it was because of
parochialism rather than because of genuine adherence to core
fascist values. The Blueshirts grew out of the Army Comrades'
Association, which consisted of Free State army veterans; a left-
leaning IRA and the Blueshirts refought the Civil War as farce on
the streets in the 1930s, to no great lasting consequence.[35]

The fact of the matter was that Irish people had had a century of
experience not with democratic government but with democratic
elections. They also had in front of their eyes the spectacle of a
working democracy in the United States and a near-democracy
in the United Kingdom. The basic cultural problem Irish people
had was an authoritarianism; those who were in power were tempt-
ed to be secretive and high-handed, whereas those out of power
tended to be truculently 'agin the government' and cynical
about the motives of those in power. Those in power had a habit
of acting without consultation and to be rather fond of intrigue.
Such cultural orientations had much to do with the Civil War; a
deep distrust of those in power fuelled the anti-Treatyites, whereas those in power put down rebellion harshly.

Much of this cultural authoritarianism seems to have come from the traditional Catholicism of the country. Irish Catholicism was austere, disciplined in a militaristic way, and predicated on the assumption that the truth was known and was uniquely in the possession of the clergy of the Church of Christ. Furthermore, the more power a priest possessed, the more wisdom he was held to possess. Knowledge and power were conflated in the culture. The idea that a bishop could be an ignoramus was unthinkable. Clerical politics were notoriously secretive. Priests had seemed at one time to possess not just religious authority but also magical powers in the eyes of many of the people. Priests had a great psychological grip on the minds of the less well educated and perhaps in particular on the minds of women.[36] John O'Leary, the famous Fenian, once remarked to the young William Butler Yeats that in Ireland, to get anywhere, one must have on one's side either the Fenians or the Catholic Church. Yeats, as a Protestant, would never of course have the Church on his side; he would therefore have to throw in his lot with the rebels, which, for a time, he did.[37]

As will be argued, the fact that the Catholic Church, despite some deep intellectual reservations, came down on the side of Irish electoral democracy was to be crucial to the development of a voter-driven and open polity in Ireland. For a generation after independence the Church was to defend the system in Ireland, at a time when Catholicism internationally, because of the fear of communism, had commonly gravitated to the support of authoritarian and fascist regimes. International Catholicism did not abandon its liking for authoritarian political systems until after the Second World War; it is only very recently that the church has become a positively democratising force, particularly in the Spanish-speaking world.[38] Even then many Catholics simply exchanged their old predilections for rightist authoritarianism for a sympathy with left-wing anti-individualism.

In pre-war Ireland, eminent Catholic ecclesiastics tinkered with corporatist ideas and sometimes denigrated the ideas of democracy; they were, however, in a minority. This did, however, encourage a subconscious contempt, which still exists in Irish Catholic circles, for ideologies that emphasise the sovereignty of the common man and for points of view that look sceptically at theories of elite rule or aristocracy in its Greek sense of rule by the best or most morally aware. Evidently only the Catholic Church could produce those who were most morally aware, in the eyes of Catholic ecclesiastics; it followed that an Irish democracy would be tolerated only in so far as it obeyed this moral elite. Fortunately, perhaps, the democracy of partitioned Ireland tried to live up to this ideal for a time.

Another and perhaps central reason for the stability of Irish democracy was the fact that the independent Irish state inherited the results of a rural property revolution that had occurred in the 1880s. Irish democracy was buttressed by the support of yeoman farmers of recent creation, who wished for no social upheaval and who had a strong collective consciousness of the magnitude of their achievement; the bold tenant farmer had, by his own bravery and by the collective action of his fellows, turned himself into the compleat petty bourgeois under the benign eye of Parnell and the ambivalent eye of Davitt. Property and belief formed a great glue: an alliance between the farmers and the church resulted in a central bloc in Irish society that brooked no great political innovation.[39]

A further cause of the stability of early Irish democracy was partition, which hived off from what amounted to a new country that part of the island that posed a social and political problem that the new system might not have been able to handle. There existed in Northern Ireland a settled community of Protestant faith, with a strong military tradition and a firm determination never to be absorbed into a Catholic state where they would be outnumbered four to one; to put it in the terms of the 1990s, a united Irish democracy would have had at best the problems of Czechoslovakia, at worst those of Bosnia-Herzegovina.

Of course the new state also had the often-mentioned advantage of having taken over bodily the British legal system, the revenue and the general administrative apparatus, most of which organisations were staffed by native Irishmen and had been so for a generation. It was the existence of this resource that made the assembling of the new Free State's apparatus in such a short time possible, as the civil servants promptly gave their allegiance to the new regime. The fact that Home Rule had been anticipated for decades made this shift psychologically easy; instead of John Redmond they got William Cosgrave and, later, Eamon de Valera. The second shift was no more difficult than the first.

After all, even when on the run from the British between 1919 and 1921, Michael Collins was being advised on financial problems of government by a senior civil servant, Joseph Brennan.[40] Many civil servants were members of Sinn Féin or even of the IRA. Collins was able to penetrate the British apparatus in Ireland by turning its own officials against it.[41]

Another reason for the victory of democracy was the willingness of the Free State leaders to listen to senior authority. Collins in particular, seventy years younger than his revered west Cork farmer father, seems to have been peculiarly receptive to the counsel of old age. In particular, he listened carefully to the advice of Tim Healy, the leader of the anti-Parnellites, one of the first of the old 'imperialist' Irish Party to jump ship and ally themselves with Sinn Féin after the 1916 Rising. Furthermore, Healy was well informed, acute, and able to convince the younger man. Irish Party veterans came over to Sinn Féin in large numbers and were to leaven the republican lump in 1922 by accepting the Treaty.[42]

In a sense, then, independent Ireland had everything going for it except extreme wealth. The question then suggests itself, why was there an immediate threat to the nascent Irish democracy in the form of the anti-Treaty IRA, by mid-1922 armed to the teeth? Why was a civil war necessary to preserve the infant state? The answer seems to lie in the collective experience of a generation of young men who came of highly authoritarian personal backgrounds, who were politically inexperienced, who had exaggerated personal expectations, and, as has been suggested, combined authoritarianism with hostility to authority. They had also tasted power at local level as IRA commanders, and liked it. Furthermore, there was much mutual distrust among the rebel leaders. I explore this explanation in more detail later in the book.

The conflict was clearly not about partition, which was scarcely mentioned in the Dáil debates on the Anglo-Irish Treaty of 1921. Both sides declared publicly that Northern Ireland was not to be coerced physically to join their new polity. The Civil War was deeply unpopular with the majority of the population and was, in a sense, an anomalous event. It involved only the elites and their immediate followers, the new political class. The split did not truly involve the general population, unlike that of 1891, which had destroyed Parnell a generation previously. This was so because the Catholic Church, while siding with the pro-Treatyites, kept its lines out in many different ways to the anti-Treatyites, and made peace with them subsequently; crucially, de Valera was a pious Catholic, whereas, by way of contrast, Parnell had been a Protestant guilty of a public sexual misdemeanour. Also, and most importantly, Parnell died immediately after his crisis, whereas de Valera survived and prospered. For the dead Parnell there was to be no forgiveness; for the long-lived de Valera there was to be not only forgiveness but an apparently unconditional popular pardon for his mistakes of 1921–22. De Valera was a hero, and heroes were to be forgiven their few trespasses. As I shall argue, Ireland was ready for democracy, but some of its elites and activists were not quite so ready.[43]

The Irish experience suggests that democracy flourishes best when both economic circumstances and cultural orientations coincide and create favourable circumstances for it. A determination to create an Irish democracy existed not only in the minds of many senior Sinn Féiners but also in the minds of senior civil servants, businessmen, labour leaders, and churchmen. Admittedly, in Ireland the cultural organisations, the church, the family, the school system and the press had a greater task 'selling' democracy to some people than might have been the case in a richer and materially more egalitarian country. As it was, the 'selling' was only partially successful; despite the exhortations of some priests and the words of the journalists of the mainstream papers, Irish democracy also had to be forcibly imposed, not on the general population but on a section of the nationalist elite and their followers. As shall be argued, the conquest of Leinster, Munster and Connacht by the Free State army in 1922–23 resembled a liberation rather than the invasion by fascistic 'Green and Tans' it was claimed to be by so many noisy republican and leftist propagandists in Ireland, Britain, and America.

2

Revolution and Democracy in Ireland, 1913–23

Between 1913 and 1923 the island of Ireland went through a violent political revolution, much as did large parts of eastern and central Europe at that time.[1] The fundamental cause of these revolutions was the Great War of 1914–18, which weakened or destroyed the great multinational European empires of the nineteenth century and replaced them with a patchwork of parochial nation-states carved out from their territory. These successor states have had varied political histories since 1918, and their fates have been the subject of much historical scholarship. They have been of perhaps particular interest to students of democracy, communism and nationalism as mass political phenomena.

The Irish part of the story is well known and has often been told, from nationalist, unionist and socialist viewpoints. Occasionally it has also been told from strange combinations of these general perspectives. The outcome of the events of that ten years was the dismemberment of the British-ruled Kingdom of Ireland in 1920–22 and its replacement by the two political entities now known as Northern Ireland and the Republic of Ireland. Northern Ireland remained part of the United Kingdom, whereas the rest of the island became an independent state within the British Commonwealth, styled at that time the Irish Free State. The Free State, renamed Éire/Ireland in 1937, eventually left the Commonwealth as the Republic of Ireland in 1949.

Because of the insistent nature of the violence in Northern Ireland since 1969, attention has more recently been focused on the politics of Northern Ireland rather than on those of the Republic. The North has been regarded as a problem, which it is for practical and practising politicians, whereas the Republic has been regarded as relatively unproblematic for politicians of this kind. The fact that the academic and journalistic literature on Northern Ireland in the last twenty years has been at least ten times the size of that on the Republic gives the impression that the North is somehow intellectually more interesting, as distinct from being rather more troublesome, than the Republic. Modest northerners will demur, and alert southerners will grumble.

In the little universe of the comparative politics of the British Isles it is the Republic that is not only the little-known case but also a case of wide potential significance. Its potential interest is partly practical: what happens in Northern Ireland is, for better or worse, partly determined by what goes on in the Republic; the two states are intertwined, and each is similarly closely connected to Britain. In fact the very existence of the Republic, and its relative economic, political, diplomatic and cultural success or failure, hugely influence the internal political dynamics of Northern Ireland.

From the point of view of the political scientist, the Republic is of interest for many other, theoretical reasons. In particular, as argued earlier, it is one of the few new states that emerged in the aftermath of the First World War that succeeded in maintaining democratic institutions from its date of foundation in 1922 to the present day. The dramatic and violent circumstances of its birth contrast starkly with the peaceable and humdrum politics that have evolved there since 1923. The only parallel case in Europe is Finland, whose birth throes were, at least at a superficial level, eerily similar to, and far more violent than, those of newly independent Ireland: perhaps eight thousand people suffered violent deaths in the island of Ireland during the ten years between 1913 and 1923, but in a few months in 1918 twenty-five thousand people were killed in Finland, a country with approximately the same population.

The new Irish state was also the only part of the British Isles to create a fully entrenched written constitution and to develop a sophisticated tradition of judge-made law similar to that of the United States or the Federal Republic of Germany. This was largely to be the achievement of Eamon de Valera and is one of his lasting legacies. To put this achievement in perspective, the last English attempt at creating a written constitution was the Cromwellian Instrument of Government, written three-and-a-half centuries ago and still-born because of the Lord Protector's abundant contempt for it. Behind the Constitution of 1937, however, lies the Constitution of the Irish Free State of 1922, the unacknowledged model for the 1937 document; de Valera's constitution pretends not to be a 'Free State constitution' and claims to be a constitution for all of Ireland but is in reality as much a constitution for a partitioned Ireland as its predecessor. Perhaps it was more partitionist, in the sense that it took less regard of the existence of a separate unionist political identity in the North.

In this chapter and later in this book I examine in a comparative context the emergence of democratic and non-violent government in what is now the Republic between 1921 and 1923, in the aftermath of the unionist defiance of London in 1912, the Easter Rising of 1916, and the Anglo-Irish War of January 1919 to July 1921. A particular theme is the slow and patient creation of a civic order and of free political institutions in a context of violent revolution, collective hysteria, and the breakdown in disorder of the British scheme of things in both parts of Ireland.

THE EMERGENCE OF IRISH DEMOCRACY

Within a year of the Anglo-Irish Treaty of December 1921, the guerrilla army that had contributed so much to that achievement, the IRA, was in armed revolt against an elected Irish government. Ten years after that again, these guerrillas became the elected government themselves, in a remarkable turnabout. The Free State, under Arthur Griffith and Michael Collins and later under William Cosgrave and Kevin O'Higgins, defeated the IRA, notionally under Eamon de Valera and actually under Liam Lynch. Ten years later de Valera, as leader of Fianna Fáil, was prime minister, and had become so by legal and democratic procedures.

This transition to competitive electoral democracy regulated by the rule of law that occurred in the twenty-six counties of 'Southern Ireland' in those years has been treated by many historians as an inevitable and unproblematic series of events. In fact Frank Munger, an American political scientist, commented at article length some decades ago on the apparently curious fact that Irish people took the changeover in government of

1932 so much for granted, given the bloody events of ten years previously. Munger argued that Irish politicians were unusually able people who were able to overcome the setback of civil war in 1922–23 and build a stable civic order in unpromising circumstances.

Parenthetically, the creation of the Free State has been treated as an act of unforgivable treachery to the national cause by extreme nationalists and by many sympathetic to what might be described as the de Valera or Fianna Fáil school of historical revisionism. Again, to vulgar Marxists the end of the Civil War and the establishment of the Free State in 1922–23 was of course the Irish Thermidor, the victory of the moneyed classes over the forces of revolution and the people: it constituted the pseudo-democratic triumph of bourgeois reaction and the defeat of ordinary working people. By extreme secularists, liberals and unionists it has been seen as a pseudo-democratic takeover by a national version of the Catholic Church, which controlled the minds of the people and thus, indirectly, controlled the behaviour of elected politicians. To hard-line republican nationalists the Free State was a British-dominated puppet regime whose rulers were well paid by their British paymasters for their national apostasy and betrayal of the revolutionary republic of 1916–23. In some versions the entire population of the republic was similarly condemned for its slavishness and unworthiness. This last viewpoint still survives in parts of Belfast and Boston.

In fact the emergence of what was then termed the Irish Free State and has since been transmogrified by a long constitutional evolution into the Republic of Ireland was, first of all, a triumph for electoral democracy, a co-operative effort of those in Sinn Féin who became 'Free-Staters' and the leaders of Irish Labour who were intellectually able to see through the emergent tyranny of the socialist Russia of the era. These Irish revolutionaries also had a well-deserved contempt for the Marxist-Leninist ideological notions of the Soviet Union's Irish intellectual dependants and agents.

Furthermore, the emergence of Irish democracy, with its strange alliance between a quasi-fundamentalist Catholicism and the classic values of Anglo-American liberal democracy, was quite a close-run thing. This is, ironically, despite the fact that the opposition of de Valera and much of the IRA to the Free

State and to the partition settlement implied by the Anglo-Irish Treaty was deeply unpopular.

Militarily, things were not as one-sidedly in favour of the Free State in early 1922 as is sometimes assumed. This fact has been forgotten, or rather smothered in floods of ultra-republican ink; in early 1922 the new Free State army scarcely existed, and the IRA had rearmed and was riding high. The new army of the Irish Free State was untrained and unofficered, by way of contrast. A coup against the new Provisional Government and the dismemberment of the Anglo-Irish settlement at the behest of a small IRA junta was not impossible in early 1922. As Paddy Morrisey, a well-known Dublin commander, remarked years later,

> my opinion is we could have beaten them with our caps that morning [in May–June 1922]. The F/C [Four Courts] garrison if they came out could have beaten anything surrounding them is my opinion: the best men of the I.R.A. were in there and then were locked up for the rest of the [civil] war.

Ernest Blythe, a prominent member of the pro-Treaty government shared, from the other side, Morrisey's opinion of the military capacity of the IRA. In December 1922 he remarked in the Dáil that the attack on the Four Courts was essential to preserve parliamentary democracy.

> As a matter of fact, if we did not take the action we took then [in June 1922], so far from Irregularism falling to pieces, they [the IRA] would have carried out a *coup d'état* and there would have been no Dáil Éireann sitting here now.

Peter Hart's fascinating and horrifying study of the Cork IRA strongly suggests that the best fighting men stayed anti-Treaty, with a few exceptions, in particular the coterie of gunmen surrounding Michael Collins. The hard core of the old IRA had a strong collective loyalty and thought of themselves as sovereign. 'They had organised themselves and armed themselves and paid their own way.' They saw themselves as having created the Republic, and no-one had the right to give it away, democratically or otherwise.

The superiority of the brave guerrilla soldier over the average citizen was a key theme in anti-Treaty mentality. Kevin O'Higgins seems, somewhat inaccurately, to have blamed de Valera for creating this mentality; in fact de Valera seems to have been as much its prisoner as its creator. In justifying the draconian measures adopted by the Free State in crushing the anti-Treaty IRA, O'Higgins said of de Valera in the Dáil on 8 December 1922:

> Outside you have a President who was defeated in his candidature for the Presidency, even in that Second Dáil he talks so much about, a President who fitly enough chooses as his Council of State, for the most part, men who were refused a mandate from any constituency, men whose representative characters were taken from them by the electors of the country, and fitly enough that President and that Council of State has a thing which it calls an Army, but simply has degenerated into a combination of Apaches, a combination.

The anti-democratic elements in Irish political culture were quite widespread and had much to do with legitimising armed resistance to the democratically elected Irish government in 1922–23. I admit immediately that the general ideological assumptions that nowadays legitimise electoral democracy in the West and, increasingly, elsewhere, held sway in the Ireland of the immediate pre-independence period. The principle of using the mechanism of election was long established and was used routinely in sporting clubs, social organisations, and political associations. As far back as the middle of the eighteenth century, Whiteboy captains were appointed by vote of their comrades. The principle that power should ultimately lie in the hands of the people rather than in those of an aristocracy or a monarch was generally accepted. Furthermore, the Irish, both Protestant and Catholic, were relatively well educated and lived in a country with something approaching what would have been the equivalent of a 'First World' standard of living and with a well-developed administrative structure. Lawyers, with their grasp of the rules of the game, as distinct from the morality of specific political actions, were culturally powerful. The problem of democracy in Ireland was that most Irish people, whether Protestant or Catholic, were majoritarian rather than pluralist democrats; crucially, they disagreed on which majority was to be sovereign.

Nationalists insisted on the supremacy of the separatist or quasi-separatist majority in the thirty-two counties; unionists, whether Irish, 'Ulster', or British, similarly argued for the majoritarian rights, in their local area, of the unionist or quasi-unionist minority. Some in what is sometimes comically referred to as 'mainland' Britain denied the right of any Irish 'faction' to disrupt the consensual order of the two countries to the detriment of the general welfare or of that of the British Empire.

On the other side, extreme nationalists often had deeply ambiguous attitudes towards electoral democracy, thereby echoing the imperialists. Even among the nationalist majority, attitudes towards the new idea of universal-suffrage democracy were, behind even the majoritarian rhetoric, ambiguous. Admittedly, all Redmondites and the vast bulk of those who supported a republican form of independence for the country agreed that some form of parliamentary democracy was the appropriate governmental form to use. This was true of those who, like Patrick Pearse or Kevin O'Higgins, supported the idea of a constitutional monarchy; it was true of the underground and conspiratorial IRB; and it was also true of most of the socialist left. The Catholic Church also accepted the idea, despite its Vatican-inspired hankering after corporatist ideas and its distrust of secularised political systems inspired by the experience of Pio Nono.[2]

However, the fact that the church was organised in a highly non-democratic fashion attenuated Irish people's wholehearted acceptance of the principle of election; the church regarded its authority as coming not from the people but from God. The wisdom of the church was ultimately derived from divine authority and was transmitted from the Pope down through the bishops to the lower clergy and ultimately to the people, who were implicitly envisaged as being at the bottom of the heap. A common self-image of the priest was that of a Good Shepherd; naturally, this imputed something of the character of sheep to lesser human beings. A religion that structured human political society in such a way was bound to be less than reverential towards doctrines of democratic popular sovereignty. Certainly the international Catholic Church was deeply ambiguous about the coming of democracy elsewhere in Europe and was commonly to flirt with various fascist and other right-wing authoritarianisms in the inter-war years.

Sensitivity to this ambiguity towards democratic ideas occasionally showed itself. Between 1919 and 1921, Alfred O'Rahilly, a well-known Catholic spokesman and one of the drafters of a proposed constitution for the new Free State, published a series of articles in the Jesuit periodical *Studies* that claimed at great length that the Catholic Church had actually invented democracy. In the introduction to the 1921 article he averred rather testily: 'The current Protestant view is that democracy was introduced by the Reformation; and unfortunately this travesty of history is accepted as a commonplace by Catholics.' In a 1919 article he remarked that 'the institutions and the mentality which constitute modern democracy are a heritage from medieval schoolmen.'

It is difficult not to suspect that much Catholic acceptance of nominal electoral democracy was due mainly to the fact that the Irish majority could usually be trusted to obey the injunctions of the clergy; the majority of the people were manageable. Democracy, therefore, was for Catholics a tolerable rather than an ideal form of government, and Irish people sometimes displayed a profound grasp of the mechanics of representative government combined with a dislike of the principles of freedom of speech and assembly that classic democratic theory would assert are an essential part of the democratic process. Irish Catholic approval of democracy was sometimes combined with a conditionality: there were truths that the majority had no right to flout. This conditionality was to be a prime cause of the Civil War.

Electoral democracy in western Europe was, furthermore, not the revered object it has tended to become since 1945. Modern electoral democracy, with all its emotional shallowness and compromises, appeals more nowadays because of the hideousness of the proffered alternatives: the murderous totalitarianisms of left and right that were touted by many twentieth-century intellectuals. The fantastic murderousness of Nazism and the even greater murderousness of Lenin and Stalin have laid the romantic revolutionism of both left and right to rest for the moment. Francis Fukuyama's 'end of history' has indeed come in some sense, and the battle has perhaps become one of public, or statist, modes of collective action as against private action or private property principles.

At the time of Irish independence, however, capitalism, socialism, various forms of right-wing authoritarianism and electoral democracy were the rivals. Romantic styles of political thought were still fashionable, and Karl Popper's *The Open Society and its Enemies*, with its crushing rejoinders to the totalitarians, lay twenty years in the future. The much-touted vocationalist and corporatist theories of many ideologues of the period had not yet been subjected to the critiques of modern economists, which point to the tendency of such systems to lead to stagnation and elite oligopoly.

Furthermore, in 1918 'bourgeois' electoral and representative democracy did not yet look all that good. Distrust of parliamentarianism and distrust of competitive electoral politics had deep cultural roots, particularly among key groups of political leaders in Catholic, clerical, unionist, nationalist, republican and socialist circles. Attitudes existed that later were to express themselves as an open distrust of the wisdom of ordinary people, a belief that voters were easily fooled, and a conviction, one that gained notoriety later when heard from the mouth of de Valera, that the majority had no right to do wrong.

James Connolly, for example, was deeply uneasy about electoral democracy as he had seen it operate in Britain, Ireland, and the United States, and with good reason. Like Robert Michels, Vilfredo Pareto, Gaetano Mosca, and Moise Ostrogorsky, the then fashionable chief theorists of democratic elitism, he saw democracy as prone to takeover by small, self-interested and corrupt cliques: the organised minority would always win out over the unorganised majority in electoral politics, because the minority would have the inside track and the initiative. Connolly was a syndicalist and had picked up many of his ideas from the Industrial Workers of the World (the 'Wobblies') during his years in America. In Connolly's view, the organised industrial action of the workers was a far more authentic expression of democracy than was public election. The latter was a useful adjunct of the former, little more.

> The real battle is the battle being fought out every day for the power to control industry and the gauge of the progress of that battle is not to be found in the number of voters making a cross beneath the symbol of a political party, but in the number of these workers who enrol themselves in an industrial organisation with the definite purpose of making themselves masters of the industrial equipment of society in general.[3]

Electoral democracy was, he admitted, an essential means to that end, an end envisaged as replacing such arrangements with more authentically democratic syndicalist forms. In bourgeois society the structure of property relations was such as to make oligarchy inevitable, regardless of the formally democratic appearance of public institutions. Connolly's perception of democratic institutions in capitalist society as inherently liable to corruption by Tammany Hall was life-long. His attitude was similar to the diagnoses of the academic political scientists of the period, referred to briefly above. According to Connolly and the democratic elitists, the voters were easily managed by misinformation, manipulation, threats, and outright bribes. Concerning a Scottish municipal election in 1894, for example, he remarked:

> The socialists did not send any carriages for their lady supporters; they did not have committee rooms outside the polling booth, and waylaying unfortunate voters, rush them in, and then escort them between tall hats and frock coats, to record their votes in favour of the rights of property; they did not tell Irish Catholics that Mr Conservative was a Freethinker, who wanted to overthrow the Church, and then tell old Scotch women of both sexes that Mr Conservative was an Irish Papist who wanted to introduce the Scarlet Woman; they did not seek the support of the Unionists by telling of the letter of recommendation from a leading Edinburgh Unionist; and seek the support of the Home Rulers by calling to their aid every quondam Home Ruler, or leader, who could be induced to sell his name, and voice, and birthright for the ill-smelling pottage of Liberal promises.[4]

For so many Irish, and perhaps particularly those on the left, British Liberals and Conservatives were Tweedledum and Tweedledee, and their public quarrels over imperial crises, European power struggles and free trade had little to do with the real interests of the mass of British working people; electoral democracy was, in effect, a seedy sham.[5] To put it in slightly anachronistic terms, their view of representative democracy tended towards the Leninist; it was in the name of a similar doctrine of political vanguardism that Lenin shut down the Russian parliamentary assembly in January 1918 and murdered the infant Russian democracy, a tragedy from which Russia has not yet recovered. In British Ireland, representative democracy was seen as being even more of a sham than it was in Britain, as the Irish members at Westminster were permanently in opposition and were nearly always politically impotent. Competitive electoral democracy in an independent Irish republic, Connolly argued, could be expected to have not much more to do with the interests of ordinary people as long as bourgeois property relations remained intact and the workers remained unorganised or were organised only by professional politicians who had their own rather than the workers' interests at heart.

Connolly's critique of capitalist democracy was a powerful one and echoed the opinions of many observers of the nascent democracies of Europe and America at that time. Socialist and communist critiques of electoral democracy often echoed Connolly's view in other parts of Europe as well. Significantly, Connolly's political writings were hugely influential in left-wing circles, not just in Ireland but throughout Europe and America.

An aesthetic, as distinct from a hyperdemocratic, dislike of conventional electoral democracy was also fashionable among many intellectuals. W. B. Yeats, for example, yearned for the preservation of aristocratic values and even the reinstitution of some kind of nobility in the post-revolutionary Ireland of the future. His naïve flirtation with something that looked like fascism in the 1930s was a belated echo of this idea. He was fond of citing Goethe's famous remark to the effect that the Irish reminded him of a pack of hounds tearing down a noble stag. However, he neglected to point out that Goethe's noble stag was the Duke of Wellington and the pack of hounds was O'Connell and his Irish Party in the House of Commons. Wellington was, after all, the victor of Waterloo and therefore the liberator of Goethe's Germany from Napoleonic tyranny.

James Joyce, perhaps the most democratically minded of the great Irish writers of that extraordinarily gifted generation, had a 'Parnellite' perception of the Irish people as malicious and slavish:

> This lovely land that always sent
> Her writers and artists to banishment
> And in a spirit of Irish fun
> Betrayed her own leaders, one by one.

'Twas Irish humour, wet and dry
Flung quicklime into Parnell's eye . . .

The insurrectionists of Easter Monday 1916 embarked on their rising partly because of that precise belief: a few brave men would have to show courage and self-sacrifice so as to wake the Irish people up from its spiritual coma, its slavishness, and its cowardice. Pearse clearly saw himself as an Irish Messiah sacrificing himself for the sake of the moral regeneration of a spiritually enslaved people. However, he was not alone. In a less visionary way, the other 1916 leaders possessed a similar self-perception. The idea of a moral elite also appealed to many in the IRA of 1919–22, a volunteer force deeply imbued with the values represented by the 1916 men.

One soldier of the IRA who went anti-Treaty in 1922–23, Christopher S. ('Todd') Andrews, recalled his own mentality at that time in a remarkably honest and self-revealing memoir. He described himself as having not so much a contempt for electoral democracy as an incomprehension of it in early 1922. This was the period in which the Republic was giving way to the Free State, and the two wings of the IRA were beginning to shape up for the Civil War of 1922–23. The anti-Treaty IRA had already indicated that they would not acknowledge the right of the Dáil to disestablish the Republic and bring in the Free State. One of the leaders, Rory O'Connor, in a notorious remark, made it clear that the IRA intended to push the politicians aside and govern as a junta. This did not shock young IRA soldiers of Andrews's generation.

In the spring of 1922 the idea of a military dictatorship in itself had not at all the frightening connotations it has now. Mussolini had not marched on Rome, the word 'fascist' to the limited few who had ever heard of it had no untoward significance. Hitler had only begun the long haul to power, while Stalin had not yet undertaken the liquidation of the Kulaks or the show trials of the Old Bolsheviks. Equally, democracy had not been, as it since has been, elevated to the position of a goddess in the public mind. 'The democratic process' were words which would have fallen on uncomprehending ears in the Ireland of 1922. What the people understood by military dictatorship, as propounded by Rory O'Connor, was that they were liable to be pushed around at the whim of young IRA commanders.[6]

Andrews exaggerated, perhaps. As shall be argued later, many of the elites came to an understanding of the fundamental principles of electoral democracy. Cosgrave and O'Higgins, in particular, saw themselves during the Civil War as putting down an organised attempt by mutineers to prevent the holding of elections in 1923. This self-perception has considerable validity. On the other hand, the IRA of early 1922 saw itself as a more authentic corporate representative of the Republic and of the Irish people than Dáil Éireann. After all, the first Dáils, those of 1918 and 1921, had been elected rather irregularly. The First Dáil was the assembly of Sinn Féin, a political party, rather than a parliament containing all Irish parties; the surviving remnants of the Irish Party, the Unionists and unionist Labour all boycotted the First Dáil. Only one Republican Labour TD, Richard Corish of Wexford, sat in the First Dáil. The election of 1918 had been in many ways non-competitive, and there had been considerable intimidation by what was becoming the IRA. There was also a considerable amount of impersonation and stuffing of ballot boxes. Separatist leaders openly admitted subsequently that the elections of 1918, 1921 and 1922 were doubtful expressions of the popular will. The first 'normal' Dáil election was to be that of 1923.

Most importantly, the dramatic events of 1916–18 had the effect of making the 1918 election something of a stampede of a newly enfranchised electorate, much of it consisting of young, poor and male first-time voters. The Second Dáil, that of 1921, afterwards sacred to extreme republicans and to Eamon de Valera in his unreconstructed phase as the last legitimate parliament of the Irish Republic, was actually not elected at all; Sinn Féin nominees, generally the choice of a small caucus centred on Harry Boland, Michael Collins, and local IRA leaders, were given walkovers in the twenty-six counties. Thus, despite the extravagant claims subsequently made of its superior legitimacy to the Third and subsequent Dáils made by de Valera and the IRA, the democratic mandate of the Second Dáil, though clear enough in Republican legality, was psychologically weak.

IRISH DEMOCRACY AND THE PUBLIC BAND

In some ways, the IRA seems to have come to see itself as a military analogue of the democratic syndicalist workers' movement recommended by Connolly. The IRA commanders generally were elected, at least in the early years of the organisation, and their delegate conference did seem to see itself as being in some sense a representative assembly, one with greater moral claim to rule than had Dáil Éireann; the Second Dáil was to be the creature of the IRA rather than its ultimate ruler.

The new revolutionary parliament was therefore culturally artificial, not least in the minds of the IRA soldiers. It could be argued that the Dáil was essentially the IRA's creation, rather than the IRA being the loyal army of a government elected by the Dáil. It was natural enough for the IRA to see their own historical mandate as being superior to that of the Dáil, descended as the IRA was from the 1916 events and from the Fenian-IRB tradition. Thus, for the republican Jacobins of the dissident IRA of 1922, the more psychologically satisfying political mandate seemed to belong to their militant organisation rather than to a parliamentary assembly of doubtful provenance and moral stature. The local militant organisation, based on the solidarity of young males, had old roots in Ireland, certainly going back to the Whiteboys and Ribbonmen of pre-Famine Ireland and expressing itself innocently in times of peace as recreational groups such as football clubs, wren boys, straw boys, mummers, and the like. Peter Hart puts it in the Cork context as follows:

> These men shared very real convictions and ideals, but it seems clear that, for the majority of volunteers, the decision to join was a collective rather than an individual one, rooted more in local communities and networks than in ideology or formal political loyalties. Young men tended to join the organisation together with, or following, members of their families and friendship groups. The 'boys' who 'strawed,' played, worked and grew up together became the 'boys' who drilled, marched and raided together.

David Miller has labelled the Ulster version of this collective political mentality that of the 'Public Band' or volunteer tradition

of local defence, common in peasant societies all over Europe
and certainly very strong in Ireland since the middle of the eighteenth century.[7] The 'Jacobinism' of men like Andrews and the
'syndicalism' of men like Connolly combined easily with this
folk tradition of collective political action and with the tradition
of young male solidarity.

In the aftermath of the First World War, Ireland was not
alone in witnessing a recrudescence of Public Band traditions.
In Germany and Italy in particular, a partial reversion to
Hobbesian conditions encouraged the growth of local vigilantism.
The Freikorps organisations of post-war Germany, for example,
were derived from male solidarities built up during the war and
formed the basis for enduring Stahlhelm, Hitlerite and communist units. In Ireland, Public Band psychology tied in perhaps
particularly neatly with traditions of male solidarity and comradeship. The continuing agitation and fighting of 1918–21 was
psychologically very satisfying for young men of this sort; bravery,
loyalty to each other, steadfastness in adversity and self-sacrifice
witnessed by the awed or fearful eyes of one's male comrades and
the admiring eyes of the young women earned one the approba-
tion of the other members of the Public Band. The IRA man as
a figure of popular glamour was born. It was this collective
Gemeinschaft of youth, deriving from deeply rooted traditions of
agrarian and sectarian agitation and of local defence, that the
ratification of the Anglo-Irish Treaty on 7 January 1922 shattered.

All of a sudden, outside entities such as 'the politicians', 'the
clergy', 'the press', 'the bourgeoisie' and, later, non-Sinn Féin
political parties such as Labour and the Farmers' Party moved in
on what was becoming a political and rational-legal process for
the first time. Nationalist politics was in danger of ceasing to
consist of an endless process of collective, heroic and comradely
resistance to British power. Andrews puts this feeling very well,
in remembering the day the Treaty was approved by the Dáil by
a narrow majority.

> I was shattered less by the vote than by what I had seen and
> read of the [Dáil] debate. For years I had lived on a plane of
> emotional idealism, believing that we were being led by great
> men into a new Ireland. Now I had seen these 'great men' in
> action to find that they were mostly very average in stature,

some below average, some malevolent and vicious. The only one that retained any residue of my absurdly high esteem was de Valera . . .[8]

The significance of people's height, as distinct from their moral or physical courage, is unclear; possibly we have here an echo of the deference the young male solidarity group would have had for physical prowess and even simple physical size. It is not irrelevant to note that both Andrews and de Valera were exceptionally tall men, whereas Cathal Brugha, for example, while being almost proverbially physically brave, was short. Incidentally, on 10 January 1922, Seán MacEntee, anti-Treaty and west Belfast, rebuked William Cosgrave for allegedly sneering at his physical height; it seems that, in a society that was essentially peasant, physical size and social and even cultural prestige tended to coincide. From being great men, according to Andrews, the leaders of Dáil Éireann fell to the menial status of mere politicians, in a culture that had been accustomed to a distrust of and even contempt for electoral politics ever since the fall of Parnell in 1891.[9]

Furthermore, it was obvious even in early 1922 that the voters, once permitted their day of collective sovereignty, would ratify the Treaty by an overwhelming majority. Older people and even Protestants would be permitted to vote, regardless of the contribution they might have made, or not made, to the war effort. In June 1922 the voters proved to be perfectly willing to ignore the Collins-de Valera electoral Pact of May 1922. What is striking is the republicans' refusal to acknowledge that the voters had a right to reject a patently undemocratic conspiracy between the pro- and anti-Treaty factions of Sinn Féin to prevent a clear verdict on the Treaty.

The bishops of the Catholic Church roundly denounced the anti-Treatyites' intransigence, and the press was almost unanimously pro-Treaty, as were the local authorities elected on a rate-payer franchise in mid-1920. Many younger and less senior clergy, however, sympathised with the republicans, often sharing their collective mentality. Monks of the Franciscan and Capuchin orders, politically radical in Ireland as elsewhere in Europe, seem to have been particularly attracted to republican ideas. Republicans declared the voters to have been misled by the priests and the media and as being simply passive, manipulated creatures, if not positively venal servants, of the pro-Treatyites. The voters were seen as victims of what the fundamentalists described as the slave-mind syndrome, in the words of Seán MacBride and many other national radicals on many later occasions. In the words of Liam Lynch, chief of staff of the anti-Treaty IRA, in early 1923, the people 'were merely sheep to be driven anywhere at will.'[10] Interestingly, this image echoes that well-known Catholic image of the appropriate relationship between the clergy and the laity referred to earlier. Republicans knew better than the ordinary people, who should be their flock and follow them obediently. Republican political culture was contemptuous of electoral politics and of the unheroic mentality of the ordinary citizen. Republican political culture also had a fantastically inflated view of its own virtue, wisdom, and right to rule; the Catholic Church of the period had taught the radicals thoroughly.

An honest and self-critical analysis by Ernie O'Malley, a famous IRA soldier, in December 1923 as he lay recovering from hunger-strike in Kilmainham Jail averred:

> We are and have been slaves and so have the slave mind. The open fighting of 1920–21 and some of the fighting of 1922–1923 has helped somewhat to eradicate slavish defects but at heart we are still slaves and have slaves' meannesses and lack of moral qualities. It is inevitable. All enslaved nations have ever been the same. The fact that now and then every thirty years or so a 'red coat' or peeler has been killed, or as in the recent 'war' a signal cabin (unoccupied) gallantly attacked or a few sleepers with attached length of rail dug up, at the point of a bayonet, does not matter. Even though there are such outstanding deeds the mass cannot rise to them save in a certain form of enthusiasm. I'm afraid it will take a big length of time to make up for the personal loss of the '16 group. Pearse and his group set out to minister to the spiritual side of the nation. They were replaced by Collins and Mulcahy neither of whom . . . were spiritual; they had genius for work, though.[11]

Here, Pearse and company are seen as political priests, ministering to the spiritual health of the nation and doing so by precept and by personal example. The ghost of a certain style of aristocratic thought is clearly visible behind O'Malley's imagery.

It is a style of thought that is fundamentally anti-democratic and also profoundly arrogant in its tacit assumption that the ordinary people did not understand their own best interests, could not be trusted to vote the 'right way', and were essentially fitted only to be slaves and underlings.

Fundamentally, the voters, lawyers, priests, journalists, the 'bourgeoisie', the farmers, trade unions and all the other elements of civic society had moved in on the moral territory that the Public Band of the IRA had staked out for itself, a thing that the IRA felt they were not entitled to do, because they did not share in the moral community that the Public Band constituted in its own eyes. Throughout the revolutionary period, informal and personal agreements tended to take the place of formal and rule-bound relationships and understandings. Personal friendship, mutual trust and admiration were essential to the collective working of the movement. Physical bravery was particularly valued, even when it shaded over, as it often did, into blood-lust and murderousness. Distrust, dislike and contempt would have made collective action impossible, and there is ample evidence of a repressed mutual distrust existing between the leaders long before January 1922. Desmond FitzGerald remembered that in 1921, during the period between the coming of the Truce in July and the signing of the Treaty in December,

> apart from the difficulties of the situation, the fact that the leaders were bound together by the most intimate bonds of friendship obviated the need for strict forms. Friendly conversations took the place of formal dispatches or minutes.

Another, British observer noted that at a lower level many IRA did not want to go back to fighting in August 1921, when knives were beginning to be sharpened:

> The news of the hitch in the Peace negotiations has been received with considerable uneasiness. The general public are in favour of accepting the terms, and have not got enough spirit to insist openly that the 'DÁIL' should close with the offer.

Land had been offered to IRA men, and 'fear of losing this land is the main reason why the IRA wish to accept only an Irish

Republic and nothing else.'[12] Thus, residual land-hunger among rather small groups of men in an undisciplined rabble-army, as much as personal distrust among elites or elaborated ideological differences, generated the energy for a futile and half-hearted civil war. The war, such as it was, had little to do with the social concerns of most Irish people and was, in a curious way, ignored by most of the population, who treated it rather like a large riot or faction-fight rather than as a genuine war between large and representative sections of the nation. It is clear that the reception for the Free State army in Munster and Connacht in late 1922 was a welcoming one and fuelled by relief at seeing the backs of the IRA.

Although several anti-Treaty writers and de Valera himself have represented the attack on the Four Courts as a treacherous surprise attack that the anti-Treatyites had not anticipated, many observers who watched the tragedy unfold from mid-1921 expected an unavoidable split among the victors emerging early on. Some smelt violence in the air, others did not foresee it. J. J. Nolan, for example, a professor in University College, Dublin, toured the south of Ireland in August 1921, when the men of the south were busily rearming themselves under cover of the armistice with the British. He predicted civil war, and communicated this insight to the Dáil government. Significantly, this was long before the final form of the Treaty was decided. The *Freeman's Journal* reported on 7 October 1921 that there appeared to be 'pre-concerted attempts to create trouble' and to disturb the atmosphere of peace in many parts of the country.[13]

Another observer, who possessed a very different vantage point, was Batt O'Connor. O'Connor was well known in the movement and was intimate with de Valera, Collins, and the Donnybrook IRA and Sinn Féin set of the period. A Kerryman, he had spent five years in the United States and returned to Ireland, setting himself up as a building contractor in Donnybrook. He built much of petit-bourgeois Donnybrook and also the famous house, 36 Ailesbury Road, with the hidden room. It was from this house that Ernie O'Malley attempted to escape during the Civil War in a famous incident. O'Connor had 'formed fours' with de Valera during the early years of the Irish Volunteers and claimed to know his character very well. He had an unreserved admiration for him. In a private letter that he wrote on 12 December 1921 he commented that a renewal of the war with the British was now impossible. The reason was that the British had ceased their attempt to control the country by military and paramilitary force, the army, Black and Tans and Auxiliaries being confined to barracks. Popular support for renewed fighting was minimal, unlike the period 1919–21, when an authentic mass support for the IRA campaign existed and was being continually augmented by the high-handed behaviour of the British authorities. In effect, Irish society was reverting to a peacetime mentality after four years of popular anti-British solidarity. O'Connor prophesied a split and interpreted de Valera's probable behaviour as that of a tragic hero and not, as has often been subsequently claimed, an act of treachery against brave comrades.

> De Valera will reject the terms, but this does not say he will get a majority to vote with him and this means he will resign and this will be deplorable. Won't it be terrible if the country lose the service of such a noble man. He has no peer in Ireland this is admitted on all sides . . . the offer is certainly very good and it will be hard for the country and its representatives to reject it.

As a man friendly with the leaders of what were shortly to be two bitterly opposed sides, O'Connor admired Collins and Mellows while evidently worshipping de Valera, as did many others. It did not occur to him that the division within the Public Band that the Treaty would provoke might start an uncontrollable escalation into open warfare. De Valera's own conscientiousness at this time was widely accepted, even by people of pro-Treaty conviction. For example, Edward MacLysaght, an eye-witness of these events, and William O'Brien, an intimate of de Valera, thought simply that de Valera was mistaken in his rejection not only of the Treaty but of the entire Free State. His honesty was not questioned, however; in this they agreed with O'Connor. Michael Hayes recalled that at that time de Valera was 'respected, admired, almost adored. To many he appeared as the personification of the patriotic fervour of the period.'

Others were more worried about the loyalty of the IRA than about de Valera's probable actions. On 16 December *An tÓglach*, the official paper of the Army, specifically ordered the IRA to obey the Dáil in terms that reflect an underlying and well-founded uneasiness about the IRA:

> The Army is the servant of the nation and will obey the national will expressed by the chosen representatives of the people and interpreted through the proper military channels. Whatever that decision may be, the soldiers and officers of the Army of Ireland will accept it in the true spirit of disciplined soldiers, loyal to the nation in defence of whose rights and liberties they have been enrolled, and will obey their orders cheerfully and unflinchingly whatever the consequences . . .

Exchanges of fire between IRA and British army personnel continued sporadically throughout the Truce. Furthermore, IRA soldiers were in many areas becoming uncontrollable. Drink, parties and joyriding in 'commandeered' cars became major distractions. During the Truce many unofficial murders occurred, some of them evidently the work of local IRA. Many of the murders were clearly sectarian. In the twenty-six counties, between 1919 and 1923 an unknowable number of Protestant civilians, perhaps as many as thirty, many of whom were not involved in politics or violence, were murdered by local IRA. Many more people, both Protestant and Catholic, were driven from their homes and forced to emigrate, at least temporarily.

The IRA's controllability and political loyalty were profoundly suspect. On 6 January 1922, Liam Lynch, the senior anti-Treaty IRA leader in the south, wrote to Richard Mulcahy, one day before the final Dáil vote on the Treaty and therefore in an attempt to intimidate the deputies:

> It is with deep regret that I have to acquaint you that while at all times I shall do my utmost to carry out your orders, maintain general discipline and above all insist on Truce being maintained, I cannot carry out any order against I.R.A. principles during the present Treaty negotiations when such principles stand the danger of being given away by our government.

Many pro-Treaty people viewed the attitudes of the anti-Treatyites with genuine incomprehension, an incomprehension that later turned to contempt and hatred. Collins, for example, was bewildered by de Valera's fine distinction between the Treaty and his own documents 2 and 3. These were the documents in which de Valera tried to walk a fine line between the Free State and the Republic, between dominion status and complete, isolated independence: the doctrine of 'external association' with the British Commonwealth and Empire. De Valera seems to have put forward some such proposal to Collins at some stage in mid-1921. During the Treaty debates, Collins, at lunch with Michael Hayes, said emphatically about de Valera:

> How could one argue with a man who was always drawing lines and circles to explain the position; who, one day, drew a diagram (here Michael illustrated with pen and paper) saying 'take a point A, draw a straight line to point B, now three-fourths of the way up the line take a point C. The straight line AB is the road to the Republic; C is where we have got to along the road, we cannot move any further along the straight road to our goal B; take a point out there, D [off the line AB]. Now if we bend the line a bit from C to D then we can bend it a little further, to another point E and if we can bend it to CE that will get us around Cathal Brugha which is what we want!' How could you talk to a man like that?

De Valera was, of course, caught at the fault line between the emergent democratic civic order and the moral community represented by the Public Band. He was to condemn the Treaty out of hand, and went with the anti-Treaty IRA. To anticipate events, he ended up nominal president of an IRA republic but actually a captive of the IRA.

The IRA convention of 26 March 1922 took place against the express orders of the President of the Dáil government, Arthur Griffith, and was, in republican terms, a mutiny; however, it saw itself as defending a republic that the Dáil majority had betrayed. It decided to prevent an election taking place as long as an alleged threat of war was being made by the British. In parenthesis, it should be noted that Collins emphatically denied that the British ever made such a threat; the original allegation came from Robert Barton after he changed sides on the Treaty.

Three southern leaders, Seán O'Hegarty, Florence O'Donoghue, and Tom Hales, did, significantly, dissent from the IRA decision.

Mellows remembered that O'Hegarty 'expressed the view that the Free State was inevitable.' Mellows went on to write that the three 'waverers'

> declared they would not obey any orders designed to prevent the elections. They were officers with great ability with great influence in the 1st Southern Division [of the IRA]. There was little use preventing elections in some places if they were to be allowed to take place in others.

The three mutineers within a mutiny were closely in touch with Mulcahy and the Beggar's Bush forces of the Provisional Government. Desperate attempts to patch up the irreparable breach continued throughout April and May.

On 12 April the *Freeman's Journal* despairingly reported a slide into civil war and pleaded with the anti-Treatyites to obey the Dáil government and the evident wish of the majority for peace and compromise.

> Ireland faces the prospect of a civil war, a war not between Irish and British, not between Orange and Green, which would have been evil enough, but between the comrades-in-arms of yesterday, whose differences are not of principle or aim, but merely of method.[14]

De Valera slid into incoherence at times in mid-1922. On 15 April, at a public meeting, he declaimed a denunciation of reason in politics that has since been mercifully forgotten:

> Young men and young women of Ireland, hold steadily on. Those who with cries of woe and lamentation would involve you in a disastrous rout you will soon see rally behind you and vie with you for first place in the vanguard. Beyond all telling is the destiny God has in mind for Ireland the fair—the peerless one. You are the artificers of that destiny. Yours is the faith that moves mountains—the faith that confounds cowardly reason and its thousand misgivings. Yours is the faith that begot the enterprise of Easter 1916. Young men and young women of Ireland, the goal is at last in sight. Steady, all together, forward. Ireland is yours for the taking. Take it.

Here de Valera is speaking to the Public Band rather than to the Irish people, and in terms that clearly reflect the dislike of sceptical reasoning that permeated Irish Catholicism at the time; reason, being only the weak weapon of mortal human minds, could not give you the truth. Truth could only be understood through faith, which was a gift from God and therefore superior to human reason. De Valera was transposing a religious belief system into the world of secular politics.

According to Liam Deasy, de Valera met the men of the south the day before Collins was killed and asked them to surrender, either because of a genuine wish for peace or because he thought defeat was inevitable. He seems to have been extraordinarily ambivalent in his thinking, and his behaviour seems to reflect this. He nearly said as much. For example, on 6 September 1922, nine momentous months after ratification, he met Richard Mulcahy secretly in Dublin in a priest's house. This was an extraordinary thing for either man to do, as each was now a leading figure on opposite sides in a civil war. However, the conflict in some ways resembled an enormous and vicious family quarrel rather than an ordinary war, a quarrel within which many leading figures desperately tried to achieve compromise. Mulcahy put it to de Valera that the IRA had mutinied against the Dáil and that the civil government had to control the military arm. De Valera patently did not control the anti-Treaty IRA. He said, either on that occasion or on another at nearly the same time:

> Some men are led by faith, others are led by reason, but as long as there were men of faith like Rory O'Connor taking the stand that he was taking, he [de Valera] was a humble soldier following after.[15]

De Valera was already showing signs of his legendary ability to speak simultaneously to the men of faith and the men of reason, to address the two sides of the deeply divided Irish political mind. In chapter 5 I will offer a picture of this divided political culture. De Valera later developed an unrivalled ability to live at the same time in the pre-political and romantic psychic world of the Public Band and the rational-legal world of civic politics and to combine in himself the twin political principles of passion and cunning. He could indeed look into his own heart and see the will of the Irish people. In 1921–22 he was learning fast, but not quite fast enough to save Ireland from a crippling civil war. He had not yet quite discovered politics, as distinct from the romantic posturing that had passed for politics in pre-Treaty Ireland.

THE DISCOVERY OF POLITICS

The Anglo-Irish Treaty gave dominion status within the British Empire and Commonwealth to twenty-six of the thirty-two counties, containing at that time nearly three-quarters of the population of the island. Northern Ireland, already operating as a working political system since 1920, was included in the new Irish Free State but was to retain its 1920 status until the Free State came into legal being at the end of 1922, a year after the signing of the Treaty. Before the year was up, Northern Ireland was to have the right to choose between joining the Free State and retaining its 1920 status as part of the United Kingdom. To anticipate events again, Northern Ireland chose not to join a country that was not only Catholic and presumably hostile to the Protestant community but was also apparently sinking into chaos. Instead, it opted to set up a Protestant-dominated sub-state in which Catholics were heavily subordinated to Protestant popular power, commonly expressed in Public Band terms. Murderous pogroms against Catholics, often encouraged by persons in authority or even perpetrated by the police, happened in 1920–22, and vicious retaliation by the IRA also occurred. However, events in the North rapidly became separated from the fundamentally different contest that was going on in the twenty-six counties.

In effect, the Treaty gave the twenty-six counties independence under essentially republican democratic institutions. However, this fact had to be disguised from British royalist and imperialist opinion. Unfortunately, this exercise in deceit also succeeded in convincing many Irish that the independence that had been won was illusory. There was an oath in the document, later to be watered down somewhat, which the anti-Treatyites untruthfully labelled the 'Oath of Allegiance' in a marvellous lie of silence that has become institutionalised in Irish popular culture. The oath actually required Dáil deputies to swear allegiance to the Constitution of the Irish Free State and to swear *fidelity* to the

British monarch in his capacity as head of the British Commonwealth. This oath was, of course, to be the rock the movement split on. The symbols of monarchy in the Treaty, there to comfort English opinion and to deceive it as to the status of the new polity, actually succeeded in deceiving much of Sinn Féin and the IRA, who saw, or claimed they saw, a puppet state being erected on Irish soil.

The Dáil and Provisional Governments of early 1922 were utterly dependent on the good will of the IRA, which was far more loyal to itself than to any notional parliament, whether 'Free State' or 'Republican'. All de Valera's later casuistry about the Second Dáil as the last true Dáil could not disguise this. Andrews remembered:

> On a country-wide basis the IRA were in the main anti-Treaty. They began to remember that they were Volunteers with an executive which was their governing body; they owed allegiance to the Dáil only as the government of the Republic. There was an alternative course of action to be resorted to if the Dáil failed them.[16]

Actually, the IRA were more evenly divided than Andrews remembered, and many became studiously neutral in the dispute. Some of the IRA, especially in the south and part of the west, behaved as if they owned the country by dint of moral status, being fighting men; their political authority was derived, of course, not from popular suffrage but from their demonstrated or putative courage and loyalty to the republican cause. The absence of British pressure during the Truce period demoralised much of the IRA. No more fighting was expected, to be in the IRA was very prestigious and even profitable, arms were coming in to the country, but discipline and training slipped. New, unblooded recruits, the 'Trucileers' or 'sunshine soldiers', queued up to join. The Treaty, and the claims made by Griffith and Collins on their loyalty, made their already uncertain civic spirit even weaker. Andrews remembered that 'discipline was rapidly deteriorating in the local units of the IRA.' People began to feel unsafe 'in the enjoyment of their property and their freedom of movement.' At the same time the vast bulk of the population contentedly assumed that the peace of 11 July 1921 was permanent.[17]

The acceptance of the Treaty not only shattered the Public Band, it also started a long process by which groups and individuals began to emerge from a pre-political condition into an often reluctant and painful realisation of the necessity for a political process and a further realisation of the desirability that this process be an open, law-bound and democratic one; a true republic possessed such a politics by definition. The growing conviction of the urgent necessity for creating a democratic political order in the midst of the growing and seemingly unstoppable disorder in 1921–22 was eventually to result in desperation on the part of the pro-Treaty leaders, ensconced in power by the dual mandate of the republican Dáil Éireann and the British-created Provisional Government of Ireland provided for under the Treaty.

This desperation led to the use of force to suppress the mutinying IRA in Dublin in June 1922 and subsequently in the rest of the twenty-six counties. Most notoriously, the government executed out of hand four well-known anti-Treaty leaders, held prisoner since the fall of the Four Courts. This was a reaction to the gunning down in the streets by the IRA of two pro-Treaty deputies. To be an active member of the Dáil was to be physically in danger, and it appeared as though the entire ramshackle structure of the nascent Irish democracy might collapse under the guns of the IRA. Oddly, being under threat added to the prestige of being a Dáil deputy and encouraged people to take the new politicians rather more seriously; the political culture of the period rather admired physical bravery.

In reaction to the first executions, Liam Lynch issued a directive on 30 November 1922 that ordered the IRA to kill all members of the Dáil who had voted for the executions, to burn down their houses and those of their supporters, all aggressive and active Free State army officers, and all former British officers and men who had joined the Free State army since the signing of the Treaty.

Nearly eighty captured republicans found in arms were executed after courts-martial by the Free State in 1922–23. In Kerry, some horrific murders were committed by the Dublin Guards of the Free State army, a military formation whose core was Michael Collins's old active service unit. This unit was, incidentally, much disliked by the rest of the Free State army, which generally treated prisoners well and also got on well with the local population.

A Hobbesian sense of the necessity of imposing political order to permit democratic life to begin in the Free State gripped the minds of William Cosgrave, Kevin O'Higgins, Richard Mulcahy and Ernest Blythe in late 1922.

Their fears were not unrealistic. The IRA, theoretically defending the Republic against Irish traitors, was under no civil government's control. It was run by its local commanders and was now far more heavily armed than it had been during the Anglo-Irish war. Under cover of its political status, many individuals and units engaged in looting, house-burnings, land-grabbing, murder, and, occasionally, rape. There was considerable illegal property transfer during the conflict, and a tacit amnesty for most crimes had apparently to be made subsequently by the Free State.

FROM GUERRILLA REPUBLIC TO CIVILIAN FREE STATE

The events of 1921–23 saw the beginning of a domestic Irish politics of a kind that had never previously existed. The transition from the non-politics of a British dependency to the politics of independence was extremely painful, long drawn out, and confused. It was also accompanied in the later 1920s and afterwards by an elaborate rhetorical campaign designed to disguise the fact that the defeated anti-Treaty forces were gradually accepting Free State democracy. During the first, most crucial phase, from July 1921 to May 1923, one regime faded out and another gradually asserted itself among conditions of great social and constitutional disorder.

In what passes for republican political theory, the central institution of the underground Irish 'state' of 1919–22 was indeed Dáil Éireann, subject only to the consent of the people as expressed through elections. This assembly had, in January 1919, proclaimed the independence of a semi-imaginary but very determinedly imagined nation-state styled, in Irish, Saorstát Éireann (literally, Irish Free State) and in English, Republic of Ireland. The 1916 proclamation had, however, used an alternative and older term, Poblacht na hÉireann. David Lloyd George spotted this linguistic ambiguity and offered the Irish the title of 'Irish Free State' to avoid any obvious republican symbolism while giving the Irish the substance of what they wanted.

Under the 1919 constitution of the Republic, copied from the British model of the period, the Dáil was evidently sovereign, subject only to the ultimate authority of the people as expressed in elections. The Republic was not mentioned in the constitution, and it could not be argued logically that the Dáil had no right to disestablish the Republic and replace it with the Free State. Under the 1919 constitution the Dáil could do, in effect, whatever it liked. Furthermore, it could not bind itself by passing a law or decree; all such ordinances were instantly reversible by a vote of the Dáil. In any event, the cultural reality was that republican 'law' counted for little and the solidarity of the Public Band for much. The Public Band *was* the Republic, in its own eyes at least. Michael Hayes, writing decades later, recalled:

> It is to be remembered that the Army was an unpaid volunteer force which was in existence before the Dáil, and which, as a condition to coming under its jurisdiction had insisted on all the members of the Dáil taking the oath of allegiance to the Republic.[18]

If the deputies were far-sighted enough to take the 1919 oath in Irish, they would actually have been taking it to an Irish Free State, linguistically speaking. However, the true language of nationalist politics was English. Incidentally, the notepaper, signed by de Valera, that was used to give the Republic's plenipotentiaries their credentials was headed *Saorstát Éireann/Respublica Hibernia*. Names meant less than they seemed to mean.

The real problem was, as argued earlier, the increasing uncontrollability of the IRA during late 1921 and early 1922. Cathal Brugha, as Minister for Defence in the Dáil government, tacitly acknowledged that this was so by acceding during the Truce period to the suggestion that the IRA, a territorial, volunteer guerrilla force, be replaced by a regular, non-territorial, professional army. This crucial decision, by which the Public Band was to be replaced by a force controlled by civilians responsible to the Dáil, marks the beginning of the transition to genuine statehood from the semi-imaginary underground republic of 1919. The new army was to be governed by rational-legal principles rather than by local anthropological links of loyalty. This decision also marks the beginning of the slide into civil war and occurred long before the Treaty was signed. It is worth some closer examination than it has normally been given by historians.

Richard Mulcahy, chief of staff of the IRA, was contacted by Brugha in early November 1921 about the proposed new army, and it was tentatively scheduled to come into existence on 25 November 1921. Brugha asked Mulcahy to become chief of staff under his Ministry of Defence. Mulcahy agreed. This decision was confirmed at a joint meeting of the GHQ Staff of the IRA and the Dáil cabinet on 25 November 1921. Significantly, Arthur Griffith and Michael Collins were in London at the time. Austin Stack was to be deputy chief of staff, thus demoting and humiliating Eoin O'Duffy, who reacted shrilly to being replaced by an ally of de Valera who was manifestly less competent. De Valera, the prime minister of the putative Republic, got up and, in a 'half-scream, half-shout', declared: 'Ye may mutiny if ye like, but Ireland will give me another army.'[19]

De Valera thought that the men of the west and the south were willing to resume fighting the British if he ordered them to do so. Totting up the figures, and weighing the personalities and abilities of the new GHQ Staff (Mulcahy, Stack, O'Duffy, Collins, and Brugha), he presumably saw instantly that he would not be able to control this new post-IRA Irish army, eventually to materialise as the army of the Irish Free State in January 1922. De Valera himself thought little of the intelligence of Brugha, although well aware of his physical bravery. Brugha had continued to earn his living as a chandler throughout the Anglo-Irish conflict and had been bypassed by Collins in the organisation. In effect, Brugha, an older man than the average revolutionary, was part-time and never quite came to terms with the fact that Collins and his cohorts were full-time at this monstrous game of revolutionary politics.

Stack was a poor administrator and had been treated by Collins with a genial contempt, a contempt that he deeply resented. Mulcahy, on the other hand, was close to Collins and an excellent organiser. O'Duffy, also an ally of Collins, was also a good administrator and an accomplished conspirator. Michael Hayes recalled that Collins and the others were good revolutionaries because they combined the abilities of soldiers and those of civil servants, keeping files meticulously and organising information about large numbers of people on all sides of the conflict. Sighle Humphreys remarked to me in the mid-1980s that whoever had put a bullet through Michael Collins's head in August 1922 had 'killed the Republic. He kept it all in his head.' Actually he also used a filing system, but she had, of course, a very good point. De Valera had realised that his allies, Brugha and Stack, were too weak as instruments to use against Collins. Stack hated and envied Collins, and Brugha was publicly hostile to him. The distrust between the two groups of men was total, and de Valera, whose ability to express or echo the passions and suspicions of others was extraordinary, was reciprocally very suggestible to those very passions and suspicions. It is also clear that he feared and resented Collins.

One very logical and understandable source of de Valera's mistrust of Griffith and Collins was the latter's secretive behaviour. Notoriously, Collins had bypassed the formal Dáil government structures and was running the finances and much of the military campaign himself. It also appears that he was, ostensibly without de Valera's knowledge, in touch with the British long before the Truce of July 1921. In old age a British historian informed him that Collins and Griffith had been talking to senior British civil servants in the spring of that year in London. De Valera muttered, 'After I had returned from America. I wonder were they double-crossing me even then, those two.'[20]

Desmond FitzGerald, using information supplied by Dan Nolan of the *Kerryman*, argued years later that Stack was particularly responsible for hardening de Valera's attitude towards the Treaty. Stack could be seen as representing in particular the Men of the South, who were to compose the core of the 'Army of the Republic', putatively resisting the 'British' army of the Irish Free State. In reviewing Frank Pakenham's *Peace by Ordeal*, a generally pro-de Valera work, FitzGerald commented that even Pakenham, who revered de Valera as a great Catholic statesman in a time of a general European crisis of Catholicism, communism, and fascism, recognised Brugha's and Stack's essentially personal and pre-political hatred of Collins. However, neither FitzGerald nor Pakenham quite came out and said what so many quietly believed: de Valera simply could not cope with Collins's decisiveness, realism, and ability to learn quickly. When the Treaty was brought back from London, de Valera, in a crucial act, denounced it publicly out of hand.

One of the delegates spoke to Stack after the Treaty was brought home. 'I did not think he [de Valera] was against this kind of settlement before we went to London.' Stack says he replied 'He's dead against it now, anyway. That's enough.' The stress was on the word 'now.' It was a cry of triumph.

Nolan was informed by Stack's niece, who was a witness, that Brugha and Stack met de Valera after the signing and before the delegates had returned to Dublin. De Valera at that juncture apparently actually supported the Treaty. According to the niece, who was acting as secretary to the meeting, Stack managed to change the prime minister's mind. If this account is true, the Civil War in a sense both started and ended in Kerry hatred; Stack was a Kerryman. The relationships between different groups involved in the independence movement can usefully be envisaged as mapped in fig. 1.

FIG. 1

Irish separatist politics, December 1921

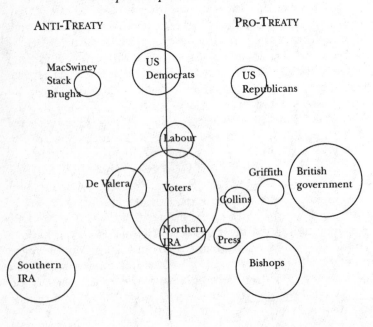

The arguments over the oath and the reality of Irish sovereignty were later to be drowned in the rattle of rifles. De Valera's decision to oppose the Treaty was, however, crucial and must have severely aggravated the violence of the subsequent year and a half. Many Sinn Féin and IRA seem initially to have taken a pragmatic approach to the Treaty, including many who were afterwards violently anti-Treaty. One epiphanic incident is a meeting between two Dublin IRA men, Liam Archer and Rory O'Connor, immediately after the signing of the Treaty in London. Archer quizzed O'Connor on his attitude to the Treaty, and O'Connor said:

> 'Oh we must work it for all it's worth,' then after a slight pause he added 'But if I could get enough to support me I would oppose it wholeheartedly.'[21]

O'Connor, of course, later became a particularly prominent leader of the would-be IRA political junta. Archer went pro-Treaty, in part because of this conversation.

> As I saw the situation deteriorate [after 6 December] and realised that O'Connor's objective was to create a situation wherein the British would have reason to return in force for the purpose of establishing 'Law and Order' and we would be plunged into complete submission again, or complete anarchy, I made my decision.[22]

The Treaty was ratified by Dáil Éireann on 7 January 1922. The Free State was not to come into legal existence until 6 December. In the interim the Republic was to continue in existence, Arthur Griffith replacing de Valera as prime minister. De Valera, as we have seen, went into an enraged opposition. Alongside the Dáil government was ranged a Provisional Government of Ireland as provided by the Treaty, with mainly identical personnel to the Dáil cabinet, the major exception being that Collins became Griffith's opposite number. This Provisional Government, with the consent of the Dáil majority, proceeded to take over the British administrative apparatus and to merge the Dáil administration with it, a long and tortuous process. Collins also became commander-in-chief of the new Free State army, which was put together rapidly in 1922 from elements of the IRA, disbanded Irish regiments from the British army, and young men with no IRA background. The IRA began to harden in hostility to the Treaty. Fear, and incomprehension, of rational-legal power was a major factor in generating the huge suspicion the anti-Treatyites had of the settlement. Hayes recalled: 'Nobody who belonged to us for generations back had ever been in authority.'

Ernest Blythe remarked with his characteristic coldness in late 1922:

> The first step towards progress is a clear recognition of the fact that, instead of being a race of super-idealists whose misfortunes are due entirely to the crimes and blunders of outside enemies, we are an untrained and undisciplined people with practically everything to learn of the difficult business of organising national life on a stable basis . . . We are marching into freedom ankle-deep in blood, and by all signs we are likely to go still deeper.[23]

The attitude towards the Irish people as being essentially unworthy of their heroic leaders, which so permeated the anti-Treaty side, existed in a rather different form on the pro-Treaty side as well. Richard Mulcahy, interestingly, was a notable exception. Throughout his life he consistently held to the view that the ordinary people of Ireland would always get their politics right in the long run, if given half a chance. William Cosgrave also very evidently shared this view. As founders of Irish democracy, Cosgrave and Mulcahy have been profoundly underrated. However, the unease about the idea that the Irish people might be capable of running their own show was also widespread. Cosgrave, for example, wanted an anonymous letter discussed at Executive Council level in February 1923, which, among other things, suggested importing German officers to train the permanent Free State army:

> I don't think it possible for a country newly started to organise itself from within. The Japs, who, of all races, are most amenable to discipline, had to be trained by outsiders, and so must we who stand at the opposite pole in regard to that quality.

In fact some Reichswehr officers were indeed imported to train the new army, and Irish army parade drill for years afterwards echoed German rather than British practice, in a typical nationalist attempt to 'look different'. German NCO rank stripes and German-style trench helmets, made in England, were made standard. However, most organising ability in the new state was native, not foreign.

Many supporters of the Treaty looked at the mental culture of the Irish with great unease. Francis Hackett wrote in 1924:

> As I see myself, and therefore my fellow countrymen, our fault is our resistance to facts . . . We insist on our idealism, to the obliteration of fact. We bully the man who dares to mention the existence of facts we don't like . . . We need our ideality to warm us up, and to enable us to stamp out our wicked opponent. And we are ready for this reason to have all sorts of secret understandings, a hierarchy of loyalties, a system of concealments and emotional understandings, which makes intellectual honesty impossible. The art of criticism, which is the political art, does not exist. Ireland is pre-political. And as long as it is loyal to men rather than ideas it will remain as pre-political as America . . . The men in prison are in the religious state still. And it will take a long time to de-bamboozle them . . . I have a splendid and passionate belief in draining the swamp of the Irish mind . . . But it is a job that can only be done by insiders. To make Ireland into a state—that is the job. And in our lifetime it won't be finished. It will take two generations. But twenty men could start it. And it will have to be done without guns.

From a very different quarter came a similar observation. Towards the end of the Civil War, Cardinal Logue announced sadly:

> The state of the country embitters what little remnant of life it may please God still to leave me . . . I never thought I should live to see so many young and promising lives sacrificed for a mere dream, and a great part of the country reduced to the ruin and desolation in which we now find it, and that by her own sons . . . Never before in the world's history did such a

wild and destructive hurricane spring from such a thin, intangible, insubstantial vapour.

An insecure and inexperienced elite found itself presiding over a population that wanted unheroic things. It was faced by an equally inexperienced 'counter-elite' that often shared its less than complimentary opinion of the population. Irish democracy was founded by unenthusiastic and rather authoritarian democrats, who combined within their minds an almost hysterical acceptance of electoral democracy and a rather bossy paternalism that contradicted their rhetorical democratic convictions. This latter trait was eventually to undo them ten years later, as the Irish democracy that they created with great foresight and courage ground them down, put them into opposition, and handed itself over to their arch-enemy.[24]

3

The Dáil Government and Local Democracy, 1919–23

To grasp the significance of de Valera's rage and frustration when he found that he had been not so much outsmarted as swamped by people who knew how to run a guerrilla war and a government of sorts, it is useful to look at the nature of local electoral democracy. Irish local government was effectively a construction inherited by the Dáil government from the British and, in turn, by the succeeding Provisional and Free State governments in 1922. De Valera's extraordinary tantrum must in part have been provoked by a sense that he had not so much been betrayed as bested by people who had a hands-on understanding of the emergent political system. At the heart of this system as taken over by Sinn Féin in 1920 were William Cosgrave and Kevin O'Higgins, both of whom were to become early pillars of the Free State government. Whereas de Valera had the allegiance of the guerrilla army, at least as long as he opposed the Treaty, the Free State had the immediate allegiance of the vast bulk of the civilian local authorities.

As 'Tip' O'Neill, the Irish-American politician and Speaker of the US House of Representatives, once remarked, all experienced politicians know that all democratic politics is, in the final analysis, local. Twentieth-century Ireland, north and south alike, has certainly offered no conspicuous exception to this generalisation. In fact one of the constants of Irish political life and of debates in modern Irish political science has been the series of desperate and only very partially successful attempts on the part of central government in Dublin to resist the pressure from local interests. I have characterised the process by which the counties gang up on the centre in terms derived from Stein Rokkan: the periphery-dominated centre. Typically, policy-makers have tried to shield the policy process by means of centralised administrative systems. The birth of the Irish state in circumstances of siege reinforced this tendency immeasurably. Despite this pronounced centripetal tendency, the pressures of localism have often succeeded in drowning any chance of rational policy-making. Furthermore, the reasons for the pronounced centralism of Irish government lie precisely in the overweening pressure from the counties on it; Irish centralism is a sign not of strength but of weakness.

Local representative political institutions long antedated the establishment of a national parliament. Eighteenth and early nineteenth-century Ireland had a dense network of local authorities, generally controlled by the local gentry and increasingly, as time went on and as the Catholic masses accumulated collective power, bypassed and rendered redundant by British-backed central authority. The culmination of this process was the abolition of the landlord-dominated local government system. Modern quasi-democratic local councils were established throughout the country in 1898–99 in a sweeping measure of reform. This simple chronological fact had a profound long-term effect on the structure of the democratic political process in the new state that emerged between 1919 and 1923. Under the Local Government Act, 1898, the old landlord-dominated grand juries were abolished, as were the Baronial Presentment Sessions. Boards of guardians, although obsolescent, were to survive until the coming of the Free State. County and 'county borough' (city) councils, elected periodically under a ratepayers' franchise that gave the vote to a substantial proportion of the adult population, were substituted for the old system in a sweeping set of reforms. At an even more local level, and subject to more central and county-level supervision, were established rural district councils and urban district councils for the medium-sized and smaller towns.

In a conciliatory gesture towards the landlord class that had just lost economic and political power, and, possibly, in a minatory one towards the owner-occupier farmers and peasantry who were taking over after the Land War, the duty of paying rates (local government property taxes) was transferred in 1898 from the legal owner to the occupier of the property. Essentially this was in recognition of the realities of post-Parnell Ireland. Farmers and peasantry became, in effect, owners of the land, but in legal theory they were still often tenantry; however, whether legally owners or tenants, as occupiers they had to pay to finance the new local democracy. They commonly did so with bad grace. Irish local democracy arguably got off to a very bad start in 1898.[1]

In the early years of the new century the General Council of County Councils established itself as a sort of unofficial Irish parliament and became, in many ways, the prototype for the Dáil Éireann of the post-1919 era. The democratisation of local government also had the effect of dividing Ireland into areas controlled, for many purposes, by the nationalist and unionist political forces that dominated the country. This control was even clearer after 1898 than it had been previously. Each worked to exclude the other from its own electoral bailiwick. In a sense, the partition of Ireland dates not from 1920 but from 1898, and the tacit, if sometimes truculent, acceptance of partition by so many Sinn Féin leaders in 1922 was derived from a long habituation to the partition of local government into Orange and Green local areas. This *de facto* partition was already traditional by 1920 and more or less coincided geographically with the much-denounced actual partition of 1920. The partition of 1920 did, admittedly, leave Derry city and large rural areas with Catholic majorities on the northern side of the frontier.

The 1898 Act also had the incidental effect of setting up a permanent antagonism between local nationalists (and, occasionally, unionists) and the British government's Local Government Board, a central co-ordinating and grant-aiding body that gave generous financial assistance to the local authorities and attempted to curb their more extravagant essays in local preference and spendthrift schemes. The Local Government Board sat in much-resented Georgian splendour in the Custom House in Dublin, a building renowned as Gandon's masterpiece.[2]

The new councils rapidly came under electoral and other local pressure to become providers of relief, employment, and patronage. In particular, the older, often more efficient system of contracting out road maintenance to private firms was rapidly replaced in most of the country by a 'direct labour' system, by which the local authorities employed workers directly.[3] With generous grants from the British government, the local councils also ran an impressively widespread local hospital system, regularly denounced as extravagant by Sinn Féin politicians angling for the ratepayers' votes. The councils also administered the widely despised workhouse system, which was held responsible, with some reason, for the general demoralisation of the local population and, historically, for much of the mortality associated with the Great Famine of 1847.[4]

Recruitment to dispensary doctor positions, clerkships and local government officer posts was controlled at local level, ordinary civil service rules often did not apply, and patronage appointments were common. At a humbler level, impoverished men often enjoyed a menial and unsecured livelihood as road gangers, workers, doormen and attendants at county and more local institutions. Rules concerning tenure and status varied wildly from county to county. Pay scales at senior level were often very high, and these posts were widely coveted. Even at the lowest levels, pay scales in local government commonly represented a substantial improvement on the normal income of farm labourers or unskilled town workers. In a relatively impoverished country, local government seemed like a lifebelt to many people, and there was considerable pressure on the councils to favour local people who had influential connections with church, business, or politics. The control over local shenanigans exercised by the Local Government Board was rather weak, in part because of the considerable political influence wielded at Westminster by both nationalist and unionist political leaders and also because of the general British philosophy in post-Parnell Ireland of letting sleeping Irish dogs lie.

Resentment of and contempt for the perceived corruption of local authorities was widespread in Sinn Féin and the other groups of nationalist and socialist radicals that emerged at the beginning of the new century. These attitudes animated much of Sinn Féin's drive towards reform, centralisation, and standardisation of employment conditions. In general, the Sinn Féiners wished to clean up what were seen, with some accuracy, as local Tammany Halls and as being unworthy of the idealistic visions of either the founders of Sinn Féin or the martyrs of Easter Week.

After the 1918 election the Irish Party's hegemony at national level was inherited by Sinn Féin, and it was obvious that the old party's domination of the local authorities was doomed to pass eventually to the new party. This duly happened in June and July 1920. The stage was set for a grand confrontation between the young, aggressive and militarised puritans of Sinn Féin and the local nationalist establishments.

The character of this confrontation was, however, transformed, ironically enough, by the British government's settled policy of denying any belligerent status to the IRA and its insistence on treating the cost of damage inflicted on people and property under the provisions of the Malicious Injuries Act. In effect this meant that damage done by the IRA, the British army and the Black and Tans could be charged to the rates, levied at county level and paid by property-owners and related to the property valuation system known as Griffith's valuation. This did not matter too much at the beginning of the Anglo-Irish War, as British exchequer grants softened the blow and ensured that the rates bills did not get intolerably high in 1919 and early 1920; understandably, the British began to get tired of subsidising a shooting war aimed at dislodging them from power in Ireland.

A crucial decision of the British government in July 1920 coincided with the victory of Sinn Féin and its Labour allies in the local elections. The Chief Secretary's office in Dublin Castle and the Local Government Board announced that the annual grants in aid payable to augment local authorities' income would be withheld if the councils did not accept fully the authority of the British government and recognise the authority of the Local Government Board. As in the matter of disarming of the police, which I deal with later, this decision illustrates vividly the utter remoteness of the British administration from the realities of Irish life. This remoteness was often echoed on the other side; in a sense, what was happening in 1919–23 was a competitive search by the British, the moderate Irish and the 'republicans' for the support of the people. The moderates were to win.

THE DÁIL DEPARTMENT OF LOCAL GOVERNMENT

Partly in reaction to this British act, the underground Dáil government set up its own Department of Local Government under the noses of the British. William T. Cosgrave became Minister for Local Government, with Kevin O'Higgins as his deputy. Cosgrave had had considerable experience with local government on

Dublin City Council. The British policy of putting war damage costs on the rates had the effect of forcing the ratepayers, on average rather more conservative in politics than the general population, to foot the costs of the entire IRA campaign. The decision had the further effect of pushing a considerable number of naturally cautious and relatively propertied people into the arms of Sinn Féin and of the Dáil government. All county and most borough councils in the twenty-six counties of 'Southern Ireland' recognised the Dáil government's Department of Local Government almost a year before the Truce of July 1921 and nearly a year and a half before the Treaty. The northern councils were enjoined or forced to transfer their allegiance to Belfast, even when they had nationalist majorities, as they had in Fermanagh, Tyrone, and Derry city.

The dramatic transfer of official allegiances of local authorities in the twenty-six counties was in part due to the authoritarianism and political incompetence of the British and to an already noticed general characteristic of British governments' political behaviour in Ireland: a propensity to veer between a complacent and open-handed negligence and an interfering bossiness, with little ability to strike a happy mean.

Cosgrave and O'Higgins found themselves, in effect, running a local government system under the noses of the Castle and the Custom House. Correspondence to the Local Government Board largely ceased, and a secret postal system was devised by Dáil officials. Letters between local authorities and the Dáil Department of Local Government were dealt with by a double-envelope system: an innocent-looking private address in Dublin was used, and in the house was a secret Dáil post office that opened the outside envelope, sorted the second envelope, and sent it on to the appropriate department by Dáil courier.

The Dáil Department of Local Government found itself fighting a two-front battle, against the British government and its Local Government Board on the one hand and against local voters, ratepayers, vested local interests and entrenched councillors and officials on the other; these local interests sometimes had the paradoxical sympathy of the government-hating local IRA, as shall be explained. The Dáil's reaction to the ensuing withdrawal of British grants to the councils was twofold: an eloquent denunciation of British thievishness and knavishness combined

with a wide-ranging set of proposals for economy in local administration. Small local 'cottage' hospitals, deemed to be 'uneco-
nomic' and 'extravagant', were to be closed down. The notorious
workhouses were announced to be demeaning and expensive
and were also to be shut down. Instead, a rather sensible system
of at-home relief ('home assistance') that preserved the individual's dignity while saving the taxpayers' money was proposed and
eventually implemented. In a country of declining population,
proposals of this kind made a considerable amount of sense;
much of the rural relief and health system had been heavily
funded by the 'killing home rule with kindness' policy of government hand-outs, and the hospitals and workhouses were
commonly half-empty. They were also commonly overstaffed;
staff apparently were commonly connections of—depending on
area—the United Irish League or the Conservative and Unionist
Party: Hibernians on one side, Freemasons on the other. At least,
this was the way it appeared in the eyes of Sinn Féin.

The Dáil also considered reforming or even abolishing the
direct labour system used for mending roads. A certain ambiguity
about this seems to reflect an acute awareness that many of the
IRA's fighting men and local Sinn Féin supporters counted on this
work to maintain themselves. An immediate problem was the collection of rates. The collection of rates by the Dáil was, naturally,
quite illegal under British law, and Dáil rate collectors were regularly arrested by the RIC and jailed. Dáil rate collection had to be
done clandestinely. The unfortunate ratepayers found themselves
serving two taxation systems. The IRA and its rather weak creature,
the Irish Republican Police, had the formal duty of enforcing the
collection of Dáil rates but tended to have other things on their
minds. After all, many IRA were themselves ratepayers or the sons
of ratepayers. However, the Dáil government succeeded in carrying on a fair simulacrum of legal and democratic local government in extremely adverse circumstances, convincing a lot of
people that the Dáil was here to stay, as indeed it was.

A general resistance to the paying of Dáil rates developed, much
of it organised centrally from Dublin by a nascent ratepayers' association. In later years a direct descendant of this organisation
was to feature in local elections until swamped, after 1934, by a
new adult franchise introduced by de Valera's lieutenant, Seán
T. O'Kelly. However, in 1919–22 ratepayer resistance was often

very strong and effective, particularly in the more remote, poorer and 'republican' counties, that is, counties with an active IRA. As already suggested, the local IRA commonly sympathised with the resistance to ratepaying and often helped to organise it, accurately reflecting the farmers' traditional hatred of taxation and reluctance to pay for government, as distinct from getting hand-outs from it. The RIC's efforts against the Dáil collectors may possibly have had the tacit approval of their military opponents in the IRA on occasion; for obvious reasons, evidence for such a structurally probable situation is difficult to find.

The Dáil department's economy proposals were implemented to a surprising degree, even before the Treaty was signed, much of the programme being initiated long before the Truce of July 1921. To a surprising extent, in the area of local government in particular, Dáil government ceased rapidly being another Irish exercise in 'let's pretend' and became an everyday reality outside Dublin and some of the bigger towns, where the old regime hung on, often with the support of labour. As British military traffic and IRA road-block operations between them chewed up the increasingly underfinanced and neglected road system, local hospitals were quietly closed down and patients evacuated to the new 'county hospitals', while the indigent were either removed to the 'county homes' that were being carved out of the workhouses or sent home and given home assistance. By the time the Treaty was signed and ratified by the Dáil in January 1922, implementation was well advanced, and local acceptance of the Dáil government was general, including acceptance of the Treaty itself; an overwhelming majority of 26-county county and borough councils formally approved of the Treaty in December 1921 and January 1922, allegedly at Cosgrave's behest but more probably because of genuine war-weariness and revulsion against the behaviour of the local IRA.

W. T. Cosgrave's role in the extraordinary achievement of taking over bodily the British local government system in the south was central and deserves more examination than it has hitherto had. A circular to the local authorities written by him was issued very early on. A version of the circular sent to Dublin County Council spelt out the situation as it was seen by him in September 1920. British policy, he wrote, entailed impossibly high rates, particularly in counties where the IRA were very energetic. A

British-owned hosiery factory in Balbriggan burned down by the Black and Tans had lodged a claim for £62,000 with Dublin County Council. There was no question of the council paying it, as, Cosgrave observed, the Dublin Union and the Richmond insane asylum would have to be closed down to pay the bill. 'The people of Ireland', he proclaimed, 'are not merely to have their throats cut [by the British], they are to be charged for the knife.' He admitted that rates were considerably higher than they had been before the June and July local elections and before the withdrawal of the British subsidies, but he averred that 'under the auspices of the Local Government Department of Dáil Éireann great and far-reaching schemes of economy and reform are being embarked upon.'[5] Irish thrift was to take the place of British extravagance; some would put it, unkindly, as Irish meanness replacing British generosity.

The double-envelope system of centre-local communication worked quite well. Occasionally there was a hiccup; on 22 April 1921, O'Higgins rebuked the town clerk of Listowel, County Kerry, a particularly troublesome county. An open opponent of Sinn Féin, she had openly addressed an envelope to him at his Dublin office. Fortunately the Post Office had been fairly thoroughly subverted by Sinn Féin at this stage. Writing to her, O'Higgins remarked, 'Whether this is due to crass stupidity or malice it is difficult to decide.' He chose to believe the former, possibly inaccurately.[6]

Mutual dislike and political antagonism commonly existed between the Sinn Féiners, both the Dublin group and the local ones, on the one hand and the local establishment, whether unionist, Redmondite, clerical, or simply local Tammany. In some cases, because Sinn Féin councillors were on the run or in jail, Irish Party and unionist councillors and officials were able to obstruct the Dáil government. In February 1921, for example, Meath County Council's secretary had insisted, in the absence of some Sinn Féin members, on obeying the Local Government Board and refused to lodge a rates cheque of £18,000 to the council's account because of its non-recognition of the British authorities. Cosgrave was extremely alarmed at the prospect of the financial collapse of a well-known Sinn Féin local authority so close to Dublin: 'It is the grand slam in Meath if this money cannot be released.'[7]

Meath and Westmeath gave particular trouble, both of them counties with a large strong-farmer presence and also large numbers of landless labourers. On 29 April 1921, Cosgrave wrote to Thomas Foran of the Irish Transport and General Workers' Union and described these two counties as ones that had given the Dáil Department of Local Government exceptional trouble, because

> the Secretaries of both Councils were not loyal to this Department, and that the County Councils have been deprived of some of their best men, some of whom are in jail or on the run renders our difficulties almost insuperable, as in almost all cases the ablest administrators are being prevented from carrying out their duties as public representatives.[8]

Cosgrave had a very clear perception of himself as a Dáil minister and saw himself as far more than a party representative. He saw, for example, the necessity of accommodating non-Sinn Féin elements in the new state. Unlike many members of the Public Band, he saw the Irish people who were not members of Sinn Féin in sympathy as people who would have to be accepted into the new political society and who had full entitlement to citizenship, whatever their politics had been. During the Truce period of July 1921 to January 1922, which had the effect of partially resolving problems of allegiance, he gave Meath County Council a slashing rebuke for firing a nurse not for any professional incompetence but rather for her Redmondite political sympathies and reportedly snobbish attitudes towards Sinn Féiners.[9]

Problems of allegiance surfaced elsewhere as well. In Monaghan, unionists resisted paying rates to a putatively treasonous Sinn Féin council in late 1920, and the Dáil rate collectors were being very successfully harried by the RIC.[10] In Roscommon a very determinedly pro-Dáil council imposed a test of allegiance to Dáil Éireann on its officials in October 1920. As in Meath, the secretary of the council jibbed at this test or oath, claiming that he was being got at by IRA or Sinn Féin councillors, 'who as he thought were trying to avenge themselves on him for giving his motor to the [British] military after Easter Week to round them up.'[11] Cosgrave and O'Higgins generally disliked putting officials under pressure of this sort, on the grounds that it was divisive and unfair to people of special ability and usefulness who happened to be caught up between political forces too big for them to handle. Also, they were acutely aware that Sinn Féin's psychological hold over the people was fragile and conditional: the victories of 1918 and 1920 were due to abnormal political conditions; come peacetime, Sinn Féin would have to deal with large numbers of people whose political sympathies were elsewhere, whether it be with Labour, farmers' interests, or unionist.

For a considerable period in 1919–21 it was unclear whether the Dáil or the IRA would be able to resist what seemed to many to be the overwhelming British military pressure on a fragile military force and on what was a rather flimsy and make-believe political structure. Much of the population, as Kevin O'Higgins admitted subsequently, professed a studied neutrality, keeping their heads down and praying for peace. Under both the British and the independent Irish governments, most of the population wished for a quiet life; there was a lot of covert hostility to the IRA, occasionally expressed in informing but finally to be expressed in the Dáil elections of 1922 and 1923. The welcome given the Free State army and the Civic Guard in 1922–23 described in chapter 4 is ample testimony to this generalisation.

During the Anglo-Irish War, in some cases at least, local officials were clearly waiting to see who would win and played both ends against the middle. The situation in North Tipperary, for example, was described with bitter contempt by a Dáil inspector on 2 January 1921 (dated 1920 in the letter). Even Sinn Féin people, he reported, were afraid to take over from the Local Government Board and obey the Dáil Department of Local Government until they were quite sure there would be no British retaliation. 'Our rate collectors to a man have ratted.' Cosgrave and O'Higgins could not expect too much of the local slavish subculture and were advised not to overlook 'the leaven of Cromwellian blood in North Tipperary.' The inspector wrote despairingly that despite the strenuous efforts of Dáil officials and the heroism of the Public Band,

> young men will not jeopardise their lives. Middle aged and old men will not jeopardise their cash. The towns are hopeless as far as the monied element goes. We may let the road-[mending] men go let the unions go smash but there is no

administrative effort in such proceedings and then we smash
the movement it has taken us 18 years to build up.

He felt that he had, since being inducted into the Irish-Ireland
movement by the legendary poet figure William Rooney two
decades earlier, 'wasted the best years of my life in Sinn Féin.'[12]

The Dáil department's response to reports of this kind was a
circular to the local authorities that amounted to a morale stiff-
ener, probably written by O'Higgins: the banks would probably
try to bribe the councils to go back to their British allegiance,
but the representative councils of the Irish people should stand
firm. Even a general financial collapse would be preferable to the
'moral collapse of a surrender to enemy regulations.'[13] Evasion
was often resorted to as a tactic of resistance. In Wexford in
November 1920 a British attempt to order a council through a
mandamus writ was anticipated and countered, on Dáil department instructions, by the council's hiding the books.[14]

Rates collection remained a chronic, general and apparently
insoluble problem. The IRA felt that they had far better things
to do than to enforce an unpopular levy, and, as mentioned earlier, in many counties the soldiers of the Republic had sympathy
with the resistance to paying any taxes, even to that embattled
Republic. Being a Dáil rate collector could be uncomfortable. In
Carlow a collector got eighteen months' jail from the British
authorities in March 1921.[15] Some local authorities simply gave
up. Kilrush, County Clare, assessed by the Dáil inspector as one of
the worst urban district councils in Ireland, actually handed over
its street-cleaning functions to the local ratepayers' association.[16]

Even during the Truce period of late 1921 the local IRA found
themselves reluctantly enforcing the collection of rates. The
Dublin Farmers' Union openly defied the Dáil collection and
challenged its legality in late 1921.[17] In Donegal, Dáil justices and
IRA officers were actually the leaders of the anti-rates campaign.
In Galway, by way of contrast, the IRA and the Dáil justices were
on opposite sides, but the justices were easily intimidated by the
local anti-rates IRA. A distressed rate collector reported that, in
the Maam area in particular,

there seems to be a sort of propaganda against the collection
when illiterate ratepayers are told and believing that I am

receiving £1,700 for the collection of rates and several other silly stories.[18]

Galway seems to have had the most determined IRA resistance to ratepaying. Parenthetically, County Galway had a poor record in the Anglo-Irish war and was despised by the Clare IRA. The Connacht IRA was particularly liable to be affected by agrarian and other economic sentiment.[19] Listowel, County Kerry, a persistent trouble spot in the eyes of the Dáil, was one of the worst defaulters and put up a very widespread and effective campaign against rates. Even as far away as Kerry, the campaign was engineered directly from Dublin by an open organisation during the period of the Truce. In March 1922, as civil war loomed, a rate collector was threatened with death in north Kerry, and the Farmers' Union were seen as being particularly successful in fomenting resistance to ratepaying in that area. The chairman of the county council, a well-known Gaelic Leaguer with the nom-de-plume of 'An Seabhac', although sympathetic to the Dáil government and to the Provisional Government, did point out to the Dublin authorities that, with the withdrawal of the British grants and the enormous extra expense caused by the fighting and destruction, the rates had grown 'beyond reason', and there was some justice in the farmers' attitude.[20]

Eastern counties, more prosperous and more tranquil than the south and west, were generally more co-operative. The major exception to this generalisation was afforded by the counties of Dublin and Meath, close to the organisational centre of the anti-rates campaign, well organised, and highly literate. Leitrim, in the far north-west and impoverished, was seen as a hopeless case by some Dáil officials. It was the poorest of the twenty-seven administrative counties that were to form the Free State, and much of its IRA resembled an agrarian society or even a criminal gang more than a disciplined guerrilla army. The IRA in Leitrim were certainly involved in the anti-rates agitation. Leitrim's roads resembled quagmires by mid-1921. In October the county surveyor reported:

Our inspector had to defend himself by firing over the heads of a crowd at an anti-rate meeting which he attended in the hope of being able to explain things to the satisfaction of the agitators.

Even by Irish wartime standards, the roads of the county were a shambles and commonly impassable. The other local services went unfinanced. Leitrim's only chance was to be, in effect, conquered by the Dublin government, an advance expedition of forty men being immediately required to seize property in lieu of rates payments. Dark and almost wistful thoughts of expelling Leitrim from the new state surfaced occasionally.[21]

The neighbouring county, Longford, was 'bankrupt' as early as January 1921.[22] Mayo, a remote and destitute county, gave little trouble, on the other hand.[23] In Monaghan, a border county, a financial crisis occurred in late 1920 because of unionist and nationalist resistance. Cosgrave took the Monaghan situation very seriously and informed the councillors that they should have come to Dublin to see him immediately to explain the situation. It was 'vital' that the Dáil underground government, having taken over the local government system, not be seen to fail because of finance. If necessary the Dáil, although financially strapped itself, would engineer a loan.

> You will please keep this item of information to yourself. I mention it to show you how absolutely vital it is considered that the public bodies stand firm.[24]

Queen's County (Laois) struck a supplementary rate to compensate for the British grant but was forced to ask the Dáil for a loan in late 1920.[25] In Sligo the collection system appears to have been corrupt, and eventually the Dáil fired a considerable number of local officials. One crooked official had in fact been fired years previously, in 1908, but had been reinstated because of pressure from 'the Bishop and Priests'. Eamon Coogan, the Dáil inspector, wrote to Cosgrave in September 1921:

> With a few honourable exceptions, the personnel of all public bodies here is of a very poor calibre. I do not know of any adjective in the English language which would sufficiently describe for you the hopeless inability, ignorance and I might almost say superstition of these representative gentlemen.

Coogan's presence in Sligo, with the Dáil behind him, was widely resented by the local elites. He was being watched, he reported, and feared to post mail locally. The local IRA were illegally demanding pay derived from a special rate for enforcing rate collection. The Jinks family seemed to control everything. In May 1922, Cosgrave wrote a scorcher, even by his own sturdy standards, informing Sligo County Council that an 'IRA rate' would be illegal under Dáil law; the Public Band was not to be publicly financed by the local authorities, although in some cases the IRA leaders either controlled, or had a significant presence on, the local authorities. The situation was speedily resolved; by May 1922 the pro-Treaty 'Beggar's Bush IRA'—the nascent Free State army—had firmly occupied the town of Sligo. The rural areas were still controlled by local IRA of uncertain loyalty at best or under the determined anti-Treatyite control of Frank Carty.[26] In South Tipperary, the famous 3rd Brigade similarly demanded a supplementary rate to finance their activities, allegedly to pay for a new IRA-created local police force, the 'Irish Republican Guards'.[27] The name was evidently copied from that of the Civic Guard/Garda Síochána of the Dáil-cum-Provisional Government, then in training in Dublin.

THE REFORM PROGRAMME OF THE DÁIL GOVERNMENT

On the economising side of the Dáil's policy, a wide-ranging hospital amalgamation scheme was indeed drawn up rapidly in late 1920 by county committees and submitted to the Dáil Department of Local Government. Cosgrave and O'Higgins pressed ahead enthusiastically with it, running into stiff and predictable local resistance. Only Roscommon, where Sinn Féin was particularly strong, actually completed its programme of amalgamation and centralisation on time and before the British finally agreed to the Truce. However, in many counties remarkable progress was made in 1920–21 in enforcing Dáil policy, despite the presence of the British army, the officials of the Local Government Board, the RIC, and the Black and Tans. Ernest Blythe, in an interview published on the day the Free State came officially into being (6 December 1922), summarised the achievements of the Dáil in this area very pithily. His emphasis was, as ever, on economy, thrift, and avoidance of big government.

There has been great saving in the administration of the Poor Law and other departments . . . The position with regard to local government is something like this: during the struggle with the British the necessities of the case as well as the freedom from legislative tangles led to very considerable changes, particularly in relation to the Poor Law. Reforms that have been urged for a long time, and which would have been dependent on legislation to come into effect, were undertaken. In all but three counties the workhouses were abolished, county homes and county hospitals were substituted and outdoor relief was replaced by a system of home help.

Cosgrave and O'Higgins had their work cut out even in conditions of warfare in pushing their programme through the counties in 1920–22. In Carlow a strong fight was put up against amalgamation by the local representatives and officials, the programme only being finally implemented after the signing of the Treaty. Tullow and Bagenalstown (Muine Bheag) hospitals were then duly abolished. Donegal carried out the amalgamations during the Truce, in part because the local IRA were both anti-rates and pro-Treaty.[28] Cork local officials, inevitably, saw the entire programme as being a scheme devised by people in Dublin against what is geographically the largest county. Resistance was strengthened greatly by local patriotism and the obvious fact that 'nobody wanted to part with his own institutions.' Nevertheless, the scheme went ahead. An ingenious, neat and pious way of saving the ratepayers' cash was found by the simple device of closing down state-financed and state-run industrial schools for orphans and handing the children over to religious orders.[29]

In Kerry, Listowel hospital fought a stout administrative battle against its own abolition.[30] During the Truce a large section of the local IRA came out against the Dáil amalgamation scheme and also opposed the enforcement of merit examination systems of hiring for local government personnel. In December 1921, the local IRA broke up a competitive examination in Killarney held to determine who should be appointed secretary to the new Kerry County Home. The examination papers were destroyed. The IRA felt that the spoils of victory should go to the brave men who had fought for freedom and not to the 'slackers and shirkers'. An IRA handbill announced:

Thus we make no wonder when people say that the Conscientious Objectors would be just as well paid in the end as well as those on active service who did all that was possible to achieve Freedom. NOW we have come to the only conclusion feasible that this examination should not go ahead at present and the only way to give effect to our decision is i.e.— Destroy the Papers.[31]

Incidentally, the examination was later held, guarded by pro-Treaty IRA, and an IRA veteran was eventually appointed. Reportedly, he got second place: the man who got first place did not take the job, for reasons best known to himself and to the Kerry IRA. The ubiquitous Coogan, roving Dáil Department of Local Government trouble-shooter in the west, commented acidly: 'A nice start for the Free State in County Kerry.'[32] In February 1922, Coogan was ordered to take over in Kerry and sort things out. Shortly afterwards, however, he was transferred to the new and mutinous Civic Guard, where we shall see him performing a similar function.[33] In the relatively civic county of Kilkenny the Dáil offer of an ambulance to compensate for the closing down of Callan hospital was treated with contempt by local luminaries in early 1922. In the same month, however, the Dáil fired all Callan local government officials.[34]

In Leitrim, the locals tried Fabian tactics. The clerk of Manor-hamilton Union suggested in August 1921 that the amalgamation proposals be shelved 'until the National question is finally settled,' an event that seems likely to be coterminous with Tibb's Eve.[35] Cosgrave wrote back one of his characteristically well-organised broadsides in early September:

I have to point out that if this was the spirit of the people Dáil Éireann would not have set up civil departments and proceeded to take over the civil administration of the country. It has, however, done so, and in doing so has acted strictly on the mandate it received from the electors. The 'great National question' would never be finally settled if those who were elected to act in the name of the people simply sat down and waited for the enemy to evacuate, and yet in substance that is what the resolution of your Board recommends. You quote English Statutes ignoring the fact that the sole legislative authority in this country is Dáil Éireann, and that Dáil Éireann in adopting the English Local Government Act, and regulations therein, did so 'subject to such modification and alterations as might from time to time be promulgated by the [Dáil] Local Government Department.' Those Representative County Committees which have formulated schemes of amalgamation in various counties have been set up on definite instruction of this Department, and the schemes they formulate, if and when they receive sanction of the Department, will be duly enforced. The Department is determined to rid the ratepayers of the burden of maintaining a number of petty and expensive institutions all through the country. I would remind you that while these schemes of Amalgamation aim at the reform of the present degrading Poor Law system, they are also schemes of economy.[36]

A classic example of the kind of 'extravagant' local facilities provided by the British and so resented by the young puritans and Tammany-bashers of Sinn Féin was afforded by County Monaghan. The county is quite a small one in both territory and population and had apparently only three hundred sick and destitute people to deal with. However, the county managed to run not only a central workhouse but also four county hospitals under the munificent British system. The Dáil's inspector, in late 1921, concluded inevitably that there was no need for a workhouse and that there was no need for a hospital outside Monaghan. The little hospitals in Carrickmacross, Castleblayney and Clones could therefore be closed down. The workhouse would be converted into a smaller county home, and home assistance would replace what was left of the workhouse's functions. Clones and Carrickmacross were only a short rail distance away from Monaghan, and even the chronic localism of Irish society would presumably be able to cope with inter-parish voyages of that length. The inspector reported in an upbeat tone in September 1921:

I stated among other things [to the councillors and officials] that they might not shed any crocodile tears over the poor. Already alterations were in hand for improving the workhouse and these would be followed up by a system of Electric

Lighting and other internal improvements in the way of pro-
viding seats, heating apparatus, improved diet, etc., and that it
was a great mistake to think that it was altogether in the interests of economy—economy was only a secondary consideration, the primary one being better conditions and comfort
for the poor both inside and outside the Workhouse [*sic*].[37]

As mentioned earlier, Roscommon was the only county to
push ahead with the elimination of the workhouse system and
the hospital amalgamation programme and to have it on the
verge of completion before the Truce. The scheme to amalga-
mate local government unions, which had had responsibility for
the poor at local level, as essentially superfluous under the new
political order was drafted by October 1920 and went into theoretical effect on 1 December. Roscommon town workhouse had
three hundred inmates, Boyle hospital ninety, and the other five
hospitals scattered around the county averaged a pathetic thirty-
five inmates each. Home Rule may not in fact have died of British
kindness in Roscommon but certainly showed signs of having to
swim in a sea of British money before the Anglo-Irish War. The
Dáil department estimated that Roscommon workhouse could
easily have coped with 850 inmates and patients. In fact, under
the amalgamation it would be required to handle far less than
700. By mid-1922, as the Civil War was starting, the workhouse
had already been converted into a county home and was working
well but needed physical improvement and repair. The system was
already coming up against an enemy that was to become traditional: the penny-pinching habits of the new Department of
Finance.[38]

Sligo contrasted sharply with its neighbouring county,
Roscommon. Sligo was far more determinedly anti-amalgamation,
anti-Dáil and anti-Treaty in organised sentiment. The county's
local government institutions were seen by Dáil officials as far
more corrupt than the average in the emergent state. The local
government unions, rendered functionally obsolete under the
Dáil scheme, defied the Dáil order to dissolve themselves not
because of any loyalty to the British Crown or because they
adhered to die-hard republicanism but because officials feared
losing their jobs under the new scheme. The mayor of Sligo was
anti-Treaty, and the local IRA was strong and anti-Treaty. The

IRA was dominated by that well-known warrior, Frank Carty, and was noticeably present in the county council.

County Sligo seems to have behaved as though it were the model for Flann O'Brien's satire on local government, *Faustus Kelly*. At one stage, in December 1921, Dromore West Board of Guardians wished to have their clerk appointed to the new county home. The writing was on the wall for boards of guardians in general, as the Dáil department had openly declared its intention of abolishing them as superfluous. Dromore West's idea was to bypass Dáil authority and resist the consequences of amalgamation, which were, in particular, the loss of local power over job preferment. Direct IRA interference in Sligo politics was intense and was quite evidently directly connected with a fear of not getting a slice of the action in the form of local service jobs once the new Free State machine got a grip on the local system and imposed meritocratic procedures. Money was demanded, as noted earlier, by the IRA for enforcing Dáil rate collection in late 1921, which had been denounced as illegal by Cosgrave. By June 1922, however, the Free State army had moved in on the town, a shooting war of sorts was going on in the Nephin mountains, the Jinks family had been either tamed or co-opted to the Free State, and the streamlined county home and county hospital system were reportedly running smoothly.[39]

James M. Kennedy, a local official at Thurles, a Sinn Féiner and an intimate and life-long correspondent of Mulcahy's, supplied a lurid picture of political life in north Tipperary as it was just after the Truce. In a letter to Cosgrave, sent through Paddy O'Keefe, joint secretary of Sinn Féin, he gave the usual description of Thurles Urban District Council being crippled by the fact that the best Sinn Féin councillors and officials had been on the run from the British and had therefore perforce permitted the 'twisters' to get their way. The Clerk was 'funky and incompetent'.

> No minutes sent to Dáil for some time. This is now attended to and they will be sent henceforward regular. Public body officials in district, with few exceptions, are opportunists and no good, being utterly selfish . . .

Local boards were, he reported, run by the few, and these were not the best, the best being good Sinn Féiners and therefore in hiding from the British authorities. Officials had taken advantage of this to evade Dáil instructions and impede the economy drive.

> The orders of An Dáil re economy were deliberately ignored and I failed to see any press reference to An Dáil's circulars being ever read. Am very doubtful if Clerks of Public Boards in this district are to be trusted. They are 'twisters' with the side they think will be strongest. Rotten crowd. Local papers of districts very weak, perhaps not unnatural.
>
> People most anxious for wipeout of Workhomes and if nothing else can do it few would regret the use of petrol for the purpose. Rate collectors . . . a rotten lot. Are almost openly hostile. Public opinion against them.[40]

As mentioned earlier, the contract system of road maintenance, generally in use before 1898, had been fairly generally replaced by direct labour systems, whereby local men would be employed directly by the county council. This had the dual effect of cutting out traditional businessmen, unionist and/or Protestant in many areas, and creating a considerable source of petty patronage to the advantage of the new local councillors. Many Sinn Féin observers felt that the system was inefficient even in time of peace. In Kerry (as usual, perhaps) the extremely well-organised ratepayers pressed loudly for a return to the old contract system in September 1921. The county surveyor, however, demurred from this proposal, insisting that the real problem was not so much the principle of direct labour as the low quality of the supervisors and the generally abysmal organisation of work. In the Kingdom of Kerry, ancient arguments between Plato and Aristotle—as to whether one should have government by virtuous men or virtuous laws—surfaced in 1921; the ratepayers seem to have favoured law, the county surveyor, men.

The county surveyor of Kerry also informed the Dáil authorities that there were far too many idle gangers, some of them illiterate, physically unfit, or suffering under the oppressive condition of having other economic interests, such as a farm or a shop. By late 1921 the entire road system in Kerry had collapsed, and only 50 out of 480 road workers were still in the county council's employ. Furthermore, the now unemployed majority's threat to black the fortunate working minority was likely to wreck what was left of the road-mending system of County Kerry.[41] Chronic local unemployment of young men fuelled the Civil War in many areas.

In general, local authorities that the Dáil Department of Local Government had in its gunsights as candidates for abolition tended, naturally enough, to be particularly difficult from the Dáil's point of view. Athlone Board of Guardians, a doomed body if ever there was one, remained loyal to the British authorities right up to the Truce, evidently aware that the new regime was going to exterminate them, institutionally speaking. In June 1921, Cosgrave, generally ecumenical about questions of allegiance as long as he thought people were doing their job, took the trouble of rebuking this obsolescent body.[42]

Quite independently of questions of allegiance, in the poorer counties in particular the roads deteriorated steadily throughout the period of the Anglo-Irish War. By August 1922, J. P. Punch, county surveyor for the relatively prosperous county of Carlow, was complaining bitterly that what money there was was not being used to repair the road system but was rather being used to employ men in a way that amounted to a species of outdoor poor relief. In Ireland generally, it should be said parenthetically, road work was traditionally regarded as a form of charity or as a political 'fix' rather than as a real job. Council employees themselves reportedly sometimes destroyed roads and bridges by night, ostensibly for military purposes associated presumably with the IRA of de Valera and Liam Lynch but actually for the purpose of generating more daytime work for themselves, according to Punch.[43]

By November 1921 the Leitrim roads were in 'shocking condition' because of the well-organised and widely supported rates strike and the resulting bankruptcy of the local authorities. In richer and more politically amenable counties the situation appears to have been relatively tolerable, the Carlow situation of misapplication of public money for a kind of public relief being more typical; roads were essentially regarded as excuses for employing large numbers of unskilled people, commonly connected with one or other popular political organisation, whether it be the United Irish League, the Hibernians, the Unionists, Sinn Féin, or the IRA.

A well-voiced complaint from County Limerick submitted to the Dáil Department of Local Government in January 1922 contained the claim that road workers were paid a lot more to do a lot less than were the local landless labourers and that this was a major source of local rural proletarian unrest and discontent.[44] Direct labour suited the unions, as they had a direct input both into the local government system and into the pro-Treaty party. It can be convincingly argued that the later Fine Gael-Labour coalitions, so anomalous in the eyes of students of comparative politics, were born during the Anglo-Irish war. In Laois, for example, the direct labour system used was seen as being particularly inefficient. However, a proposed cut in road workers' wages from 40 shillings to 35 shillings (£2 to £1.75) towards the end of 1921 caused trouble. Local council financial difficulties were used to justify the cut, but Foran, the union representative, pointed out to Cosgrave that similar cuts had not been suffered by the council's own senior officials.[45]

A general and sometimes intense distrust for the personnel in local government in the minds of the revolutionaries was commonly coupled with a contempt for the Edwardian Irish political system's characteristic plethora of small, parasitic and idle local representative bodies. Sinn Féin, very much a party of youth, had its roots in a puritan and patriotic reaction against the Irish Party, which, in the view of the separatists, had demoralised and corrupted political culture and contributed mightily to the psychological enslavement of the Irish people.

Eamon Coogan was vitriolic about the calibre of both local politicians and local officials in Kerry, and An Seabhac essentially echoed his judgments, although in a calmer and more measured tone. Coogan reported to Stack in February 1921 that only three or four of the local representative councillors elected in Kerry in 1920 'bother their heads'. These few, together with 'our chief officials do all the work and shoulder all the responsibility.'[46] Coogan was even blunter in December 1921:

> I have had to report before the apathy of public bodies towards reforms and their reluctance to co-operate with me in effecting tangible reforms. For aiming at the latter, I have been accused of being too materialistic. Incidentally, I must say, therefore, that to such people as my accusers the constructive policy of this [Dáil] Department [of Local Government] is too materialistic and lacks the fine qualities and ideals of those more

progressive reformers in Kerry who have spent their time since 22 June last [when the Truce was agreed between the British and the Irish] building castles in the air from the County Council offices in Tralee.

Coogan also reported with some asperity that the Honourable Albina Broderick, a prominent connection of the Midleton landowning family, had now 'Irished her name' as Gobnait Ní Bhruadair and still 'ruled the roost' in Kerry local politics, much as she had under the old dispensation. Coogan felt that Kerry political culture was essentially depraved. Politically active people in the county were liars, intriguers, and blackmailers. They were, he wrote, 'wolves'.

This species [of wolf] do not eat their prey, they slowly consume man's energy by the venom and poison of their tongue. This tongue has often been mistaken by ignorant people for 'brains'.[47]

THE RECONSTRUCTION OF LOCAL GOVERNMENT

As already noted, county permanent officials were generally recruited by locally devised systems, and there was relatively little of a standardised national system of recruitment of local civil servants. Eventually, under the Free State, qualifications and standards of remuneration were made uniform throughout the political system and were, essentially, set for the entire country by one central authority. This centralised system came to be much resented. The 'clean up the system' impulses of Sinn Féin persisted, however, under the Free State. A central Local Appointments Commission was set up in 1926 and eventually had the effect of slowly but decisively 'revolutionising the local government service.'[48] In effect, a national, standardised set of criteria for local officials was devised and enforced, thereby bypassing local networks of cronies. It also meant that permanent officials could transfer easily from one county to another, as criteria for rank and promotion were identical. Eventually this was to evolve into a pecking order of counties regarded as most or least desirable to be in by able senior local government officials, with Cork at the top and some midland counties at the bottom. The general effect was of a streamlining and modernising of a system that had been heavily penetrated by local vested interests and that functioned adequately mainly because the British had been willing to pay the bills.

This entire, mainly benign institutional evolution was to be systematically denigrated by the political forces that evolved into the new Sinn Féin, the 'new IRA' and the Fianna Fáil of de Valera in the 1920s. This was due to their shared commitment to the *a priori* view that the government of the Free State was a cat's-paw of the unionists, the British government, and, of course, the local privileged classes. After 1932, Fianna Fáil rapidly fell silent on the entire issue. The new party slowly realised but never admitted that it had, out of bitterness and envy, been peddling a mean-minded set of libels and now was stuck with the contempt for the new state that it had itself helped to orchestrate. This contempt was now, naturally, turned on itself, as de Valera stepped into Cosgrave's shoes. An immediate reaction to this moral dilemma was a rapid retreat into noisy Catholic piety, best symbolised by the Eucharistic Congress of 1932. Eventually, de Valera's natural dignity and his political creativity had the effect of reversing substantively this version of traditional scepticism about representative politics.

To return to the foundation years of 1921–22, local government institutions as inherited from the British were commonly seen as superfluous and corrupt by the Free State government. The tone was, as we have seen, set by the Dáil government but is well epitomised by Ernest Blythe's contemptuous reply, in his capacity as Minister for Local Government in October 1923, to Macroom Rural District Council's threat not to function until Republican prisoners in Mountjoy had been released:

> I am directed by Mr. Blythe to state that from his knowledge of the work done by An Comhairle Liomatáiste Maghromdha [Macroom District Council], he does not consider that any important public interests will suffer as a result of its refusal to function.[49]

Blythe had a point. By that time, most of the functions of the smaller local authorities had been centralised at the county level, and there was literally nothing for the smaller local councils to do in a society that had been steadily and determinedly depopulating itself for two generations and that still looked far more to its clergy than to its representative politicians for local civic leadership.

The great split of 1922 came on top of centre-periphery tensions of this kind. Local powerful people, whether unionist, nationalist, Sinn Féin, or Labour, lay or ecclesiastical, resented 'Dublin' interfering in the way in which they regulated themselves. 'Dublin' could be controlled by the British or by Sinn Féin; in both cases it was alien. The further one went from Dublin the more energetic, in general, the resistance became. Meath went to law; Kildare acquiesced; Kerry fought and schemed; Sligo connived and fought; Leitrim sank. This locality-centre tension was reinforced by tension between the post-British civil service, most of it 'patriot' in persuasion, and the interlopers from the Dáil 'Sinn Féin' bureaucracy. Generational hostility also occurred. In general, a chronic mutual distrust characterised the Sinn Féin elite, which was in process of dissolution in early 1922.

For example, Blythe even distrusted the Dáil civil servants he had inherited as Minister for Local Government and had had to bring in to his new synthesised Department, put together from both Irish (Dáil) and British ('Castle') elements. Because of the split, Blythe distrusted both sets. Furthermore, he was an outsider in four ways: he was a Northerner, a Protestant, a Sinn Féiner in the eyes of the Local Government Board personnel and a pro-Treatyite in the eyes of the crypto-republicans who lurked in the ranks of the old Dáil service turned Free State.

Blythe's solution to his own problem was simple in its Machiavellianism and also displayed a profound, humorous and cynical understanding of the psychology of these ambitious young, mainly Catholic, outsiders-turned-insiders now within sight of the glittering prizes—the levers of power and influence in a small and hungry country. According to himself, Blythe took up the staff lists of the Dáil transferees and altered their salaries, one-third upwards and one-third downwards, at random. He later reminisced proudly:

A deep and lasting split occurred amongst the [ex-Second] Dáil officials immediately. Concerted action became impossible and no overt attempt was ever made by them to act in common against the [Free State] government.[50]

The split intensified the pro-Treatyites' contempt not only for those among the other side whom they saw as the main creators of disharmony but also for the perceived opportunism of the officials of the local authorities, many of whom were covertly anti-Dáil and subsequently anti-Treaty. James Kennedy wrote to Mulcahy from Thurles on 20 June 1922, on the eve of the Civil War. The split had so divided good Sinn Féiners from each other that they were being pushed out by non-nationally minded people, 'utter rotters and a low bosthoon'. The idealistic Sinn Féin of 1919–22 was utterly dead, and Sinn Féin had been defeated by Mé Féin.

Idealism is gone, selfish sections will now go on top and tricksters opportunists worse than the old Irish Party are coming to the front, pushing away the old crowd who worked unselfishly and were animated with national aims rather than personal aims. Ireland's sun has set for generations and on top of all this ingratitude for which Ireland was ever noted, we will in continuation of the reaction become more English than ever.

Even though he was himself very much in favour of the Treaty, he had already come to the conclusion that the Treaty had not been worth the moral collapse it had triggered. Ireland's martyred dead were 'fools', and the Irish were a 'hopeless people'. Consciously or otherwise, he echoed the remark made of the Irish by the Spanish commander at Kinsale in 1603, Don Juan del Águila, 'Christ did not die for these people.' From Kennedy's point of view, Mulcahy's stubborn optimism about the latent but strong democratic spirit of the Irish people was incomprehensible. Sinn Féin had disintegrated, the days of practical, non-idealistic politics had arrived, the idealists on both sides were fighting each other, and the cynics and opportunists had been allowed to take over.

You [Mulcahy] and such as you and there are a few of you in both camps would do well to realise how poor and uncertain it is to rely on the people, how thankless it is to work for them

and how futile it is to save a people who having really made
for the first time a long sustained struggle, are now in the
depths of a reaction which will influence them for generations.[51]

Mulcahy was always far more optimistic than his friend about
the merits of the people and consistently expressed a belief,
even after years of Fianna Fáil's putatively accursed rule, that
the Irish people were fundamentally sound both morally and
politically. Kennedy, on the other hand, looking at things from
the worm's eye point of view of local government, expressed
envy of his optimism in terms worthy of Joyce or Froude:

> I believe we are an inferior race, temperamentally unfit and
> no effort can save us. We are a mean people, theatrical and
> narrow, posers and humbugs, ungrateful and malicious, a
> race of 'saints and scholars' without real religion or real edu-
> cation. There are fine fellows and fine women too but they
> can do nothing but sweat in vain before they are stoned and
> then shot. They'll get monuments thirty years after.[52]

The impulse behind the centralising and streamlining of
local government was powerful and was not to expend itself in
1923. On the contrary, the Irish state, consistent with its begin-
nings in the Dáil government, was to impose central controls
and standard practices on local government. In large part the
new controls wiped out patronage and outright corruption. The
reformism was due to a genuine hatred of the traditional Irish
Tammany Hall machine politics, but in part it was due to a fear
of a recrudescence of the Public Band in political dress, a fear
that was characteristically Cumann na nGaedheal's but was also,
in a curiously covert way, also a fear of Fianna Fáil's later on.

Neither side truly believed in secular participant local democracy and both foresaw that such participation would, if unfettered,
lead to a widespread corruption of public life. Local government was a British invention, expensive, anti-national, and
incompetent. The virtuous, as the two sets of Sinn Féiners saw
themselves in their different ways, felt themselves under an
obligation to clean out these Augean stables and, in particular,
take away from the local councils powers that might otherwise

be wielded by unsuitable people. Irish democracy was to be heavily shaped by the idea of embattled heroes in power struggling against a perceived collective moral mediocrity ultimately originating in a popular slave culture.[53]

These unenthusiastic democrats were qualified in their attachment to democratic ideas and were not prepared to trust the people with the powers to run local affairs, as distinct from the right to vote for a relatively remote central assembly sitting in Dublin. The Irish democratic state was eventually to end up perhaps the most centralised democratic state in Europe. Centralisation of this kind is a characteristic outcome of revolution; similar centralisations followed on the French Revolution and, in a more extravagant fashion, on the Russian Revolution. Revolutionaries, whether nominally democratic or otherwise, like to keep the reins of power in their own hands. Democracy is all right as long as the voters can be trusted to vote the right way; in the Irish case, both priests and patriots agreed on this guarded acceptance of electoral democracy.

Local authorities, however, could not be expected to function properly under either local or central control as long as the real centre of local power lay elsewhere, as it certainly did during the period from July 1921 to late 1922 in large areas of the twenty-six counties. The Public Band, in the form of the local IRA, was commonly the real 'local authority', and eventually Cosgrave and his allies were to steel themselves to the task of eliminating it and ensuring that Dublin's writ would run everywhere, in practice as well as in theory. For that, military force was to be required and blood was to flow; the characteristically Irish combination of extravagant farce and hideous local tragedy had to recur.

4

The Creation of a Democratic Public Order, 1922–23

As the previous chapter has indirectly illustrated, an immediate and central cause of the conflict between the two sets of Sinn Féiners was the contrast between two sets of people equipped with very different levels of administrative ability; to generalise heroically, many prominent pro-Treatyites simply tended to be better at 'running things', whereas many prominent anti-Treatyites tended to be rather better at romantic indignation or small-scale military action. Those who supported the Treaty do seem to have been more 'modern' in mentality than those who opposed and to have seen the modern world as one to be embraced, although with many reservations, rather than resisted and rejected.

Envy of, anger at and bewilderment about innate skills amounting to rational-legal ability of the kind evidently possessed by Collins, Cosgrave and O'Higgins were huge factors in generating the suspicion the anti-Treatyites had of the settlement; Collins was seen as being too clever by half. De Valera, Brugha and Stack found themselves bypassed by the pro-Treaty people; Collins ran finance, gun-running, and political assassination; Mulcahy commanded the IRA, insofar as that body could be commanded by anybody; Cosgrave and O'Higgins had effectively wrapped up the local government system, the key to the emergent electoral democracy; by comparison, Brugha was a part-timer, Stack had little control over his department, and de Valera found himself almost to be a figurehead without real executive power.

Scarcely had the Treaty been signed than a small group centred on Griffith, Collins, a west Cork 'mafia', the IRB and Collins's old active service unit rapidly started putting together a regular army free from Public Band links. They also started to create a police force, armed at first on the model of the RIC and disarmed subsequently. They also eventually assembled a new judicial system, some of it taken over bodily from the British through the device of the Provisional Government, but much of it of new invention. Furthermore, and very importantly, the new government had its hands on the revenue services and the customs and excise system. Much of this apparatus was quite new, and some of it derived from the Dáil system. De Valera and his allies watched while what they had thought of as their own project was apparently taken away from them as they were gradually marginalised in the early months of 1922. This process of marginalisation had, of course, deeper roots; the Treaty merely accelerated what had been going on for a year and a half before December 1921.

Another reason for the division was the Public Band's youthful hostility to age and to 'politicians'. The people Cosgrave and O'Higgins were dickering with in the local authorities were in many cases exactly the people the Public Band resented and despised most. The fact that O'Higgins, Cosgrave, Coogan and other Sinn Féin executives also despised them but felt they had to work with them *pro tem* cut no ice with the Boys of the Column— the Public Band. The local representatives were seen with some accuracy as corrupt, rich, the establishment, controlled by the big farmers, the grocers, and the publicans, and, above all, older. Local politicians were often seen as, or at least declared to be, gombeen men and cowardly, compared with the clean, brave and patriotic young men and women of the IRA and Cumann na mBan. The Free State was going to be the political system of the gombeens, it was argued, not that of the Public Band. An ancient alienation from government transferred itself to the local authorities and from them to the Provisional Government and the new Free State.

A SOCIETY WITHOUT ORDER

In a famous comment, O'Higgins later described the new Provisional Government, heir not only of the underground Dáil government but also of the British concessions under the Treaty, as a group of young men under siege by a culture gone temporarily hysterical in a country that had reverted to a Hobbesian state of nature.

To form a just appreciation of developments in Ireland in 1922, it is necessary to remember that the country had come through a revolution and to remember what a weird composite of idealism, neurosis, megalomania and criminality is apt to be thrown to the surface in even the best regulated revolution. It was a situation precipitated by men who had not cleared the blood from their eyes, and reinforced by all the wayward-ness of a people with whom, by dint of historical circumstances, a negative attitude had tended to become traditional. With many it was the reaction from a great fear. With others it was fanaticism pure and simple. With others still it was something that was neither pure nor simple, an ebullition of the savage, primitive passion to wreck and loot and level when an oppor-tunity seemed to offer to do so with impunity. Instincts of that kind are not an Irish monopoly. They are universal to human nature, but in the conditions which exist in modern civilized states they are, for the most part, successfully held in check, manifesting themselves only in occasional isolated outrages of a revolting character or in sporadic local outbreaks, easily countered by the organised forces of the State. But in Ireland in 1922 there was no State and no organised forces. The Provisional Government was simply eight young men in the City Hall standing amidst the ruins of one administration, with the foundations of another not yet laid, and with wild men screaming through the keyhole. No police force was functioning through the country, no system of justice was operating, the wheels of administration hung idle battered out of recognition by the clash of rival jurisdictions.

The *Freeman's Journal* of 17 January 1922 editorialised, giving a similar picture of the post-British situation. The Castle had been handed over to Collins the previous day:

The power that it enshrined was surrendered yesterday to Ireland's men. They are now masters of the administrative machine. It would be expecting too much from human insti-tutions, and even human nature, to expect that, after the changeover, things will move smoothly from the start. The machine is not merely of British manufacture, but completely out of gear. In fact, it is more or less a wreck as a result of the conflict with the people. Moreover, its chaotic condition merely reflects the chaos to which it has reduced Ireland . . .

Administrative ability was rare, unrecognised, resented, suspected, and misunderstood as underhandedness, and tended to generate an extraordinary level of resentment. The contrast between attitudes towards means and ends, and the fact that much of the split over the Anglo-Irish Treaty concerned differences over means rather than ends, echoed this general condition. Both Mulcahy and Collins had been initiated into the problems of large organisations in that flower of Victorian bureaucratic science, the British Post Office. Michael Hayes reminisced:

> But I think also required of a revolutionary is great attention to detail. Collins and Mulcahy were very much like that. They kept files like civil servants. And dug things out at a particular moment when they wanted to . . . That is one quality that a revolutionary in Ireland lacked [previously]. The Fenians were a complete failure. Partly because their leadership was divided between Dublin and New York, partly because they didn't do their homework. Collins did all the details for example.[1]

Both knew how to file, an ability that the romantic *littérateurs* could not deal with and whose practitioners they denounced as bourgeois, irreligious, or aesthetically insensitive, depending on philosophical prejudice. Michael Collins had an extraordinary memory for people and for detail, not only because of his administrative abilities but also because of his vast range of acquaintance and his ability to gain people's affection and personal allegiance. Collins's knowledge of the Dublin and London underworlds and of the sailors' world that linked Ireland and Britain made him a real-life Scarlet Pimpernel but made him a figure of suspicion to de Valera in particular. Another factor that fostered the mutual distrust that grew up between the Public Band and the Provisional Government was the almost total localism of the IRA. IRA guerrillas knew their own tiny areas intimately but were vague about the rest of the country. It is also possible that they projected their own local military success or failure onto the rest of the country. If things had gone well in south Tipperary, then there was no honourable reason why things should have gone less well in north Down or in Sligo. Thus a local IRA squad that had acquitted itself well against the British would perhaps be particularly apt to push for a resumption of fighting.

Women, although almost never active in the fighting, played an invaluable role behind the scenes as messengers, nurses, food producers, and shields: in the Victorian culture of the period, searching or attacking women was taboo in the minds of most men on both sides. Policemen often refused to search women; young women were commonly used by the IRA to carry Mills bombs, guns, and documents. In a more general sense, women had a certain psychological hold over men. De Valera's relationship of mutual dependence with Cathal Brugha, Mary MacSwiney, Austin Stack and the prominent 'republican women' was curious: an alliance of the steely political purpose of one man and the aggression, hysterical energy and rage of the rest. The general political effect of this relationship between de Valera and the republican *enragés* was catastrophic, and again the true split occurred long before the much-denounced Treaty.

The 'republican women' arguably caused a lot of the damage; most importantly, all women TDs voted against the Treaty. Furthermore, the psychological hold that women had on certain men was very powerful in this particular instance. The essentially technical subordination of women to men was counterbalanced in Victorian culture by an exaggerated sensitivity on the part of men to women's opinions of them. The white feather presented by women to men out of uniform in English city streets during the First World War is one classic example of this species of moral blackmail. Liam Archer, whose meeting with Rory O'Connor we have already witnessed, had a brother who 'went' anti-Treaty; Liam subsequently blamed 'the wife'.

Peter Hart, in his recent study of the IRA in County Cork during this period, has documented the enormous influence mothers appear to have had on the political formation of young IRA volunteers. A sympathetic outside observer, the correspondent for the *Manchester Guardian*, observed as early as August 1921 that Dáil deputies were far more moderate and pragmatic in private than they were in public; they were continually looking over their shoulders at their own supporters, and seemed particularly intimidated by their womenfolk. Mary MacSwiney apparently terrorised some of them by sheer force of personality.

She challenged every member of the [Dáil] cabinet to assure his determination to stand out for the Republic. One after another, they did so—quailing, one ventures to suggest, before the accusing forefinger of Miss MacSwiney, whom no one would dream of charging with inconsistency.

P. S. O'Hegarty, a useful if biased contemporary inside observer, wrote in 1924 that the women revolutionaries were often far more extremist than the men. The women TDs had all voted against the Treaty, regardless of their private opinions, he averred; they voted together to show female solidarity and under the influence of de Valera.

It is women who were largely responsible for the bitterness and the ferocity of the civil war. In the whole period of war, both of the 'Tan' war and the civil war, the women were the implacable and irrational upholders of death and destruction. They never understood the political situation and they never tried to understand it—not indeed that the majority of men were any better in that respect—but the women jumped to conclusions without any consideration whatever, save their emotions, and once having done so, never afterwards looked facts in the face or attempted a re-examination of the situation.[2]

At the end of 1921, Batt O'Connor remarked on the actual superficiality of the divisions in the party. He also noticed that the divisions were far sharper at the top of the movement than they were lower down or in the general population. He made very similar observations to those of O'Hegarty about the role of the republican women:

There is not much real division noticeable at all among the people but the women are 'holy terrors,' they are mud-slinging and name-calling, and spitting and froughting [*sic*] to the mouth like angry cats, and always casting up about their relatives that died for Ireland.

He added, with considerable prescience considering the studiedly male composition of Irish parliaments during the subsequent generation:

I think the Irish people will not be in a hurry to elect women to represent them, they have never stopped canvassing and wire pulling to get members of An Dáil to vote against the Treaty.[3]

This perception was a popularly held one; O'Connor was by no means an untypical male chauvinist amid a nation of sexual egalitarians but a shrewd observer. The anti-Treatyites were later to be dubbed the 'Women and Childers Party'. Michael Hayes remembered that some Dáil deputies would have voted for the Treaty were it not for pressure from their wives: 'Many of the women were frantically anti-Treaty.' When de Valera decided to oppose the Treaty, the republican women seem indeed to have been particularly quick to conclude that Collins was a traitor. Several prominent women opponents of the Treaty alleged that Collins had been bribed by being offered the hand of a princess of the house of Windsor. One of the women TDs said rather defensively during the Treaty debate:

When it was found that the women deputies of An Dáil were not open to canvass, the matter was dismissed with the remark: 'Oh, naturally, these women are very bitter.' Well now, I protest against that. No woman in this Dáil is going to give her vote merely because she is warped by a deep personal loss. The women of Ireland have not appeared much on the political stage. That does not mean that they have no deep convictions about Ireland's status and freedom. It was the mother of the Pearses who made them what they were. The sister of Terence MacSwiney [Mary MacSwiney] influenced her brother and is now carrying on his life's work. Deputy Mrs. Clarke, the widow of Tom Clarke, was bred in the Fenian household of her uncle, John Daly of Limerick.

An early triumph for the anti-Treatyites was the victory of their side in the women's arm of the IRA, Cumann na mBan, which voted overwhelmingly against the settlement. In late February 1922 the Sinn Féin ardfheis was held in Dublin, and a similar victory for the anti-Treatyites occurred. The *Freeman's Journal* commented that the women's delegates were particularly antagonistic to the settlement and noted also that the women tended to come very disproportionately from the towns.

There is no sex bar in Sinn Féin, and women are on exactly the same terms as men. There will be as a result of this many women delegates, but it is a curious fact that practically all women delegates come from the cities and towns of Ireland. By the real country clubs few, if any, women have been elected; in fact it is notable that while in town clubs women often share the officer posts with men, in the country they are seldom even members. This is probably due not so much to sex antagonism as to the fact that farmers' wives and daughters have to work too hard and continuously on the farms to have time for politics.

An article by Anna Joyce some days later pointed out that the pro-Treaty women had dropped out of Cumann na mBan and that the almost unanimous vote gave an illusion of female solidarity. Women, she opined, were less politically experienced and not as well educated as were men. It does look as though the subordination of women to men in Irish Victorian culture was materially counterbalanced by a psychological dependence of many of the men on their womenfolk. The 'Mammy's boy' syndrome, long a joke in Irish culture, seems to have had some reality behind it; much of the unreality of republican political ideas seems to have been derived from the political emotionalism of inexperienced girl-friends, wives and mothers filtered through psychologically intimidated young warriors and politicians. Certainly the extreme male chauvinism exhibited by both male and female voters for a generation after the Civil War must be partly connected with a dislike of the idea of women having political power that was, possibly, in turn partly derived from the bizarre behaviour exhibited by so many newly emancipated women in the period 1919–23. A similar wish to control young men, which was certainly very visible in schools of the same period, may be partly similarly derived from a fear of the young men 'getting out of hand', as they had very definitely done between 1913 and 1923. The genies of youth and sexuality had been put back in the bottle by church, state and voter after the Civil War; the stopper was to be kept firmly in for a generation after 1923— a classic post-revolutionary reaction. However, in 1922 the young men and women were still making the running, organising political clubs, drilling, agitating, making speeches, and publishing little newspapers and pamphlets.

There is considerable evidence that the Sinn Féin ardfheis of February 1922 was rigged by those opposed to the Treaty. The *Irish Independent* reported:

> Correspondents in different parts of the country call attention to the very strenuous efforts of anti-Treaty advocates in their endeavour to influence the Sinn Féin Cumainn, who are now appointing the delegates to the Ard-Fheis to be held on February 7. That meeting of the Ard-Fheis is to decide what the future policy of the Sinn Féin organisation is to be and on which side—for or against the Treaty—the machinery and funds of the organisation are to be utilised in the coming General Election [of 16 June 1922] on the Irish Free State issue.
>
> Undoubtedly the Provisional Government and many leading supporters of the Treaty have been very much handicapped owing to the vast amount of work they are confronted with in taking over all the British Government services and departments in Ireland, and consequently they had not the time or opportunity of the opposition party amongst the Cumainn.

A strange combination of Dublin radicalism and rural antinomianism gripped the anti-Treatyites in 1922. The *Freeman's Journal* commented as early as 14 December 1921:

> Opposition to the Treaty of Independence is evident in Dublin to a much greater extent than throughout the country.
>
> That is not to exaggerate the amount of dissatisfaction in the capital, which is more vocal than powerful. Men who have just returned from the Midlands and the West are astonished to find a minority in Dublin opposed to harvesting the fruits of the struggle.
>
> In the West particularly, including the counties of Limerick, Galway and Clare, the Treaty is an accepted fact, and the people are all looking ahead. They are discussing the constitution of the Provisional Government which will immediately follow ratification, and the date of the evacuation by the British Army.

Personal hatreds and envies seem to have become uncontrollable, and not all of it was between the two sides. Secret animosities lurked within the pro-Treaty group as well. Blythe allegedly quoted O'Higgins as remarking in late 1921: 'That crooked Spanish bastard will get the better of that pasty-faced blasphemous fucker from Cork.'[4] On the other hand, however, many participants retained contacts and friendship with the other side through the entire period. Frank Aiken, for example, refused to commit his IRA force to the Anti-Treaty side, tried to stay 'neutral anti-Treaty', kept his lines out to both sides, and was to admit publicly and repeatedly that the people were pro-Treaty, even though he disagreed with them personally. Others refused to be involved at all and gave up politics temporarily or permanently. The year 1923 was to see an extraordinary surge in religious vocations among both men and women, as large numbers of politicised young people gave up the secular world for the sacred.

Disorder increased throughout 1922 and early 1923. The establishment of the Irish state coincided with perhaps three thousand violent deaths during this period.[5] At the time, theft was more commented on than killing, reflecting the mores of the time. An early symptom of the coming conflict was a concerted series of bank raids on 1 and 2 May 1922. The biggest hauls were £18,000 from Ennis, £20,910 from Tipperary, £18,285 from Clonmel, and £10,000 from Ballina. Bank raids totalled £167,000 between 1 January and 22 July 1922. On top of that, Customs and Excise yielded £73,000 to the IRA in illegal cheques.[6]

Free State gossip credited Republicans close to de Valera with keeping large sums for themselves to start businesses and buy themselves large houses. The 'Belfast Boycott' was used as an excuse for a large proportion of the local population to strip goods trains from the North in Tipperary. Popular hostility to banks helped to rationalise the raids; one of Seán Moylan's IRA, a bank robber in County Limerick, remarked, 'Sure it's only a venial sin to rob a bank.'[7] The absence of any reverence for civil law as distinct from religious precept is classic. Many people do not seem to have cared much, and subsequently showed themselves quite happy to vote for well-known thieves. A Garda report of 1929 on County Clare concerning the occasionally murderous activities of local IRA remnants reminisced on the colourful past of certain Fianna Fáil county councillors who had allegedly set themselves up in business for life on the proceeds of bank raids. A prominent member of the council had been expelled from the IRA after being tried by Seán MacBride and Moss Twomey. He had used raid money afterwards to set up a motor business, 'and this is the man who holds forth on good government.'[8] The remnant IRA appeared to disapprove of this more than did the citizenry of County Clare.

Almost certainly, popular support for the Free State was generated by a wish for orderly government and disgust at the fanaticism and criminality of many of the IRA and their supporters. An *Irish Times* reporter, in a fascinating eye-witness dispatch, observed in central Dublin in early July 1922, soon after the siege of the Four Courts:

> For the first time in our history a Government using force to put down an insurrection has had the overwhelming support of the common people. As one moved about in the back streets, it was possible to gather the general feeling. Certainly there was some support for the Irregular cause, and what support they had was of a vociferous quality. It was apparent, however, that its mainspring was Sentiment and personal ties of kinship between the declaimers and the defenders [the IRA]. For every vehement harangue there were twenty solid and silent opponents, who only vented an occasional growl of disapproval to show their real opinion. When it came to deeds, not words, the kindly attentions paid to the troops wherever they were quartered showed their own personal popularity and the popularity of their cause.

During the Truce, considerable quantities of arms had been appropriated by the IRA, and the Civil War IRA was far better armed than the IRA of 1920. Besides IRA violence, many politically unattached criminals took advantage of the situation. A pro-Treaty TD and another Free State sympathiser from the south wrote to Mulcahy in early January 1923, describing the south of Ireland as being under an IRA terror rule, whose main object was to smash the new state by physical destruction of the infrastructure and by looting. Murder, he reported, had become unnecessary, as owners of land would not dare deal with landgrabbers.

> Not only is there a variety of interests and motives [among the republicans], but there is a variety of methods. Homes

and farms are burned in a wages dispute; haggards are burned in a land dispute; trains are attacked; Post Offices robbed; Banks raided, individuals robbed without any patriotic pretences or in the name of the Republic, men are murdered for personal reasons or in the name of the Republic and so on.

Making the civilian population unwilling to resist was an effective way of wrecking the Free State. However, republican atrocities also had the effect of making people end up being indifferent to Free State ruthlessness, and the electorate seem to have consented quietly to the executions. O'Higgins commented at this time that opposition to the government was only partly due to the Treaty. Much of it, he argued, was due to a general reaction from the selflessness of 1919–21. There was also a sense that anyone who had done his share was entitled to an easy life afterwards. 'Leavened in with a small amount of idealism and fanaticism' there was a good deal of 'greed and envy and lust and drunkenness and irresponsibility.' What was needed was 'executions in every county; prevention of outlawry, and elimination of legitimate grievances.' The Free State would have to 'kill the active Irregular, tackle the passive Irregular, make friends with the rest.'

As I have already suggested, the Free State army, as it gradually conquered Munster and Connacht, was clearly welcome to the majority of the people. An unnamed prominent Cork figure claimed as early as 21 July that the army would be welcome in the IRA-occupied south. Such a welcome was not always worthily motivated. The taking of Waterford barracks by the Free State on 23 July, for example, was greeted with great cheering and an orgy of looting by the population. There were night-long celebrations when the IRA were driven out of Claremorris, County Mayo, on 24 July. At the end of July the Free State army was welcomed by huge crowds in Tipperary town. This was in part due to the fact that the IRA had burned down such factories as the town possessed, thereby throwing many out of work. Unlike the IRA, the Free State army was relatively controllable by its hierarchy, and the IRA had, in the absence of payment, maintained themselves at the expense of the local people. A dead IRA man in Mayo was found with £800 in his pocket, an enormous sum for that time. Unlike the British army or the IRA, the Free State army did not generally kill civilians, whether on the grounds of suspected political affiliation or, for that matter, out of simple murderousness. Clonmel gave a particularly enthusiastic welcome to the Free State army, as did west Clare and Mayo. In Clonmel on 11 August,

> amid scenes of enthusiasm, Commandant-General Prout, with the column of national troops, to which I have attached myself, entered Clonmel . . . The people thronged the streets, and gave cheer after cheer for the victor of Kilkenny and Waterford. The soldiers were shaken by the hands, and doors were thrown open for their welcome. Captain Mackey, a native of the town, had a remarkable reception. He was raised shoulder-high by the people, and borne triumphantly through the streets.[9]

The fact that much of the new army was made up of young men of the type who had been British army volunteers a few years earlier may have had something to do with the enthusiasm shown by people in a garrison town like Clonmel. There does, however, seem to have been a genuine relief and a widespread perception of the army as a liberator.

ESTABLISHING PUBLIC ORDER: POLICE

To recapitulate briefly, the IRA had become increasingly restive after the 7 January vote. On 13 January, Mulcahy already felt obliged to warn James O'Donovan, GHQ director of chemicals, that the Dáil was still the elected government of the Republic and that supreme control of the army was vested in that civilian assembly and not in the IRA leadership. The Republic, he assured O'Donovan, was to stay in being until disestablished by the voters and replaced by the Free State.

Meanwhile, under the Provisional Government, the Dáil ministers, wearing their Provisional Government hats, proceeded to take over the British government apparatus in Ireland. The British forces proceeded very rapidly to evacuate the twenty-six counties, and Collins moved rapidly to put his sections of the IRA into green uniforms. The new ministers showed considerable energy and ability in taking over the government. As already narrated,

Blythe was quick to paralyse the small group of Dáil civil servants transferred to the new synthesised Department of Local Government. As the last chapter argued, this department was crucial in that it had actual legal control over the local administrative apparatus, and Dáil authority was generally accepted by the local representative bodies.

The power to tax slipped smoothly into the hands of the Provisional Government. The real problem was the complete absence of any effective agency of enforcement, now that the RIC was not only demoralised but being stood down. The RIC, which had begged the Castle government some years earlier to permit its own disarmament, had been destroyed as a consequence of its being really a gendarmerie rather than a constabulary. The new government, after an initial fumble, was not to repeat that mistake. By early 1922 the only regular police force still functioning after a fashion outside the docklands of Dublin was the unarmed Dublin Metropolitan Police, which was to be taken in bodily into the new Civic Guard, soon to be renamed the Garda Síochána.

Contrary to myth, the name of the new police force was the normal journalistic term for an unarmed police and appears to have had little to do with Catholic ambitions to ape the Spanish *Guardia Civil.* The DMP's authority was, during the War of Independence, dependent on IRA say-so. The Irish Republican Police was a cipher. The rural RIC, armed as it was, was regarded by the IRA as a legitimate target: many policemen were murdered by the IRA between 1919 and the Truce of July 1921.

However, the new Free State regime had a crucial cultural ace-in-the-hole: the taboo on killing unarmed men and women who could not reasonably be seen as spies or informers. It was on this taboo that the new government was eventually to trade in creating its new police force in 1922–23.

Meanwhile the country was unpoliced, and uncontrollable gangs of young men roamed at will and burned out unionists, shopkeepers, and those they regarded as either political anathema or agrarian enemies. Post offices and banks were raided for enormous sums. A Hobbesian state of nature seemed in prospect, not only in the eyes of the rich and privileged but also in the eyes of the poor and vulnerable. Murder, rape and robbery became unpreventable and unpunishable as the British hastily evacuated and the Irish were left with a 'government' that was to a great extent still one of make-believe and based on the transient will of the Public Band rather than on electoral decisions or on a political culture that accepted rational-legal standards.

Nationalist radicals had always disliked the RIC, which had policed most of the country since the early nineteenth century and done so obediently and with a discipline that was quasi-military. The RIC's problem, quite apart from being armed, was that it was required to keep an eye on political activity, defined by the authorities as including not only subversion but also nationalist activities such as those represented by the GAA and the Gaelic League. On top of this, the RIC was required to keep an eye on the new trade unions and on organisations such as the Ancient Order of Hibernians and the National Foresters.

The RIC clearly saw the falsity of their position once the Irish question exploded in everybody's face after 1912. It wished to be converted from a gendarmerie to a genuine constabulary. As mentioned already, during the First World War it quietly asked the British government that it be disarmed and converted into a rural equivalent of the DMP. Not only was the request refused but the fact that it had been made was censored by the British authorities under the Defence of the Realm Act. After the War, the *Freeman's Journal* complained that Dublin Castle had prevented the papers from publishing

> the protests of the rank-and-file against the diversion of the police from their proper duties as a civil force; and their suggestions for their own security. The most serious of these suggestions was that they should be disarmed of military weapons. The possession of these weapons was, the police themselves said, only a source of danger to them and an invitation to attack. If there were no weapons in the police barracks, they declared, there would be no [IRA] raids.[10]

Instead, of course, the British government's reaction to the IRA campaign was to militarise the RIC further and eventually to attempt to stiffen it with British military veterans in the form of the Black and Tans, an uncontrollable paramilitary force and one that became more uncontrollable, exasperated as these ex-soldiers were at the 'unfair' guerrilla tactics used by the IRA. With the demise of the British regime, a policing vacuum opened up, Austin Stack's Department of Home Affairs in the Dáil government deserving Collins's withering contempt.[11]

However, the central idea of an unarmed and non-political police force stuck, as did the idea of the policeman as civilian law-enforcer in contrast to the heavily militarised RIC. The idea seems to have been directly inspired by the existing example of the DMP, the unarmed and apolitical city constabulary that had early made its peace with Sinn Féin and the IRA. Under the Treaty the RIC was disbanded and the function of policing was handed over to the Provisional Government. Significantly, the DMP continued to function under the new regime.

Interestingly, the new government's first reflex was to establish a new version of the RIC for areas outside Dublin, complete with rifles but on a more modest scale. This was prompted not only by the familiar example of the RIC precedent but also by the outbreak of armed criminality that accompanied the collapse of the British regime. The unrest prompted Collins to organise a special police squad, 'Oriel House', ex-IRA converted hastily into a CID whose main purpose was to protect the Dáil and Provisional Government. In the beginning it was nominally under the control of the Provisional Government's Department of Defence and rapidly earned itself 'an unenviable reputation for toughness, unscrupulousness and violence.'[12] At the end of 1922 it was transferred to the Department of Home Affairs. After the Civil War this now notorious unit was disbanded because of its uncontrollability and occasional murderousness.

The Civic Guard formally came into being on 22 February 1922. The first Commissioner was a pro-Treaty Dáil deputy, Michael Staines; the principle of separating the legislative from the executive functions had not yet quite caught on. The original decision to set up an armed police force, a decision whose wisdom was disputed from the beginning, was soon reversed. As the political climate deteriorated in early 1922, it became clear that anti-Treaty elements were attempting to penetrate the new force, most of whose members were, after all, IRA veterans. In the temporary depot at Kildare a self-appointed committee consisting of anti-Treaty IRA veterans seized the armoury and the camp on 24 April. They alleged that preference was being given to RIC veterans in the appointment of officers. In point of fact, relatively few RIC were brought into the Civic Guard, precisely because of the resentment this would have generated. The seizure of the depot was tolerated by a remarkably patient government until Staines and his fellow-officers

> were literally chased out of the Depot and of the town of Kildare. They describe how they were pursued by a threatening mob containing many members of the Civic Guard and how they had to run for their lives and take shelter, after many adventures, in the house of the Parish Priest for the night.[13]

Part of the problem was indeed the resentment orchestrated by anti-Treatyites against the small number of RIC veterans, mainly Collins's spies and lieutenants, combined with early retirers who had taken the Dáil side in the War of Independence. Essentially, this resentment was worked on in the interests of the anti-Treaty IRA. Most importantly, this coup in Kildare was specifically recognised by the government as 'the first overt act of hostility' against it by the IRA.[14]

The ironic and benign outcome of this episode was the standing down of the infant Civic Guard and its immediate re-establishment as an unarmed force along the lines suggested years earlier by the RIC to the Castle government. Selective re-enlistment into the new unarmed version of the Civic Guard went ahead rapidly. Some RIC veterans were used to 'stiffen' the force, and 'foreign' advisers were also used. The new force was to be only about two-thirds the size of its predecessor, and the guards were not to be concentrated together in large barracks as the RIC had been. The idea of the isolated village bobby was finally to be applied in Ireland. In particular, the new force was to be absolved of responsibility for 'political' and 'military' duties of the kinds that had burdened the RIC. For the moment, these duties would be carried on by the new army; later they were to be transferred to the Special Branch of the Garda Síochána in 1926, just in time to investigate, unsuccessfully, the murder of Kevin O'Higgins in 1927.

The essential distinction between the unarmed apolitical Civic Guard and the older RIC stuck. To kill an unarmed policeman became a taboo, even among the IRA. A new, post-British division of labour between the police, the army and what was to become the Special Branch was being worked out by trial and error. The new force was to be heavily centralised, however, in part in reaction to the Kildare events.[15]

The Public Band was a local phenomenon, based on ties of kinship and faction. The new Civic Guard had immediately to cope with the strength of these traditional local loyalties.

> In the Civic Guard there was one very dangerous feature which we can best describe as parochial allegiance—following the lead of somebody because the members happen to have fought with him [in the IRA] or were from the same district. As far as possible an officer should not have a man from his own district under his direct charge. It is not fair to either.[16]

The old RIC rule that prohibited a policeman from serving near his home place was reproduced for the Civic Guard. Police pay was regarded as very high. Much of the unrest in the new force was due less to discontent than to lack of training and youthful high spirits. Young peasant boys who had been away from the discipline of home and who had not been subjected to a true military discipline took time to be licked into shape. Ernest Blythe recalled talking to a sentry at Government Buildings in June 1922, shortly before the Civil War began. A fusillade of shots was heard nearby, and Blythe jumped to the conclusion that the anti-Treaty forces had launched their long-expected attack. The sentry said casually, 'Oh, it's nothing. It's them Civic Guards. They were paid last night.'[17]

Eoin O'Duffy replaced Staines as Commissioner. By May 1922 the RIC had withdrawn from outlying areas and had ceased to function in the twenty-six counties. The Civic Guard was formed firstly at the RDS grounds in Ballsbridge but was soon moved into the old RIC depot in the Phoenix Park. During the second half of 1922, while the Civil War rumbled on, squads of guards were ordered to report to their sergeants around the country. This everyday process is rendered bizarre by the fact that a war of sorts was going on at the same time. Essentially the new force followed in the footsteps of the Free State army as it gradually occupied the country and pushed what was left of the IRA south and west, rolling up the Republican 'front' in Munster and Connacht.

The new policemen were popular, especially in the context of a society that had been without normal policing for several years. The guards were recruited from the IRA and the DMP. Discipline came to be inspired by RIC and British army precedents and was inevitably somewhat soldierly, which comported oddly with the force's assigned role as an unarmed 'civilian' constabulary. Essentially it was, and still is, a constabulary with some of the organisational characteristics of a gendarmerie. Quiet understandings were reached with the local IRA in many areas; the guards were to occupy themselves only with non-political crime, ensuring that public houses closed on time, that thieves were arrested, and that rapists and other criminals were suppressed. A blind eye was turned to the Public Band: that was army business. The IRA eventually accepted this tacit bargain, leaving the Civil War to be fought out between the Free State army and the IRA. One guard recalled that during the Civil War

> we used to meet IRA with arms in Elton [County Limerick] and we said good night to them and they said good night to us.[18]

Civic Guard stations were commonly raided by the local IRA, but normally the new policemen were physically unharmed. Sometimes their uniforms were taken from them. Commonly, the Guards achieved local approval by being involved, as the RIC could not have been, in the Gaelic games favoured by both Free Staters and IRA.[19]

The attitude of the anti-Treatyites to the new and untried police varied. Very early on, the Civic Guard was denounced by the IRA ruling junta as a 'new RIC', but this tack was gradually abandoned when it became obvious that it was a very different kind of force, symbolised physically by the disarmament of September 1922 and by the shift in uniform colour from quasi-military RIC green to policeman's blue. Many IRA merely despised the new force. By October 1922, Liam Lynch and the GHQ of the IRA had, with their usual republican astigmatism towards the logic of Irish politics, decided that the Guards had refused to be armed because of their cowardly fear of the IRA. IRA leaders first hoped to provoke the Guards into taking up arms but later accepted their unarmed status. Lynch clearly underrated the potential of the Guards, and wrote in October 1922:

If the Civic Guard are properly managed [by the IRA], they should not cause much trouble, as fifty per cent of the force are more Republican than Free State—25% are useless to either side and may be disregarded, and the remainder, owing to the fact that they may not be stationed within twenty miles of any town in which they have relatives and that they will be in a minority in Barracks with men of the previously mentioned classes, will be in no way dangerous.

In all circles of the Civic Guard there is continual mention of the fact that the I.R.A. have not taken any offensive against them, and when the time comes for them to take up political work, unless something occurs in the meantime to alter this opinion—this should account for large resignations.

There is very bad morale in the force as a whole, and in any Barracks to which they are sent there are only likely to be one or two men of experience or administrative ability owing to the inclusion in administrative circles of a large number of inexperienced Army [IRA] men.[20]

Lynch felt that the Civic Guard offered young men a 'cushy job', and the force could be regarded as harmless, by analogy with the DMP. In a sense he was quite right, and the Civic Guard could be seen accurately enough as an extension of the DMP into rural areas; in a way, the DMP can be seen as a model for the Civic Guards. On 12 December 1922 a general order was issued by the IRA not to fire on unarmed guards.[21] The acceptance by even the anti-Treatyites of the new policemen in a time of civil war was an extraordinary triumph for the Free State and reflected the political dexterity of some of the new state's leaders. It also reflected a tacit republican recognition of the unpopularity of their own cause and a dawning recognition of the illusory nature of their republic in the face of the reality of the Free State. Further, this strange stand-off between the IRA and the Civic Guard reflected the unreality of a civil war in a society that was steadily and quietly re-establishing a civil order regardless of the revolutionary and insurrectionist rhetoric of the republicans.

J. G. Douglas wrote to the Attorney-General of the Free State in July 1923 asking that the government, now that it was firmly in the saddle and had defeated the IRA, press forward with building a 'structure of order which was winning the respect of the people.'

The sending out of an unarmed police force was an act of courage and wisdom on the part of the Government, and I believe did a good deal to add to public confidence and hope for the future. The promised creation of a new judiciary at an early date together with an unarmed police force with only the military in case of extreme disorder or organised violence, all pointed towards a speedy establishment of an Irish State. My idea is that the aim of the Government should be to slowly and steadily withdraw the military rule with its abnormal powers and substitute the civil authority acting strictly in the spirit of the Constitution [of the Free State].[22]

The rapid deployment of an unarmed police force in time of civil war contrasted starkly with the emergence of an armed gendarmerie in Northern Ireland, in the form of a descendant of the RIC, the Royal Ulster Constabulary, augmented by an occasionally murderous armed part-time constabulary recruited from the ranks of the Protestant community; Catholics who joined were objects of intimidation by both sides. Unlike the Civic Guards, the RUC and the special constabularies were seen as fair game by the IRA.[23]

On 16 November 1922 the *Freeman's Journal* editorialised on the killing of a guard in County Tipperary and appealed in a curious way to the better nature of the IRA leaders to prevent any further such killings.

The Civic Guard gives Ireland what the plain people of the country have been demanding for nearly a century—a non-political, unarmed police force strictly confined to non-political duties.

In the very height of the war with the British occupation the IRA and its authorities came to terms with the Dublin Metropolitan Police even though the latter continued under British control.

The Dublin Metropolitan Police laid aside its revolvers, cut its connection with the political intelligence department, and confined itself to its work as a civil police force.

The IRA co-operated with them in laying looters and robbers by the heels.

Ever since the unfortunate division in the IRA some of the
dissentient units contributed in the same patriotic way against
the common enemies of the people.

Why should the Civic Guard not be given the same fair
treatment on the same terms?[24]

The new police force also reflected the new government's
near-fixation on the necessity for economy in administration. It
was to be far smaller than the older force.[25] A comparison of the
number of Civic Guard stations with those of the RIC in 1914
showed a very marked decrease: 797 as against 1,196 in the
twenty-six counties.[26] The parsimony of the new government,
which has already been documented for health and welfare,
extended to law enforcement as well.

The entire process of establishing the new police was aided
by the fact that the area of the Free State was in fact normally
one of very little ordinary crime. The Troubles of 1913–23 had
had the effect of encouraging a general lawlessness, and since
even the leaders of the independence movement were divided
on the issue of governmental legitimacy, the population were
able to evade or disregard the instructions of the various authorities purporting to have governmental authority.

The licensing laws were generally ignored, and illegal distill-
ing went on everywhere between 1919 and 1923 because of the
absence of regular policing.[27] The ready availability of drink,
often produced at gunpoint, contributed mightily to the discipline problems of both the IRA and the Free State army during
the Civil War. The Guards themselves were certainly not immune
to the corrosive effects of drink. Eamon Coogan, whom we have
encountered in chapter 3 wearing his Local Government hat,
transferred to the Guards in early 1922 and gave a vivid account
of a station in Corofin, County Clare, in early 1923. The police
had seized poitín and were drunk on it. Three women in the
cells turned out to have been passers-by kidnapped by the
Guards 'for a purpose better imagined than described.'[28] The
entire local complement of police was fired.

New guards were systematically urged to hold to the ideal of
the unarmed peace officer. O'Duffy, O'Higgins and others used
their considerable rhetorical talents to present the Civic Guard

as brave men, examples to the male youth of the country and undeterred by gunmen and criminals.[29] Like the Free State army, which will be looked at later, the Civic Guard, after a shaky start, gained acceptance except in areas where the surviving remnants of the IRA persisted in long-term resistance, often fuelled by agrarian passions or by criminality. Leitrim, Clare and Kerry were the most recalcitrant counties from the point of view of the police, just as they were for local government purposes. By late 1923 most of the Free State had returned to normal policing, and the full target of 800 police stations had been achieved.[30]

The Civic Guard was a brilliant improvisation. A fundamental reason for its success was the recognition by all sides that its personnel were of republican, pro-Treaty, nationalist and, occasionally, ex-unionist tradition, much as was the population in general. The *Manchester Guardian* of 31 May 1923 observed that the make-up of the Free State army, the Civic Guard and the IRA scarcely differed. The real problem was unemployment; 'there is not room in these organisations for everybody, and the present incumbents got there first.'[31] The acceptance of the new police was aided by the obvious inadequacy of the Irish Republican Police. Furthermore, republicans saw themselves as defending an Irish Republic against domestic traitors in the form of the Free State army. This entailed an ideological commitment to law and order that forced them into a grudging acceptance of the Guards as the only available source of such order. This acceptance in turn was an important turning-point in the general acceptance of Free State democracy at the general election of August 1923.

The simple device of disarming the new police force ironically gave it exactly the status begged for by the RIC representative body before the Anglo-Irish War. A disarmed and depoliticised RIC might have changed the entire character of that conflict and perhaps rendered the physical force policy of the Dáil illegitimate in the eyes of many. British rule was unpopular only in part because it was British and unresponsive to the will of the Irish voter; it was unpopular also because it was armed and untrusting. In effect, the British government in Ireland rejected a golden opportunity to civilianise its own rule in Ireland and draw the teeth of the Sinn Féin argument that the regime was really one of occupation rather than one of democratically legitimised civic rule. The Free State was not to repeat that British error, although it came close to doing so in early 1922 by initially giving guns to the Guards.

Much of the IRA in effect mutinied against the Dáil and Provisional Governments in March 1922. At the special convention held at the end of March in defiance of Mulcahy, Griffith, and the Provisional Government, 220 delegates out of a possible 600 attended and voted down the settlement. Southern and western delegates dominated the proceedings. Civil War was postponed until after the Pact Election of June, but it became obvious to shrewd observers that the Free State was going to have to defend its democracy with armed men. The Free State army was a new army, only notionally a continuation of the old IRA. As pointed out earlier, the idea of such a regular army went back to late 1921, when it was first suggested, ironically enough, by de Valera in an unsuccessful attempt to wrest control of the IRA from Collins. During the first months of 1922 the anti-Treaty IRA, its arms augmented with British rifles, probably had the balance of military advantage but was irresolute and divided internally. Otherwise, as argued earlier, it could easily have crushed the new Free State army, centred in Beggar's Bush barracks in Dublin, in the egg. It failed to take its opportunity, despite being warned that the Provisional Government was training a regular army built around the core of Collins's squad and other pro-Treaty IRA mainly from Leinster and Ulster. Another reason for the IRA's inaction was the residual comradeship felt with Collins's men and also the inherently local and decentralised nature of Public Band organisations such as the old IRA.[32]

The Free State army, unlike the armies of other British Commonwealth countries of the period, was not made up of lightly renamed versions of the old British regiments. On the contrary, these regiments were promptly disbanded. The new Irish army was actually a strange hybrid organisation consisting of IRA veterans, British army veterans, and young, inexperienced and apolitical mercenaries from the garrison towns who traditionally would have joined the British army. In many areas it was organised virtually on IRA or Public Band principles during the emergency period of the Civil War but rapidly showed signs of becoming a non-territorial, barrack-based regular force of full-time professional soldiers.

Acute tensions existed inside the army between ex-IRA and ex-British veterans, later to develop into the Army Mutiny of 1924. Comradely links persisted between many Free State army personnel and the IRA, and information commonly flowed between the lines. The existence of such leakages exaggerated in IRA minds the internal divisions in the Free State army and perhaps lengthened the period of anti-Treatyite resistance to government forces. Certainly, many republicans expected the Free State to disintegrate, as did many other observers, whether unionist or extreme nationalist.

At the beginning, the Irish army was clearly an army of the Dublin area. As late as July 1922 it had no organised presence in Sligo, Mayo, Leitrim, Louth, Offaly, Wexford, Tipperary, Waterford, Cork, Kerry, or west Limerick. Recruitment policy was carefully aimed against overloading the new force with IRA veterans. According to Mulcahy, policy involved pouring cold water on the idea that the Free State army was a 'preserve for any particular self-appointed drops of the National Cream.' On the contrary, only select, politically trustworthy IRA veterans would be taken, and the policy was to absorb into the new force

> the best of the disbanded [British] regiments in a way which will get over any stigma on us for them—and get them broken up sufficiently to absorb them.[33]

The absorption of ex-British soldiers occurred easily, despite Free State soldiers occasionally going into battle with shouts of 'Up the Leinsters!' and 'Up the Munsters!' The absorption of Collins's men was a greater problem, and they were to be disliked not only by their victims but also by the bulk of the Free State army. The real problem, however, was that the army had to be expanded enormously to take control of the territory of the new state, and its strength eventually peaked at about fifty thousand, an immense total in a small country of three million people. As a consequence much of it consisted of untrained, raw and unorganised young men, many of them illiterate and 'civilian' in character. A Free State army medical officer, writing early in the Civil War, was extremely unflattering to the new force, echoing Coogan's description of the Corofin Civic Guard station on a larger scale. Discipline was bad, with the exception of the 1st Western Battalion, some battalions of Dublin Guards, and a few companies elsewhere. The later militarily crucial South-Western Command was

> very badly disciplined, frequently mutinous, very inefficient from a military point of view, sometimes treacherous and, except in certain Barracks, dirty and slovenly.

Rifle maintenance was appalling, mud and rust making weapons commonly more dangerous to their owners than to their targets. The men were naturally physically brave but very ignorant, he reported. Officers were unable to read maps. Essentially they were ex-IRA guerrillas playing at being regular soldiers, whereas they knew, in reality, only about 'street fighting, car bombing and private assassination.' The ex-IRA Free State army officers knew no military law. The soldiers were often health hazards because of the 'filthy habits' of many of them. Sanitation was very bad, and medical orderlies were unskilled. Mess tins were sometimes used 'alternatively as sanitary utensils and for their normal purpose. The function of latrines does not seem to be understood.'

Perhaps most importantly of all, the Free State army had not yet developed a command hierarchy and was not completely controllable, although it was more controllable than the IRA. Relationships between officers and men were dangerously egalitarian, and officers were commonly obeyed only as a personal favour. Privates commonly addressed colonels by their first name; promotion was so rapid that a man starting as a corporal might find himself half way up the officer hierarchy in a matter of months.

There was also a general reluctance to see the IRA as the enemy, a disposition that, after all, the soldiers shared with their commander-in-chief, Michael Collins. There was a tendency to fraternise with the other side. The Free State army's ex-IRA officers' 'inefficiency is only equalled by their conceit.' However, an instructor at the Curragh Camp in July 1922 remarked that the recruits were indeed not fully trained troops 'but as a mob,

as material for an army, they are the finest body in Europe.'
Furthermore, they were making rapid progress.[34]

Not only Liam Lynch expected an internal collapse of the
Free State. On this, if on nothing else, much unionist opinion
coincided with republican opinion: they both despised the emergent Free State, the one because it was the creation of Catholic
rebels, the other because it was putatively a British puppet
regime. As late as January 1923 the *Northern Whig* of Belfast still
felt able to foresee such a debacle. If the Free State army's fidelity ever became untrustworthy,

> the Free State is at once threatened with complete collapse.
> The whole jerry-built structure—Constitution, Parliament,
> Provisional Government, with their 'Gaelic' decorative effects
> —would come down by the run. Like most systems of revolu-
> tionary origin, the Free State is entirely dependent for exis-
> tence on the fidelity of its military forces, and could not
> survive a change of allegiance on their part for a day.[35]

However, the more sympathetic and perceptive correspondent for the *Manchester Guardian*, Stephen Gwynn, could see
that already a counter-tendency had set in. Free State army
efficiency and discipline were improving rapidly. A well-known
Irish veteran of the British army's Western Front, W. R. Murphy,
was now director of operations and was doing 'remarkable work'
in Kerry, following on the degeneration of the Free State campaign in that county into murder of prisoners and military inef-
fectuality under the ex-IRA management of Michael Collins's
Dublin squad. Under Murphy, however, Kerry had gone from
being one of the most disaffected in the Free State to being one
of the quietest.[36] By 19 February, Gwynn felt able to say that
there seemed to be a 'marked improvement' since Christmas
1922 in the discipline and appearance of Free State army soldiers in the Dublin area. Elsewhere, things weren't as good.
However, new officers with British experience were sharpening
things up in the provinces, and the army was far more efficient
than it had been at the beginning. By 19 April, weeks before the
end of the Civil War, a correspondent in the south reported that
the army's conduct was now 'astonishingly good', considering
that 'they have as yet no tradition of respect for their officers.'[37]

It was easy for republican propaganda to exaggerate the number and role of ex-British officers in the Free State army and to represent it as a green-clad regiment of the British army. However, it had one huge advantage over the British forces of two years earlier: it was Irish, and shared with the IRA the local knowledge that the British had lost once the RIC, the eyes of the old regime, had been paralysed.

For example, an important psychological defeat was suffered by the IRA on 18 January 1923, when Liam Deasy, a well-known southern IRA commander, was captured by the Free State. It was decided to execute him. However, in return for a stay of execution, Deasy eventually agreed to sign a letter to the IRA leaders asking for an immediate end to the hopeless resistance to the Free State. Before this 'treasonous' act, however, Denis (Dinny) Lacey of South Tipperary IRA ordered the arrest of five farmers who were brothers of the Free State army's ex-IRA commanders for the area. Lacey threatened to execute all five brothers in the event of Deasy's execution. Tom Ryan, the senior Free State officer involved, recalled:

> I knew that it was possible to contact Lacey urgently through a sweetheart Miss Cooney, a Flying Column comrade of mine pre-Truce, who became Irregular and was at this time one of Lacey's key men [*sic*] . . . She was at business in Clonmel and was known to be doing Irregular work. I called to her address and gave her a dispatch to be delivered in haste to Lacey. The wording of the dispatch was as follows: I understand that Liam Deasy will be executed tomorrow. Should you, following on the event, carry out your threat to execute the five prisoners now held, inside twenty-four hours of execution confirmation—every male member of the Lacey family in South Tipperary will be wiped out. Signed Tom Ryan, Vice Brigadier, National Army.[38]

It will never be known whether or not this was a hollow threat, as Deasy was reprieved by the Free State government for quite separate reasons of policy: he offered his services as a peace intermediary. However, the closeness with which the leaders of the two forces knew each other gave the conflict a peculiar intensity and intimacy that made its occasional viciousness even more unforgivable, as perpetrators and victims commonly knew each other and had roots in the same localities.

During the war itself, discipline rapidly improved, as did efficiency. In early 1923, Denis Gwynn, writing again for the *Manchester Guardian*, was impressed by the Free State army in the Waterford area. Casualness characterised the soldiers. However, in Dublin they were actually beginning to show some signs of professionalism.

I give my personal testimony for what it is worth, but there seems to be a marked improvement in the last two months in the soldiers that one sees in Dublin. Negatively, I have not for some weeks seen any of them drunk, nor have I seen a group of them at a sentry post chatting with girls. Positively, they look smarter, more willing, more alert. They look just as good as the young British post-war soldiers who were here till last year; and I see a guard about the Commander-in-Chief's own home who could not be beaten for appearance.

An anonymous article, perhaps written by Francis Hackett, in the *Literary Digest* of 13 October 1923 observed in similar vein:

Soldier by soldier, company by company, regiment by regiment, he [Mulcahy] was increasing that nucleus of trained men into an Army. They were developing the pride of uniform and the *esprit de corps* which go with the possession of barracks and strong places, and fighting in the open.

The Free State army slowly but relentlessly broke up the IRA, imprisoning the guerrillas in their thousands. Towards the end, twelve thousand IRA members were in jails and prison camps. After many probings by go-betweens, de Valera was sent a final peace offer by Cosgrave on 3 May 1923.

All political action within the country should be based on a recognition by every party in the state of the following principles of order:—

(*a*) that all political issues whether now existing or in the future arising shall be decided by the majority vote of the elected representatives of the people.

(*b*) as a corollary to (*a*) that the people are entitled to have all lethal weapons within the country in the effective custody or control of the Executive Government responsible to the people through their representatives.

Prisoners who signed a simple promise not to take up arms against the elected government would be released, but arms would have to be surrendered first, and the Free State army would then cease fire. Rather shrewdly, the government offered to spare the wounded feelings of the Irregulars. Irish people had an acute sense of the ridiculous, and humiliation of the young men was to be carefully avoided:

The arrangements for the delivery of the arms and the place of their deposit would be made with as much consideration as possible for the feelings of those concerned.

It was promised that the republicans would be allowed to campaign freely for the forthcoming general election. De Valera jibbed at the oath one more time, and then gave up. The IRA dumped arms, but never formally surrendered. The Civil War ended with a whimper.

After the ceasefire the regular, clearly post-IRA and bureaucratised character of the new Free State army became decisive, and Public Band features such as local powerful men being commanders in their home places were done away with. Demobilisation of an army of fifty thousand was not as difficult as might have been expected. Pay was seen as low and chances of advancement, once the conflict ended, poor. Many from both sides ended up meeting each other as emigrants in the booming United States of that decade. By November 1923 army strength was down to 32,821, of whom 16,000 actually refused re-enlistment because of poor pay. Lack of promotion prospects was also probably significant. In yet another area the parsimony of the new regime was having its requisite effects.[39]

In fact the other side of the coin was more important. It was difficult to find suitable recruits for the Free State army once peacetime came. Volunteer recruits were of poor quality. Dubliners in particular were seen as 'poor specimens'. The army had suddenly achieved what was to become its traditional condition of being underfinanced and neglected, under the direct and penny-pinching gaze of the civil servants of the Department of Defence and the Department of Finance. A small, apolitical and professional army, remote in structure and purpose from the old IRA, emerged in 1923. Socially it suffered from low prestige and came to possess a modest view of its own role in the scheme of things. By September 1924 the chief of staff and army generals were complaining about being given back seats at the Tailteann Games, 'while sundry clerks and other minor Government officials and police officers were accommodated in the Distinguished Visitors enclosure.'[40] Soon afterwards the army was to lose its only major political role when the task of fighting political crime was transferred to the Garda Síochána's Special Branch. The Free State rapidly became one of the most demilitarised societies in Europe, its army being essentially a tiny internal security force combined with a squad of mounted ceremonial hussars and a jumping team. By 1927 the Free State army was down to under twelve thousand men, by 1930 to under seven thousand.[41]

The continuity with the old IRA was not organisational or structural, but there were personal links. All top posts in the new peacetime army went to trusted personnel or to technical experts; British, American and, for ceremony, Irish experts were used where they could be found. British army experts were quietly sidelined once their jobs were done. W. R. Murphy, for example, the pacifier of Kerry, was given a senior post in the DMP and virtually written out of history, presumably to his own satisfaction.

The demilitarisation of the Free State set the stage for the emergence of the Civic Guard as the main arm of law enforcement. As we have seen, its acceptance was general, and even the remnants of the IRA came to accept it as the normal constabulary. Even the transfer of anti-IRA duties from the army to the Garda Síochána in 1926 did not seriously affect these essentially cultural relationships. IRA, Civic Guard and Free State army all knew each other, in many cases by relationship or friendship. The army became politically unimportant, the Civic Guard benignly pervasive. What was left of the IRA, however, never forgot the Irish army of 1922–23: it is, after all, the only force ever to have defeated the IRA in the field.

5

Irish Political Culture and the Emergence of the Irish Free State

The Civil War of 1922–23 took place in a culture that was, ironically, very unmilitary and 'civilian', if not always exactly civic. Soldiers and guerrillas, whether serving British, Free State or 'Republican' causes, were young men of modest or very humble background who wished for adventure and escape from home; wars occurred in continental Europe, Africa, and Asia, not at home. Not only was the population unused to warfare, it was equally unused to self-government. What experience the population had had with local self-government at county level in the generation before independence was not particularly happy, as chapter 3 has suggested at some length. On top of that, the collapse of the British administration had left much of the twenty-six counties without any real civil administration at all and effectively in part under the control of self-appointed armed squads based at local level and functioning as so many tiny autonomous republics. Strangely, in the midst of this apparent chaos, certain general services continued to function, the non-financial end of the Post Office and the welfare system in particular. Even the IRA did not dare interfere with these, as they had with the railway and road systems, for obvious reasons. The parallel with post-1969 Northern Ireland, where a guerrilla 'war' coincided with an acceptance of British administration as distinct from a British government, is obvious also.

From January 1922 onwards, as already argued, the military odds were initially strongly in favour of the anti-Treaty forces, but in the longer run, time was on the side of the Free State. In January no true Free State army existed, and it took several months to create; in an extraordinary piece of administrative improvisation, the new state flung together the military organisation consisting of humble, short-contract state employees in arms that was to become the collective, and little-thanked, saviour of Irish democracy. Uniforms, vaguely influenced by German prototypes, were stitched up in Dublin factories. Early parades by the new army in its dark-green uniforms were enthusiastically cheered in Dublin. The army had no trouble in getting recruits in an underemployed economy whose wartime boom had faded.

To fob off the anti-democratic forces of the IRA, and under the influence of Collins's wish to keep the two sides together, an informal pact was made with de Valera in late February. The election that was intended to give the voters a chance of expressing their opinion on the merits of the Treaty was postponed in an attempt to heal the deep divisions in the IRA and in Sinn Féin. The IRA in effect mutinied by holding that convention on 26 March. So unsure of themselves were the new ministers of the Provisional Government that they tolerated this rebellion and virtually connived with the rebels; in many ways they shared the rebels' instincts. De Valera continually attempted to force the Government to revise the election register so as to eliminate dead people and emigrants while including women under thirty. This process would have taken up to six months to complete, and eventually the Government insisted on going forward to an election on the old register. De Valera's purpose was to delegitimise in advance any verdict the electorate might bring in. The pro-Treaty decision of that electorate in June 1922 was to be overwhelmingly confirmed a year later on a complete, over-21 register; de Valera admitted in private during the Civil War, as documented earlier, that such a decision by the voters was inevitable: people would vote for peace rather than for IRA warrior rhetoric. Had de Valera said as much in May 1922, the pattern of Irish political development would have been both different and more benign. However, the difference might not have been to his own political advantage.

BULLETS AND BALLOTS

Frank Gallagher recalled privately afterwards that at the IRA convention of 26 March 1922 'the fire eaters wanted a military dictatorship (especially Tom Barry).'[1] The presses of the *Freeman's*

Journal were smashed after the convention by Rory O'Connor's Four Courts IRA under O'Connor's instructions, because the newspaper published a truthful and unflattering account of the proceedings of this gunmen's parliament. It seems that the newspaper particularly annoyed the warriors by pointing out that only one-third of a possible total of delegates actually met in the Mansion House at a meeting that even the Dáil government, never mind the Provisional Government with which it was inextricably entangled, had forbidden. This assembly has since been apotheosised by various curious ideologues, some of whom actually accumulated political power subsequently in Fianna Fáil and other republican parties.

The occupation of public buildings in Dublin by the IRA was, incidentally, deeply unpopular, and the IRA evacuated several buildings in Dublin because of the relentless barrage of joking comment that the citizenry, well trained in ridicule as Dubliners often were and are, rained down on them. In particular, sardonic Dublin wit seems to have liberated the Ballast Office in Westmoreland Street from the armed 'culchie' countrymen of Rory O'Connor's IRA. T. M. Healy, a cunning and observant analyst, spotted this unpopularity very early. He wrote on 25 March 1922:

> I saw de Valera on Thursday and tried to reason with him. He was very civil, but I could see their plan was to stop the elections. In this they will be defeated, except in a few districts.[2]

Healy concluded privately that the young men of 1916 had done more in a few years than the old men had been able to do in thirty years. He tried to advise de Valera and became one of Collins's key political consultants, as I have noted earlier. He preferred the notionally impious Collins to the pious de Valera. Crucially, he begged Collins to 'disperse' the anti-Treaty forces at the end of March 1922 after O'Connor's extraordinary display of authoritarian obscurantism and his concomitant dictatorial outburst. Collins, sentimentalist as he was in so many ways, demurred from Healy's suggestion, with arguably disastrous results. Healy, like de Valera but more honestly and consistently, being an older and more detached man, saw clearly how deeply disliked the IRA had become since the British had retired to barracks. Collins, like de Valera, had a sneaking regard for—to use the Irish term—the hard men of the south and west who, in rhetoric at least, had won Ireland's freedom. This essentially sentimental sneaking regard was to scupper Collins permanently and de Valera temporarily in this crucial 'long year' of 1922.

The pro-Treaty Publicity Department of the Dáil government documented an increasing drift towards chaos in both parts of Ireland in early 1922. In the North, savage Orange pogroms against Catholics and almost equally murderous IRA retaliations went on. The Unionist government in Belfast in effect used British money to finance the murdering of Catholics, under the guise of policing an admittedly restless and often violent minority. However, pro-Treaty spokesmen in Dublin tried to understate the gravity of the situation and attempted, almost pathetically, to create the impression that the entire island was gradually settling down under a native government in Dublin. The opposite was, of course, the case: in the North, savage state-backed repression killed nationalist insurrection for fifty years. In the South, Dublin's vacillation and physical helplessness permitted widespread looting and murder by the IRA and private enterprise, the one not readily distinguishable from the other, to escalate. Ernest Blythe noted defensively in the spring of 1922:

> Mutiny of certain portions of the Army, the interference with public meetings, lootings, shootings, etc. . . . Certain speeches, apparently advocating civil war, followed by lawless acts by mutineers, have given the impression abroad that the Irish people are about to spring at each other's throats. This, no doubt, will be remedied when the Election puts an end to the present transition period.[3]

It is indeed quite clear that the anti-Treaty forces were terrified of a free election, because they knew very well that it would involve a humiliating landslide against them. As argued earlier, from the point of view of the moderate republicans under de Valera and also that of the fundamentalist republicans under Liam Lynch and the other IRA chieftains, the voters were slavish and intimidated into wanting peace at any price. From another point of view, it was evident that the local IRA companies had often long outlived their welcome and the voters would vote for a return to normality after years of bullying, agitation, murder, and violence.

Interestingly enough, the anti-Treatyites feared a general election not because they were ideologically communist or fascist in political opinion but because they knew they would lose, and lose very badly. The 'Irish Thermidor' of June 1922, if such it should be termed, was one of the very few such post-revolutionary events ever to be decisively ratified by popular vote, as it was in the elections of 1922 and 1923. After all, it was the pro-Treatyites who espoused the idea of majority rule; the anti-Treatyites rejected it by appealing to a theory of the electorate's expressed will being irrelevant and intimidated by various tyrannies, in particular the apparatuses of thought control represented by the journalists and the clergy.

In reality, the electorate were being bullied by nearly everybody *except* the Provisional Government and the Dáil government or nascent Free State. Furthermore, this was quite clear to both sides in advance but never really admitted by the anti-Treatyites. The proposition that the Free State government liberated southern Ireland has never been specifically addressed in official schoolbooks, mainly because the enemies of that liberation commonly ended up, after ten years of democratic competition, as the partially tamed democratic rulers of the country.

On 10 May 1922 a meeting between the two sides occurred, and they desperately tried to come up with an eleventh-hour deal 'with a view to an immediate cessation of hostilities and subsequent Truce.' Harry Boland actually suggested that the Third Dáil have exactly the same personnel as the Second Dáil and that there be no contested election, much as had happened for the Second Dáil, 'elected' undemocratically as it had been in 1921. As related in chapter 2, the undemocratic suggestion that a pact be devised was made: in effect, the anti-Treatyites wanted, and got, an agreement not to submit the Treaty to the voters and to 'fix' the result of the election in advance. Furthermore, pro and anti-Treaty candidates would be offered to the voters in a joint panel; the voters were to be instructed to vote for a joint ticket.[4]

This pact, which promised the anti-Treaty side a place in the post-election government proportionate to its pre-election strength, was fragile from the beginning. Almost certainly it would have constituted a violation of the Treaty had anti-Treatyites been permitted to sit in the Dáil and participate in government without taking the oath of fidelity. Collins remarked afterwards that the pro-Treatyites agreed to the pact essentially under duress; without the pact the IRA would have prevented the election taking place. As it happened, they engaged in extensive ballot-box stuffing; women were reportedly particularly successful at impersonation, because the culture of the era was such that men were wary of challenging women voters. IRA spokesmen such as Ernie O'Malley denounced the election as unfair, because of the age of the register and the exclusion of younger women, which was due to mechanical rather than ideological reasons, as I have suggested. Desmond FitzGerald commented on 22 June:

> One sometimes hears it remarked that the result of the election proves that there should have been no Pact. People seem to forget that but for the Pact it might have been difficult to hold the election.

The IRA were certainly not wedded to free speech or to free elections; local units allegedly burned out the houses of thirty-seven Dáil candidates long before Collins repudiated the pact. An anonymous memorandum of official origin and possibly written by Collins described the dilemma facing the Provisional Government quite bluntly. It was written in response to a report from Northern IRA and Sinn Féin leaders of 12 May 1922. This report pointed out that a split in the south would give the Ulster unionists a huge morale boost and would strengthen their political hand immeasurably. In effect, the rebels in the south under de Valera and Lynch were betraying the northern nationalists for their own local purposes, these northern spokesmen argued. The possible consequent disintegration of the new state in the twenty-six counties would certainly result, the report prophesied convincingly, in 'the permanent partition of the nation'. This report was circulated not only to Collins but to Brugha, de Valera, Griffith, Mulcahy, O'Connor, Lynch, and O'Duffy. A great historical irony is provided by the fact that the northern IRA, besieged as it was by a hostile majority, was pro-Treaty and regarded the anti-Treatyite stance represented by de Valera and Lynch as a threat to the cause of northern nationalists; the real problem, it seems, was not some southern sell-out but rather a romantic southern (i.e. Munster) militaristic mess, which duly occurred. The Provisional Government memorandum noted:

It will be a good thing if we can make peace with the [IRA] soldiers—but we cannot abandon our own position or be deflected from our own course by [anti-Treaty] politicians who are trading on the [southern IRA] soldiers' attitude. [These] Politicians have no power apart from the soldiers' threat of war.

And that war is not for Ireland or against the Treaty but simply to prevent an expression of the people's will.[5]

Collins, pushed into a corner by the intransigence of the anti-Treatyites, apparently decided to turn an initially honest attempt to avoid conflict into a deception of the incorrigible IRA local bosses. At the last moment, in a speech in Cork days before the election, he repudiated the pact publicly, advising the voters to vote for whomever they liked. Anti-Treatyites represented this as a betrayal, but it seems to have been a final explosion of Collins's essentially democratic instincts against the moral elitism of the Public Band as represented by Lynch, O'Connor, and, more ambiguously, de Valera. Furthermore, had he said nothing it seems very unlikely that the electorate would have given any other verdict than it did: for the Treaty and against de Valera's increasingly imaginary Second Dáil Republic. Collins actually said in Cork:

You here are facing an election on Friday, and I am not hampered by being on a platform where there are coalitionists.

I can make a straight appeal to you citizens of Cork, to vote for the candidates you think best of—to vote for the candidates whom the electors of Cork will think will carry on best the work that the citizens of Cork want carried on.

On the day of the election, 16 June 1922—by strange coincidence the eighteenth Bloomsday and in the year of publication of Joyce's masterpiece novel about the common people—despite massive intimidation in some areas the common people heavily favoured the pro-Treatyites, the Labour Party and the Farmers' Party with their votes. Joyce might have said, 'Here Comes Everybody.'

The voters essentially were rejecting the assertion by the IRA, in seizing the Four Courts on 25 April, that the Public Band was morally superior to the Dáil. Also rejected by the people was the proposition that the only democracy that was to count was the internal democracy of the IRA itself. This internal democracy was itself subject to a form of democratic centralism, that oxymoronic Leninist formulation so beloved of a certain kind of twentieth-century left- or right-wing *lumpenintelligent* political activist. Admittedly, democratic centralism in the IRA had to be a fiction; no-one could control the local honchos, even the leadership of the Army Council and the 'Second Dáil'.

Almost by definition, if one were pro-Treaty one could scarcely regard oneself as a member of the post-convention IRA. The executive of the IRA was powerful in theory. Blythe put it exaggeratedly when he commented:

> This [IRA] Executive had extreme [*sic*] control. It was by means of the Irish Volunteers thus controlled that the Republican Government was set up and maintained . . . The approval of the Articles of Agreement for a Treaty necessarily involved the disestablishment of the existing Republic. This caused dissention in the Army and the Country.[6]

The attitude of the IRA to the new army and police was hostile, although, as we have seen, it softened its line on the latter subsequently. The Civic Guard was denounced as a new RIC early on. In general, the IRA demanded a return to the *status quo ante* December 1921. However, the June election in effect ratified the Treaty. On 28 June, under some British pressure because of the assassination of Field-Marshal Wilson, the Free State army attacked the Four Courts, which surrendered on 30 June. No IRA were killed in the assault. Rory O'Connor, an employee of Dublin Corporation, had been apprised by officials of the immense cultural value of the Public Record Office. He deliberately mined the building and timed the mines to go off two hours after the surrender, which they duly did. Twenty Free State soldiers were injured, and the contents of the Public Record Office, containing the social, political and cultural history of Ireland, lovingly accumulated by scholars, were distributed in tiny fragments all over the city. The enormous cultural loss to the Irish nation perpetrated by these putative patriots but actual vandals has been irreversible. The Civil War then began in earnest.[7]

As we have seen, the war was fought between two amateur
armies. Collins remarked in mid-1922: 'We have no Army; we
have only an armed mob.'[8] Inefficiency, indiscipline and internal wrangling were inevitable in the Free State army, given its
mixed provenance. There was, perhaps fortunately, much truth
in the IRA claim that the government's forces were not a direct
or legitimate successor of the old IRA. As we have also seen, discipline gradually improved, and long before January 1923 it was
obvious that the anti-Treatyites were defeated. The new state
that was coming into being was, paradoxically, helped by growing unemployment in the depression that followed the wartime
boom. It was not hard to hire young men as soldiers. Later,
British army veterans were brought in to temper the IRA veterans in the upper ranks, and the Army Mutiny of 1924, which was
easily put down, represented the last attempt by the old IRA and
IRB to act independently inside the new state's structures.

The new army was rather unmilitary, in fact 'civilian' in the
eyes of many, a characteristic it has clung to ever since in the
most civilianised political culture in western Europe apart from
Iceland. The ordinary Free State soldiers of late 1922 erred, in
the words of Denis Gwynn, 'if anything, not in the direction of
militarist ferocity but of civilian slackness.' Hierarchical control
within the army was difficult to establish, because the officers and
men were socially similar; the British caste distinction between officers and men had been abolished, with confusing and, literally,
revolutionary results. The officers

> are for the most part drawn from the same class as the privates,
> are sometimes quite illiterate, and have little of the military
> experience.[9]

An almost non-military, anti-establishment sympathy for the
Irregulars on the other side was quite common in the Free State
army. An intercepted letter from a Free State officer dated
February 1923 described a demoralised army that was paradoxically victorious over an even more demoralised 'enemy'. Eighty
per cent of the officers were unfitted for their jobs because of
lack of education. They could not manage large groups of men.
The NCOs and men despised their officers. Also, the army was
allegedly thoroughly infiltrated by the IRA.

I think it is tolerably well-established that our Army is infested with spies, more especially among the officers. On one occasion I heard a discussion at this mess regarding Tom Barry. In the course of this discussion one of the officers said he hoped Tom Barry would never be caught . . . Some officers are playing a double game.[10]

Others were in effect conniving at IRA activity. Some allegedly didn't want the Civil War to end for the very unheroic, civilian and unmilitary reason that they would then become unemployed. This mixture of 'civilian' uncontrollability and fecklessness, as much as the soldiers' very occasional murderousness, was the reason W. R. Murphy was sent to Kerry to pacify the county. This he duly did, as recounted earlier, bypassing in particular Collins's old squad and the Dublin Guards of the Free State army.

POLITICAL MENTALITIES

A pseudo-legalism of ideological and political style characterised the political argument of both republican and Free State protagonists. On the republican side the oath, rather than the vexed questions of sovereignty or Ulster, was the final stumbling-block, but it did not become the primary issue immediately. It was soon evident after 6 December 1921 that some already saw the oath as the unacceptable feature of the Treaty but that others saw it as tolerable. Others again still essentially saw it as a bar to sovereign status, that is, as an oath of allegiance rather than an oath of fidelity, which is what it actually was. Some saw the Treaty as a breach of the oath to the Republic, and yet others saw it as a breach of the Republic's 'law'. De Valera's own position appeared to shift from his early 'external association' formula to a clearly uninformed questioning of the reality of dominion sovereignty and then to the issue of the oath; presumably because of the influence of Childers, his understanding of the status of the dominions in the British system was impoverished and out of date.

Central to the mind-sets of many anti-Treatyites was a simple personal distrust of the Free State leaders and a contempt for their motivations, a contempt very generously reciprocated by the supporters of the Treaty. This contempt included, on the anti-Treaty side, an increasing conviction of the utter venality of their opponents; those who supported the Treaty were after jobs and status, were sucking up to the British, wanted to become a new Ascendancy, were in Westminster's pay, as so many historical figures in the nationalist tradition had been, were traitors, were 'unspiritual', and were moral dwarfs compared with the men of 1916, who, being dead, did not have to make the moral choices of December 1921.[11]

Anti-Treaty journalism harped continuously on these themes. The Treaty was a sell-out of a heroic and undefeated cause and was immediately used to create an Irish *Dolchstosslegende* for the die-hard republicans. The Provisional Government was, it was argued, merely a British creation and was partitionist. The Second Dáil, deified and rhetorically revered by the anti-Treaty IRA, was claimed to be still in existence after June 1922, because it had never been dissolved. Little weight was given to the observation that the First Dáil had never been dissolved either: it had simply been assumed to have gone out of existence when the Second Dáil was elected in 1921. The Provisional Government, it was also claimed, was simply the result of an illegal *coup d'état* against the only true government of Ireland, that of the Second Dáil up to 6 December 1921. De Valera was particularly keen on this last argument and used it continually in the years between 1923 and 1936. He then stopped.

Back in 1922, de Valera was notionally still president of the Republic in the eyes of these people, despite his rather graceless but formal resignation from that office on 8 January 1922 in favour of Arthur Griffith. It is intriguing to observe that even today the portrait of Arthur Griffith is not included in the gallery of paintings of Irish prime ministers in Leinster House. The Catholic bishops, who supported the Treaty, were 'Castle bishops', it was claimed, conspiring with traitors and hirelings to perpetuate British rule. Worst of all, the voters, the products of centuries of tyranny, had become so spiritually slavish that they could not see that their true obligation as citizens of the Republic was to remain loyal to it and were willing to vote for continued 'enslavement' under the Free State.[12]

As early as 18 July 1922 the IRA admitted publicly that their resistance to the Free State was unpopular: 'the people generally are hostile.' However, it became evident that democratic principles of legitimacy were unimportant compared with a competing set of principles that were essentially of religious origin. The Republic had had transferred to it doctrines structurally echoing those of traditional Tridentine Catholicism: the gates of Hell would not prevail against the Church of Christ, promised the Penny Catechism. Similarly, the gates of Dublin Castle, now penetrated by Michael Collins, that allegedly most unspiritual of men, would not prevail against the Republic of Pearse. Mary MacSwiney wrote to Richard Mulcahy in late 1922:

> You are supporting men who have declared that 'what is wrong with this country is that we are too damned religious— too much spirituality about us and it's materialism that pays.'

The Free State was all about jobs for the boys, she claimed, and was a new Redmondite Tammany backed up by London. However, in the long run, right would triumph.

> You are supplying perjurers, job-hunters, materialists and driving away those who stand for truth, honour and the sanctity of oaths, who refuse to take or sanction others to take an oath of allegiance to the King of England . . . [God] has in store for our dear country that Governments can be built up on a basis of truth and justice and honesty, not as heretofore on trickery, meanness, false oaths and exploitation of the weak.

Anti-Treaty propaganda in 1922–23 tended towards high-flown rhetoric, sentimentality, and exaggeration. Its impact was limited beyond activist cadres, as subsequent electoral behaviour abundantly suggests. Conn Moloney, adjutant-general of the IRA, wrote on 22 August 1922 that IRA propaganda was falling on deaf ears.

> Propaganda against the general public will not be effective at present. Even when our Army held the South intact the people did not support our side with the prospect of victory. They will not be with us now either, not so much because they are against our ideals but because they are anxious for peace, and it is undoubtedly a disheartening situation for most of those who have wholeheartedly supported the Republican

Army during the [British] terror to find that in the hour of victory those on whom we most relied turned their arms viciously against their former comrades in traitorous combat for treacherous Imperial aims and personal considerations regardless of the nation.

The London *Times* commented on 4 April 1923, when there were ten thousand prisoners of war in the custody of the Free State authorities, that

prior suffering happens to be the least effective form of propaganda at the disposal of the Republicans, for so many to whose emotions they appeal have themselves engaged in elaborate tricks to plague British prison officials.[13]

The Labour movement by and large supported the Treaty, although with reservations. Some anti-Treatyite leaders thought that an emphasis on unspiritual but social issues might bring workers over to their cause. On 3 September 1922 the railway workers' lack of enthusiasm for the republican cause was tackled in the form of an offer of a quasi-socialist republican constitution derived from the social programme of the First Dáil. Republican propaganda did not, however, make much impact on the railwaymen, who were being put out of work in large numbers by the activities of the IRA, which included the wholesale destruction of railways and rolling stock. On 4 September 1922, Liam Lynch wrote:

It is not advisable to press this matter but their [the railway workers'] co-operation with the enemy [the Free State government] should be protested against. I wonder how they reconcile their present attitude with all their 'gas' about a Workers' Republic?[14]

Republicans were well aware of their own unpopularity and were actually pleasantly surprised at the relatively strong support they received at partitioned Ireland's first universal-suffrage election in 1923: they received one-quarter of the vote, mainly in poorer and more remote areas. These partly coincided with areas where the IRA presence was strong. Republican prisoners in jail were fascinated by the mechanics of proportional representation and were, in a grudging way, impressed by the pedantic fairness of the proportional representation system devised by the Free State government. The possibilities of Free State democracy were a shock to many republicans, who had been persuaded by republican propagandists like de Valera and Frank Gallagher that electoral democracy in Ireland was corrupt either in the sense of the ballot being interfered with or in the voters themselves being venal or cowardly. In that pre-political culture, the entire process of popular and genuinely competitive election was itself a revelation.

Republican prisoners in Newbridge military camp were being taught courses in constitutional law, local government, and Irish history, under the aegis of Dan O'Donovan, a well-known Dáil civil servant who went anti-Treaty, by September 1923. He and other lecturers suggested that the military victory of the Free State could be reversed by peaceful means. Non-violent penetration of the local government apparatus would, in the long term, deliver the new polity into the hands of its enemies. Local organisational centres were already being set up all over the twenty-six counties. The genesis of what was to become Fianna Fáil occurred in the Free State's prison camps, much as the IRA had been born in the British camps of 1916–17.

Many writers of the time pointed out publicly that the Treaty was no final solution to the Irish problem and that it was, in the words of Collins, merely a stepping-stone to freedom, or 'the freedom to achieve freedom'. However, these arguments fell on deaf republican ears in 1922. P. S. O'Hegarty, for example, in a book published in 1924 pointed out what most pro-Treaty spokesmen had pointed out: the anti-Treatyites had denounced things in the Treaty that were, admittedly, unattractive. The republican movement had

> stressed the things in the Treaty which are irksome to all Irishmen; and by drawing England's attention to those things, by making test questions of them, it has prevented any modification of them. They will all go eventually—the oath and the Governor-General and the Privy council and Partition. But some of them would have gone ere this were it not for the pseudo-Republicans, and all of them will now be somewhat overdue when they depart.

Lynch was killed in battle in early 1923. As long as he lived, his attitudes, which were profoundly anti-democratic and authoritarian, dominated the anti-Treatyite movement. His death certainly hastened the end of the Civil War. Even the anti-Treaty party itself was to be subordinated to military authority; his attitude to politicians was one of deep arrogance and contempt. As early as 30 August 1922 he declared:

> Republican Party representatives must work under our officers —we must control the whole situation there. We have been too soft in this respect in the past . . . Advisability of getting Count Plunkett to protest to the Pope on outrageous conduct and pronouncements of Bishops and Priests here against Army [IRA] campaign . . . Views and opinions of political people are not to be too seriously considered. Our aim and course are now clearly defined and cut and dried. It is certain many influences will be constantly brought to bear to deflect us from them, but these will be brushed aside.

Political illiteracy, deriving from inexperience and youth, was common on both sides. In particular there was a tendency to reduce everything to the military level. Even after their decisive military defeat, republicans clung to their imaginary Republic and commonly dreamt of a revolution that would conclude in its being re-established. The 'GHQ' of the IRA announced as late as January 1924 from its headquarters in Suffolk Street, Dublin:

> Our resistance [to the Free State] has always been constitutional. It was a constitutional duty of the soldier-citizens of the Republic to defend the Republic when attacked . . . But though armed resistance was, and is, constitutional, it is no longer expedient . . .

However, a new realism began to force itself into republicans' thinking. Some of them could even articulate a scepticism about their own propaganda, which had reached a standard of rant and surrealism high even by Irish standards: 'It is futile sob-stuff which even *we* do not read.'[15]

However, de Valera's propaganda on the illegality and illegitimacy of the Treaty and the Free State lingered on. Even in 1932, when his Fianna Fáil formed its first government with Labour support, Executive Council proceedings were labelled those of the 'First Government', thereby denying the legitimacy of the four pro-Treaty Dáils or 'administrations', to use the American term, of the period 1922–32. Oddly, it could also readily be interpreted as ignoring the legitimacy of the underground governments formed by the first two revolutionary Dáils.

On the pro-Treaty side, mentality differed radically. This was so despite a similar militarism, exemplified by the decision to attack the Four Courts and postpone the first meeting of the Third Dáil. The influence of lawyers' thinking was, however, also very noticeable on the Free State side, reflecting the emergence of a demand for lawyers' skills because of the urgency of constructing political institutions for the new state. The ideas of Hugh Kennedy, the Free State's first Attorney-General, were particularly pervasive. In Kevin O'Higgins and Desmond FitzGerald the Free State had brilliant propagandists, while W. T. Cosgrave displayed a capacity to summarise political situations shrewdly and economically. He also displayed a tart and ruthless sense of humour.

Legalism came to dominate the minds of the Treatyites, much as romantic moralism dominated the minds of their opponents. Once ensconced in reasonable jobs themselves, they were happy to install a pedantically meritocratic set of rules for subsequent hirings to the public service. The supporters of the Treaty had to prove, however, that the Free State was the legitimate successor of the state founded in 1919 and play down as much as possible the undoubted fact that the Free State had hybrid origins, being both a successor to the underground Republic and also a product of Westminster legislation.

As already suggested, the Irish language was a useful vehicle for asserting continuity, as the term *Saorstát* could legitimately be rendered in English as either 'Free State' or 'Republic'. What could not be finessed linguistically was the famous oath. The original wording of the oath agreed upon did indeed involve a declaration of allegiance to the monarch, but this was soon whittled down by the Free State's lawyers to one of 'fidelity' to the King in his capacity as head of the Commonwealth.[16] Pressure from the British forced the drafters of the Free State Constitution to moderate their essentially democratic and republican sentiments. Although the final version of the oath was far less royalist than the original one, by that time the oath had become a bug-bear and Civil War inevitable.[17]

Hugh Kennedy in particular argued passionately in early 1922 for the essentially republican character of the new state, despite the superficial trappings of monarchy included in it to pacify the British. He argued cogently that there were essentially two forms of state, that which derived its authority from the people and that which owed its authority to a grant from an external power.[18] This is discussed in more detail in chapter 6.

To anticipate, Kennedy argued that a treaty was by definition a contract between two states. Therefore it followed that Ireland was a sovereign state that had agreed, for the moment, to limit its status to that of Canada, as determined by usage. Kennedy argued that the Free State could, under the Treaty, use all the resources of international law to achieve all the advantages of sovereignty, and do so rapidly. However, the drafters of the Constitution knew only too well that these legalisms would be emotionally unappealing, particularly to the Public Band. In near-despair one unknown draftsman, possibly Kevin O'Sheil, scribbled with some passion in March 1922, when the main lines of the Constitution had been determined, on top of Kennedy's notes:

> People of Ireland, here's your Constitution, and if there's going to be civil war in the name of God fire low 'cos there's only four million of us.[19]

THE TREATY AND IRISH POLITICAL CULTURE

Jeffrey Praeger in *Building Democracy in Ireland* has argued cogently that the Civil War was not just some kind of army mutiny nor an Irish Thermidor but a profound event in the formation of modern Irish political culture. Far from being a squalid squabble between conspirators who envied and distrusted each other, as it appeared certainly to many English and Irish eyes, the conflict echoed a deep division in the Irish political mind. It was far more than a split provoked either by British intransigence or by some ruthless defence of class interest by the Irish bourgeoisie.

Praeger essentially uses Durkheim to argue that the central problem facing the creators of a new state is that of creating a new sense of community. This new sense is needed to correspond 'to the new forms of social organisation accompanying independence.' There is a need to create a sense of national solidarity where only local, kin, tribal, class or religious bonds exist—a need to create the political in its purest sense. By this is meant a loyalty to the state, which is fed by a perception that the state is truly the instrument of the community and not the enemy of the community, set 'over against' the people by a particular class, clique, or foreign power.[20] The state typically is new, weak, and inexperienced. The culture is old, strong, stuck in its ways, and pre-political; there is a weak state and a strong society, an old society and a new state. The two must get married but have problems getting on.

This Durkheimian perspective distinguishes the state from civil society but insists that the state must be understood in the terms by which the civil society itself comes to understand it. The Civil War, Praeger argues, focused on profoundly different and fundamentally 'religious' aspirations about the nature of an independent state—a new and historically quite unprecedented entity in the history of the country, despite many dreams of independent statehood going back to mediaeval times.

Kevin O'Higgins was particularly alert to the problem of inventing a true citizenship, as were many rhetoricians of the Dáil government. During the Civil War he, or someone close to him, wrote pamphlets enjoining, and almost begging, the people to support the infant state. He argued in particular that the executions of people caught in arms after the amnesty expired, and the killing of several prominent anti-Treatyites without trial, were necessary to defend the infant Irish democracy, horrifying though some of the killings might be.

> The duty of the Irish citizen today is to strengthen the State and the intelligence of the State by every means in his power . . . He who would cheat the State of its due is robbing his neighbour as surely as if he put his hand in that neighbour's pocket and stole what belongs to him. The mind that does not realise these things is part of the slave mind inherited from the days of the [British] tyranny.

Another Free State government pamphlet of late 1922 argued that even greater issues than that of the Treaty were involved. Democracy was involved. The people's right to decide through their elected representatives any issue arising in their national policy was definitely challenged, and on the result depended whether the people of this country were to be citizens or a mob coerced and intimidated by an armed [anti-Treaty] minority. The Pact failed because the Four Courts garrison had repudiated the understanding that lay behind it—in particular, the idea of parliamentary supremacy.[21]

Praeger labels the division as one between 'Gaelic-Romantic' and 'Irish-Enlightenment' values or political mentalities. Essentially, Praeger follows F. S. L. Lyons's well-known identification in his *Culture and Anarchy in Ireland, 1890–1939* of three main Irish subcultures: the Anglo-Irish, the Gaelic Irish, and the English-speaking native Irish.[22] Praeger, however, specifically notes that his categories are not intended to refer to the cultural characteristics of specific social entities, unlike Lyons's labels.[23]

Praeger's dichotomy is interesting and illuminating. Certainly the opposition to the Treaty has a definite romantic tinge to it, and it is also true that there is an almost philosophical and classical or 'Roman' tone to O'Higgins's justification for the killing of IRA prisoners, for example. However, there are certain problems with the dichotomy; in particular, it does tend to suggest a natural affinity between cultural closeness to Gaelic culture and opposition to the Treaty. The danger of this is that it encourages a tacit acceptance of the anti-Treaty position that those who accepted the Treaty were somehow less Irish and more assimilated mentally to Britain than were those who rejected the Treaty. This also echoes the ideology of the Gaelic League of 1893, which posited an almost primordial opposition between 'Gaelic' and 'English' culture and which advocated a revival of 'Gaelic civilisation' at the expense of 'English' culture in Ireland.[24]

There are serious problems with this opposition, so central to much of nationalist ideology and so willingly accepted by so many modern scholars because of its superficial plausibility. As several people have argued elsewhere, neo-Gaelic ideology was closely connected in its early years to English and continental European revivalist movements of the late nineteenth century and was, in that sense at least, exotic and 'un-Irish'. Its connection with the real Gaelic past was far more tenuous than was suggested by the barrage of nationalist propaganda of the time or of later decades.

Essentially, the acceptance of the Gaelic Romantic versus Irish Enlightenment opposition tends to encourage acceptance of the national-revivalist fiction that Irish Catholic culture was 'Gaelic', or at least less 'English' than was Irish Protestantism. In fact Irish Catholicism was very much a creation of the Counter-Reformation and was heavily affected by returned Irish missionaries who had been trained in seminaries on the Continent. Furthermore, the Catholic Church in Ireland has been English-speaking since the seventeenth century and, like the reformed version of Christianity in Ireland, used Irish mainly for missionary purposes. It is only in the late nineteenth century that the idea took hold that Catholicism and Irish-speaking could be opposed to Protestantism and English-speaking in any arithmetical or mechanistic way.

The fact is that both sides on the Treaty issue were cultural revivalists, at least in rhetoric. Most leaders on both sides who knew any Irish at all possessed a 'second-hand' English-speaker's knowledge of the language, often acquired after great effort. Even Patrick Pearse, half-English by parentage, learned his Irish as a young adult; his native language was Dublin English. The pro-Treatyite Eoin MacNeill knew far more Irish than did even Eamon de Valera, for example. Pro-Treatyites were as likely to be piously Catholic as were anti-Treatyites. Anti-Treatyites were perhaps even more likely, on average, to have non-Irish roots.[25]

Both sides were neo-Gaelic in ideology. It is true that many of the bourgeois backers of the Treaty were undoubtedly cynical about the prospects of reviving a dying culture, but it is also obvious that many anti-Treatyites and pro-Treatyites knew little about the language and used the term 'Gaelic' as a 'hurrah' word. The confusion, or identification, of the terms 'Gaelic' and 'Catholic' was not new, and it is clear that many assimilated the linguistic-ethnic term to the religious-sectarian one, either innocently or calculatedly.

The differences between the two sides were not posited on some ethnic, settler-versus-native dimension, despite attempts to frame it that way by various propagandists.[26] Rather, they were based partly on class but mainly on elite differences of a non-sociological nature; mutual distrust, envy and contempt amounted to a paranoia that had long underlain formal friendship and ties of loyalty and affection—an emotional set of collective relationships now unreconstructable. The division did, however, have a cultural aspect: it tended to follow a divide that separated those who saw the Republic as a moral and transcendental entity analogous to the Church of Christ, an entity whose citizens were duty-bound to defend it with their purses and their lives, from those who saw the Republic as a bargaining device in achieving rational-legal self-government for as much of Ireland as possible, regardless of formal political labels. Those opposed to the Treaty also tended, consciously or unconsciously, to think of the Irish nation in terms of ethnic rather than civic nationalism. The former type of nationalist ideology sees the nation as a primordial and 'natural' entity to which one belongs whether or not one wants to, by the fact of inheritance of ethnic identity: you are Irish because you were born here and because your identity has been transmitted to you by your parents, almost like your blood group or your hair colour. Furthermore, you have the duty to live up to that identity in your personal life or pay the price of being seen as less patriotic, less courageous, less noble, or simply less *Irish*.

Civic nationalism, on the other hand, focuses on the concept of the free citizen: you can choose your citizenship by an act of individual will; in principle, you can decide not to be Irish and choose to belong to some other nationality by means of a voluntary political contract. The ability of the leaders of the Free State, however reluctantly, to accept the expressed wish of northern unionists to remain British and refuse to join the new Irish state echoes their stronger attachment to civic nationalist thinking. Similarly, the denial by the anti-Treatyites of the possibility that the northerners had a right to secede from the emergent Irish nation-state was derived from their greater attachment to ethnic nationalist ideas.

As is well known, these sets of ideas derive from the argument between France and Germany over the status of Alsace-Lorraine in the late nineteenth century, and before that to contractualist versus Herderian ideas about civic and national identity. Germany insisted that the Alsace-Lorrainers were historically and culturally Germanic; if they did not feel German, they would have to be taught to be, or even forced to be, German. The French, naturally, pointed out that these German-speaking people had clearly chosen to be French.

A similar argument dominated the Irish split of 1922 and the nationalist community for two generations after 1922. The problem is that ethnic nationalism is commonly far more emotionally satisfying than civic nationalism, because it taps into apparently perennial human desires for solidarity and comradeship against the outside world and is psychologically similar to kinship or tribalism in the relationships it proposes between people. By contrast, civic nationalism looks like a bloodless lawyer's creation. Of course, this bloodlessness may be one of its greatest virtues. Seventy years later, Michael Ignatieff was to write:

> What's wrong with the world is not nationalism itself. Every people must have a home, every such hunger must be assuaged. What's wrong is the kind of nation, the kind of home that nationalists want to create and the means they use to seek their ends. A struggle is going on wherever I went between those who still believe that a nation should be a home to all, and that race, colour, religion and creed should be no bar to belonging, and those who want their nation to be home only to their own. It's the battle between the civic and ethnic nation. I know which side I'm on. I also know which side, right now [1993], happens to be winning.[27]

Ignatieff was writing in the context of his recent excursions to Northern Ireland, Yugoslavia, Germany, the Ukraine, and his native Québec. This struggle is not a new one and certainly dominated the debate over the Treaty of 1922.

In much of Irish political culture in the 1920s, republicanism came to be identified not with a classical theory of government involving the principles of representation, public debate and the rule of law, as suggested by Hugh Kennedy or Kevin O'Higgins, but rather with the idea of a moral community created by a single and irreversible plebiscite and sanctified by the blood of martyrs; Irish republicanism was not a political theory but a secular religion. The ideology of republicanism invented by de Valera and such communalist propagandists as Aodh de Blácam still exists, although now mainly in the minds of some members of Sinn Féin and the IRA. The vast majority of Irish people, whether nationalist or unionist, have always stood aloof from it, consciously or subconsciously.

While scarcely admitting it, the voters persistently and quietly accepted the validity of the arguments of the pro-Treaty side. When the Republic of Ireland was declared in 1949 and the last tenuous link with Britain was severed, it was by pro-Treaty means that anti-Treaty ends were achieved. The division of 1922 was indeed a division over means but it was, deep down, also one about ends: a national moral community versus a nation-state of citizens whose individual moral state was, subject to minimal legal restraints, a private rather than a public matter.

By way of supplementing rather than replacing Praeger's categories, I would propose 'republican moralism' and 'nationalist pragmatism' as convenient labels for the two subcultures or collective political styles. Moralism of political style tended to go with an inability to handle the political ideas of those who thought differently, and a related tendency to see disagreement as necessarily motivated by unworthy considerations. Pragmatism, on the other hand, tended to go with an indifference to political passions and with a certain political minimalism: politics was a process by which large numbers of people settled their differences non-violently, rather than being a process by which human beings became better people. Significantly, as suggested earlier, de Valera could speak both of these 'political languages'. Moralism is also associated with what I have referred to as 'communalism', which is an attitude that sees each human being as being of equal worth and to be rewarded equally, regardless of the effort made by the individual and regardless of his or her special abilities; no man, de Valera once remarked, is worth more than a thousand pounds a year. Pragmatism is associated more with individualism or the acceptance of the proposition that human beings have different abilities and energy and that inequality is inevitable and can be defended morally. The moralist's political community is local, is supervised as a shepherd might supervise his flock, is caring, values personal contact, and is profoundly distrustful of change or of individual thought. It is the political culture of a successful peasantry becoming near-subsistence free farmers and of poor people anywhere. In contrast, the pragmatist's political system is an impersonal, unloved and unloving machine that processes demands from citizens impersonally and in a rule-bound way. It is the political culture of the citizen, the bourgeois, the well-off, and the literate. It is similar to the opposition between

Hamiltonianism and Jeffersonianism in the infant United States and is certainly linked historically to that opposition; in this, at least, nationalist Ireland is rather un-European and actually 'fringe American'.

TABLE 1

Irish political subcultures, 1920s

	Republican moralism	Nationalist pragmatism
Institutions	Republic Local police Public band Egalitarianism Church-state alliance Fianna Fáil, Sinn Féin	Free State National police National army Meritocracy Church-state harmony Fine Gael, Labour
Political style	Communalism Moralism Fundamentalism General will (Rousseau) Moral elitism Romantic Transformist Ethnic nationalist	Individualism Legalism Pragmatism Will of all Voter rule Classical Empirical Civic nationalist
Policy stances	Neo-Gaelic Subsistence economy Protectionism Isolationism Zero-sum economics *Dirigisme*	Neo-Gaelic Commercialism Free trade Commonwealth Non-zero-sum economics *Laissez-faire*
Social base	*Gemeinschaft* Peasants, small farmers Unskilled worker Petty bourgeoisie Public sector Rural	*Gesellschaft* Commercial farmers Skilled worker Bourgeoisie Private sector Urban

Table 1 offers a tentative and inevitably impressionistic sketch of the two main subcultures in the nationalist community. The categories are offered as Weberian ideal-types rather than as literal characterisations of the minds of real people: they indicate tendencies or directions. As I have argued, these cultural tendencies are deep-rooted in Irish life and are still operative two generations later.[28] These divisions operate in ways analogous to religious differences, as Irish political culture, like so many other modern democratic political cultures, is heavily coloured by religious tradition. Republican moralism is closely connected with the austere and puritan Catholicism that became rooted in Irish life in Victorian times; it is inspired far more by English puritanism than it is by the semi-paganism of the old Gaelic culture, most of which died even before the Famine. As has been well documented, Irish Catholicism replicated in Ireland a version of what E. P. Thompson has described as Methodist religious terrorism in mid-Victorian England. Religious and millenarian hysteria, fomented by extravagant visions of a literally hellish afterlife for the unspiritual, affected entire political cultures in the British Isles. Quoting Karl Mannheim, Thompson reports:

> Chiliasm has always accompanied revolutionary outbursts and given them their spirit. When this spirit ebbs and deserts these movements, there remains behind in the world a naked mass-frenzy and a despiritualised fury.[29]

Republican moralism is also new but resonates well with the conformist and puritan culture that owner-occupier free farmers seem to create wherever they form a dominant sociological group in society, as in eighteenth-century New England, nineteenth-century New Zealand, nineteenth-century Scandinavia, or nineteenth-century Ontario and Québec. Because of the doctrinally monolithic character of Catholicism, however, emotional extremism could not express itself through millenarianist cults; instead it expressed itself through what was nominally a secular cause but was actually an emotionally charged political and quasi-millenarian nationalism.

Nationalist pragmatism is rooted in Irish versions of political ideas derived ultimately from the English and French Enlightenments and their Scottish and American offshoots. It is intriguing to note that a prominent pro-Treatyite who had much to do with the drafting of the Constitution of the Free State, Kevin O'Sheil, took time off in the middle of the Anglo-Irish War to write *The Birth of a Republic*, a competent popular history for Irish readers of the birth of the American republic a century and a half earlier. The book was published in Dublin in 1920. The influence of American ideas on the Constitutions of both 1922 and 1937 was pervasive and is underrated by many commentators.

Francis Hackett, an acute contemporary observer of the political scene and one who had spent much time in the United States, wrote to Desmond FitzGerald in 1924 portraying the difference between the two sides as one between what he termed the romantic and scientific spirits, in terms quite similar to those I have offered above.

> Our people, mine and yours, are separated, not by Document One and Document Two, but by Scientific Spirit—liberty, curiosity, and Doubt—and Romantic Spirit—which is altitude, certitude and platitude. They start off with a castle in the air, and end up minus two damn fine public buildings.[30]

Mary MacSwiney, a prominent articulator of the fundamentalist anti-Treaty position, put this contrast in a different way in a letter to Richard Mulcahy already cited. For her, what I have termed moral elitism was spirituality, and what I have labelled pragmatism was to her materialism. Pro-Treatyites possessed a weaker version of the Catholic religion than did those who opposed the evil English Treaty. The Free State was all about jobs for the boys (there was a streak of truth in this, but a similar observation could be made about some of the anti-Treatyites), but Ireland would eventually recall its unique historical destiny and become a beacon of holiness in an unspiritual world. In this she was echoing Canon Sheehan's *The Graves at Kilmorna*, with its monk's dream of a post-commercial, purified future Ireland.[31]

FitzGerald, ruminating on the Civil War and Irish political culture some years later, recalled the extraordinarily exaggerated expectations that the coming of independence had generated and the concomitant inevitability of disappointment. It was tacitly assumed that the coming of an Irish state would solve all problems; revolutionary nationalism had a strong streak of what Robert

Tucker, in discussing Stalinism, has termed 'transformism'.[32] This is an ideology or state of mind that denies empirical or scientifically established facts in favour of a view of good political action as being a heroic attempt to change human nature and with it human society: the victory of moralism over realism. Much of the apparent insanity of Soviet policy processes, for example, was rooted in this mental condition. FitzGerald felt that the Irish version of this mentality was rooted in the shock of the modern world as experienced by a people who were still in many ways mediaeval in mentality. In turn, this made statist and communal ideas attractive to Irish people, unused as they were to a non-communal, individualist and sceptical existence in an increasingly post-subsistence, commercialising world.

> Think of the passion that we put into the national struggle. To create a national Government, a national state. I can remember when people spoke of the wonderful things that would happen when we got Home Rule, and the ridiculous things that were expected to come with a Republic. Implicit in our intense nationalism was the supposition that with the coming of a national Government our lives would be radically changed. And how could that be unless the Government took possession of those lives . . .

The goal of independence became a Cargo Cult and was thought of in a partially superstitious fashion, much as traditional Marxists thought of the goal of communist society at the end of history. A hatred of the wealthy as being alien to the people and as having somehow derailed the achieving of the Republic also followed, FitzGerald felt. A predisposition to vote for the party that was more willing to take from the rich and give to the poor followed.

> Other countries grew into the modern world, we were uprooted and plunged into it . . . We had expected an Utopia, an Earthly Paradise analogous to that promised by the Communist religion . . . Our historio-political circumstances had established the belief in our minds that it was possible to abolish all evils by state action.[33]

The coming of independence, FitzGerald argued, led to the disaster of the Civil War and the even worse psychological damage that resulted from it. The conflict demonstrated the fact that Irish people were no more moral or spiritual than other people, despite their much-prized religiosity. A mirror was held up to Kathleen Ni Houlihan's face; the Old Lady did not like what she saw, reacted like Caliban, and retreated into moralistic declamation.

> The first thing our national freedom produced was a Civil War. This evidence of imperfection in ourselves might have been a corrective. Instead of that it gave scandal to many. They had presumed that we possessed a natural perfection. Their patriotism had been founded on that belief. When they saw that evidence of our abundant imperfection their patriotism suffered shipwreck. They washed their hands of their country. They did not seek to examine causes or to distinguish between the two sides in the strife. The phenomenon of Civil War condemned the Irish Race and nation.[34]

The demoralisation produced by the sudden descent from high moral tone to a crabbed legalism was extraordinary. The collapse led to an exaggerated opportunism that filled the vacuum. James Kennedy, in a letter cited earlier, wrote to Richard Mulcahy in late 1922 complaining that 'utter rotters like Gorey' (of the Farmers' Party) were defeating good Sinn Féiners in local politics. Sinn Féin was already 'dead', even before the real fighting started.

> Idealism is gone, selfish sections will now go on top and tricksters opportunists worse than the old Irish Party are coming to the front, pushing aside the old crowd who worked unselfishly and were animated with national ideas rather than personal aims. Ireland's sun has set for generations and on top of all this ungratitude for which Ireland was ever noted, we will in continuation of the reaction become more English than ever.[35]

Even though he had supported the Treaty he found himself feeling that it was not worth this appalling collective moral collapse. The dead patriots were fools, and the Irish were essentially a hopeless people. Like many other commentators, he noticed that women radical nationalists were more extreme and more

bitter than the men. Generally, 'we have grown callous and sceptical.'[36] Oddly, there was a common recognition of the motivations that drove people to one side or the other, and a curious
acceptance of the conscientious nature of these motivations in
many cases. This mutual recognition may have blunted the bitterness and may have assisted in reconciliation in the years after.
In early April 1922, Kennedy had remarked, 'I believe both parties are somewhat in the right and very much in the wrong.'
Kennedy offered the analogy of the Parnell split: reconciliation
occurred by the device of the leaders' studiously avoiding personal animadversions.[37]

In Mary MacSwiney's letter of 24 April 1922 to Mulcahy, similar
analyses are made, from an anti-Treaty point of view. Even if de
Valera had actually accepted the Treaty, there still would have
been a civil war, because of 'principle'. The anti-Treatyites could
no more accept the Treaty 'than they could turn their backs on
the Catholic faith.'

> No matter what good things are in the Treaty are they worth
> all this unhappiness, Dick? Do you not realise that we hold
> the Republic as a living Faith—a spiritual reality stronger
> than any material benefits you can offer—Cannot give it up.
> It is not *we* who have changed it is you.[38]

Many, perhaps most, found themselves in the middle. Frank
Aiken was merely one of the most well known. As late as 6 July
1922, Aiken was still able to hold Rory O'Connor responsible
for the fighting and appreciate the Free State point of view. He
could see clearly that if the Civil War escalated it would break
the republican tradition in the IRA, 'lessen the respect of the people' for the IRA, and slow up the process of achieving an independent republic. He was an accurate prophet.[39]

THE MORAL BASIS OF A BACKWARD SOCIETY

Irish society at the time of the founding of the modern Irish
democracy was essentially peasant, although it was evolving
rapidly into a classic western free-farmer society. It was also a
society that had an inherited terror of poverty and had rather

good levels of elementary education but very few highly educated people. The destruction of so much of the Anglo-Irish culture that occurred during the revolution exacerbated the problem any democratic government would have had: that of running the country. In some ways, independent Ireland had a serious problem of mentality.

Edward Banfield in *The Moral Basis of a Backward Society* has put the problem well; writing about a poor peasant community in southern Italy in the mid-1950s, he suggests that the essential problem is that a peasant living in an economically static society tends to see social life as a zero-sum game: if I win something, you lose, and if you lose, I win.[40] The idea that all can be gainers, even if some gain more than others, is difficult for people with the collective experience of a peasantry to grasp. The true focus of loyalty is not the nation or even the political party or local area but the family. The emphasis on the family as the basic unit of human society is a central tenet of Irish Catholic ideology; Banfield argues that in the case of his Italian village of 'Montegrano', the local version of the family-centred ethos ('amoral familism') had led to self-defeating collective policies. I have labelled the Irish version of this syndrome 'communalism', and it seems clear that de Valera was able to capitalise on it in the longer run. It may be the fact that British policy towards Ireland during the Famine years was commonly justified by classical liberalism that permanently tainted *laissez-faire* ideas in the minds of many Irish people.

Ruralism, or the wish to preserve country society and protect it against the pressures of modern commercialised society, ran through much of republican and socialist thought. Aodh de Blácam, a conspicuous spokesman for what was eventually to be Fianna Fáil and a major contributor as 'Roddy the Rover' to de Valera's *Irish Press* in the 1930s, averred in a well-known book, *What Sinn Féin Stands For*, published in 1921:

Every Irish social thinker envisages the Gaelic polity as a rural polity. The great crowded industrial cities of Britain or America are regarded in Ireland generally as horrible perversions of the natural order. Partly, of course, the Irish objection of urban concentration is factitious; but when all allowances are made, it is deep-rooted in the Irish mind. The average Irishman is not much attracted to the town. He loves rural sports and

manners. Given the choice between ownership of a city business and a farm of equal capital value, he would, generally,
decide for the farm. He cannot in the least understand that
prejudice against the agricultural industry which prevails in
England . . . The English love of cities and fear of the country
are unnatural: the results of unfortunate history. Blighted by
feudalism, English rural life has been made dull. Want of spiritual vivacity has killed the intellectual life enjoyed by the masses of Merrie England in earlier days. Personal freedom and
decent pay were offered the son of the land who chose to
turn his back on the farm life of his sires, the dictatorship of
the squire and parson, and the arid atmosphere described in
A Shropshire Lad. Had rural life been brightened by an undis-
turbed folk-culture, had the farmer been a proprietor instead
of a tenant, then the lure of the cities would not have prevailed
against the magnetism of the country. If these views be cor-
rect, then where rural life continues unspoilt by the draining
away of ambition and culture, it should be possible to build up
rural industries and employ the constructive talent of the people without segregating the craftsmen into cities.[41]

Various observers saw the Civil War as about jobs rather than
principles, and there is, as I have already suggested, a streak of
truth in that observation. In a capital-poor society the public sector
offered a non-farm living that was widely coveted. Political life was
seen as a kind of anti-economics, whereby the practical consequences suggested by the propositions put forward by classical
economic theory could be avoided. Democratic life was not
appreciated for itself but rather as a means of voting for oneself
or one's family what one was incapable of gaining through economic activity. A well-known Irish communist slogan was 'Let
the rich pay'; the problem was that by 1923 there were very few
rich left: many of them had been burnt out.

Many people understood this intuitively, and certainly it was
grasped by the Free State government. In fact Lynch's contemptuous dismissal of the possibilities of an Irish democracy also
unfortunately had a streak of truth in it. A wonderful example
of this is offered by a 'Tralee artisan', quoted in the *Manchester
Guardian* in early 1923.

It isn't de Valera and the Republicans that is to blame. It's the people themselves and the farmers. When de Valera came to the town [Tralee] to ask them to stand by the Republic there were 20,000 people came to the meeting just out of curiosity to see what he was like. There wasn't one in twenty of them that wanted a Republic or anything but peace. But when they were asked to vote for the revolution every man of the 20,000 held up both hands for fear he would be getting into trouble else. So what could De V do but go away thinking he had the country behind him? And that was the beginning of Irregularity.[42]

De Valera was not that imperceptive. However, the Tralee artisan's view of political culture was unfortunately fairly accurate. The Free State had a battle on its hands: the construction of a democracy in which political power and economic wealth were to be distinguished from each other; Irish political culture, then and now, confused the two. Hugh Kennedy wrote sadly after the Civil War in 1924:

The bulk of the people of Ireland are as unsound in their economic ideas as they were in May, 1920 . . . They still think politically. They still believe that a change of Government will reduce prices, and that there is a primrose path to prosperity. They are apparently as ignorant of the elementary doctrines of political science as they were four years ago, and what is worse, they have not learned the lesson that by work, and work alone, a man or a nation must live . . . I may be misreading the situation; I sincerely trust I am; but I am drawn to the conclusion that two-thirds of the population of the South of Ireland are still thinking as they thought from 1900 to 1921, and have still some confused idea that the abolition of the oath or even of the Governor-General would, without any effort on their part, lead to complete prosperity with lower rates, taxes, and food prices. Where I chiefly blame the Government is that they are still remote. They are so immersed in the task of governing that they do not realise sufficiently the necessity of economic education.

It certainly seems that Irish political culture was zero-sum in mentality at that time and that this was a major conditioning factor in the Civil War. If no inherited position such as farm-ownership or business proprietorship existed and if one's educational level was insufficient to get a clerkship in the few service industries or the bureaucracy, fighting in the IRA or emigration must have appeared the unavoidable choice for many young men. The new regime came rapidly to be hated by those who were in effect being pushed out of the country by dire economic circumstances or, in some cases, by direct discrimination against republicans by the Free State authorities. Pyne has demonstrated a very high correlation between areas of high emigration and areas of anti-Treaty voting for the election of 1923, areas where one might expect zero-sum and communal mentalities to be strongest. The Sinn Féin vote of 1923 correlated with the emigration rate for 1921 by what is, by the standards of Irish ecological electoral analysis, a very strong +0.75 (56.3 per cent of variation accounted for). The pro-Treaty vote showed no such relationship. Sinn Féin correlated heavily and negatively with average farm valuation (–0.62), considerably and positively with proportion of agricultural workers (+0.42), strongly and negatively with proportion non-Catholic (–0.62), and massively with 'agrarian outrages' perpetrated a generation earlier during the Land War of 1879–82 (+0.76). In effect there was a marked agrarian radicalism hiding behind the anti-Treaty cause, despite the persistent denials of it by anti-Treaty leaders.[43]

Pyne concludes that there was a clear social distinction between the supporters on each side. The Treaty was indeed supported by ex-unionists, the urban middle class of all denominations, and much of the small industrial working class that counted on the British trade for its very existence, and this was so despite the clearly working-class character of much of the IRA and Sinn Féin. However, the future boded well for de Valera: his brand of political moralism harmonised better with the political culture of the masses than did the slightly inhuman, though rational, pragmatism of Cosgrave and O'Higgins. However, he was first going to have to take into account elements of these men's ideas and combine them with republican moralism in his own 1937 Constitution.

6

State-Building after the Treaty

As we have seen, long before mid-January 1922 and long before the formal signing of the Treaty in early December 1921, as already argued, many foresaw civil war; a shrewd and observant few had seen the prospect of a split even earlier than that and had privately said so. Others believed, like Collins in his desperate, ruthless and sentimental way, that the movement could be kept together because of friendship and trust.

Others again saw the signing of the Treaty as an almost undreamed-of liberation: the bullying, the patronising and the cultural humiliation associated with the British connection were to go, and the Irish were to get their own country, partitioned or otherwise. Many hoped that the Treaty, with its promise of peace, would persuade Ulster to join the rest of the island, at least in some loose federal arrangement, as had been suggested in the Government of Ireland Act, 1920. Others saw Ulster as remote or, in some cases, secretly saw the South as well rid of the North. Others again saw the North as indigestible and too big to cope with in an all-Ireland polity.

Under the provisions of the Treaty the British soldiers, very often liked individually while being hated collectively, were going to leave. As soon as the Provisional Government took power, on 12 January, British soldiers, RIC, Black and Tans and Auxiliaries were demobilised and began to be evacuated. Despite some hitches, this evacuation occurred rapidly, with the soldiers being cheered as they marched onto the ships, leaving their girl-friends behind, in many cases to follow on later to Britain. Many a Tommy actually left Ireland with happy memories of his experiences, contrary to Sinn Féin and unionist stereotype. The new nationalist regime (Dáil government cum Provisional Government) faced a huge vacuum; there was great potential popular good will but it had no way of expressing itself until an election was permitted to take place. Dermot Foley, later to be a distinguished librarian, reminisced half a century later:

> It is hard to understand how any young Irishman of sensibili- ty could remain unmoved in [January] 1922 at the sight of a British regiment of soldiers marching out under the great arch of Dublin Castle as our own bedraggled lads marched in, heads high, to take over that fortress of imperial rule. My father, whose business as a building contractor had been ruined beyond recovery by the Black and Tans, held my arm in a grip of iron on one side and, on the other, my mother's hand lay in mine. Both were weeping copiously. Many of these hunted men had found sanctuary in our home, and the relief of that day, the overwhelming joy of it, could find expression only in tears.

As we have seen, the anti-Treatyites lost the election of June 1922 humiliatingly. It was obvious to de Valera, as also already suggested, that a similar defeat would occur in the projected election of 1923. He evidently dithered personally on the consti- tutional question, and on 13 September 1922, early in the Civil War, he actually expressed publicly regret at Rory O'Connor's repudiation of the Third or 'Free State' Dáil in favour of an evidently oxymoronic IRA democracy. This did not stop him accepting office under a shadowy anti-Treaty Second Dáil, one that rejected the right of supporters of the Treaty to be of its membership. De Valera had, however, evidently already con- cluded that the republicans had not the military strength or the popular support to fight the Free State. Furthermore, they apparently had, he felt, no 'popular mandate'.

De Valera also struck, in private, a modest note about his own electoral attractiveness: 'We will be turned down definitely by the people in a few months in any case.'[1] This remark contrasts inter- estingly with equally private observations made to various people later in which he repeatedly claimed that the new regime was undemocratic, bullying, illegitimate, and not committed to the principle of free elections. It does look as though de Valera, while denouncing the new regime as collaborationist, pro-British, dicta- torial, *coupiste*, and anti-democratic, well knew that Cosgrave was no dictator and was going to ensure free elections—elections that de Valera and his allies were, incidentally, going to lose and, according to de Valera himself, lose badly.

Popular indifference to the entire Free State versus Republic issue was evident from the beginning; it was an issue debated by revolutionary ideologues and by few others. The vast majority of the population accepted the settlement of 1921–22 with a very sane mixture of satisfaction, relief, and indifference. The Civil War was fought over an issue that most people cared little about and that most people saw, accurately, as pointless and unreal.

For the pro-Treaty leaders, messy and irregular as the election of June 1922 had been, its result gave them an ideological and legalist rationale for a Treaty of which they were not themselves over-fond but that they saw as a great breakthrough in Anglo-Irish relations. The people, in the view of the pro-Treatyites, *had* the right to do wrong, to misquote de Valera for Cosgrave's purposes. The Dáil Constitution of 1919 mentioned no republic; under it there could therefore be no legal objection to the disestablishment of the republic that the establishing of the Free State necessarily entailed. There could only be a moral and essentially non-legal objection to the breaking of the oath to the Republic that the Dáil deputies of January 1919 had made, arguably at the unconstitutional behest of the IRA.

Incidentally, de Valera himself had repeatedly interpreted that oath as a declaration of general intent to achieve independence under whatever constitutional forms were feasible. The brute fact of the matter was that under 'Dáil law', never mind British law, the Republic's existence was subject to nothing more substantial than the will of the Dáil's majority and, behind that, the notional will of the people as expressed in rather questionable electoral circumstances in 1921. Beyond that again, the population had the very begrudgingly acknowledged right, not mentioned in the 1919 constitution, to follow the Dáil deputies with its votes in disestablishing the Republic in favour of the Free State.

THE IMPOSITION OF FREE STATE DEMOCRACY

Democracy was essentially imposed forcibly in Ireland, against the wishes of a section of a new and inexperienced political class, much of which saw itself, rather than the voters, as the rightful rulers; Collins repeatedly referred to the people as 'our masters' during the Treaty debates, and to state that bluntly was an unwelcome proposition. Democracy was also imposed in accordance with the wishes of a large, if disorganised and not particularly 'republican', majority of the general population. The Third Dáil, its first sitting put off for two months by the Civil War, finally met on 9 September 1922, without the anti-Treaty deputies. Cosgrave described it accurately and intriguingly as being a synthesis of the Dáil tradition and the legacy of the Treaty and deriving its legitimacy from both sources; it ended the curious symbiosis of the Dáil government and Provisional Government that had been necessary under the provisions of the Treaty.[2]

The fact that the new politicians were, by and large, veterans of guerrilla warfare weakened their claim to political legitimacy, and they sensed this themselves. 'Law' offered the pro-Treatyites a way out, a psychological defence against the ideological arguments of the anti-Treatyites. 'Law' could, of course, only be supplied by lawyers, which accounts for the rapid post-Treaty political ascent of lawyers such as Patrick MacGilligan, Hugh Kennedy, and Kevin O'Sheil. The relative absence of lawyers in the pre-Treaty elite and their conspicuous presence in the early Free State elite is a crucial contrast; lawyers knew how to build law-bound states. The ideology of legalistic and unromantic electoral democracy became a cornerstone of their political position. An acute and unsympathetic Northern observer, Lord Londonderry, commented in August 1922 in a letter to the Free State's first Attorney-General, Hugh Kennedy:

> Mr. Collins has a record which, in his desire to become a statesman, is not very helpful. He achieved his position amongst his own followers by being one of the leaders of a campaign which Sinn Fein called war and which I call assassination. He has maintained his position by challenging the British Government and by succeeding in compelling the British Government to make terms, and terms of a character far exceeding the wildest hopes of Mr. Collins or any of his supporters.[3]

The wish to placate the republicans by the use of legal formulas that resembled the 'Jesuitical' formulas of Catholic canon law was, as we have seen, strong in Free State circles. Hugh Kennedy strove in particular to devise constitutional formulas that would both satisfy the British government and, in his innocence, convince de Valera of the practical reality of the Free State's independence. It seems that the only way in which de Valera could be convinced of the Free State's independence was to be handed personal control of it.

Kennedy's sometimes desperate though often brilliant intellectual efforts were to be of no avail. Childers had convinced de Valera—or rather de Valera had consented to be convinced by Childers—that the status of Canada, in the concrete circumstances of Ireland, would be impossible to maintain against the might of Britain. Why this was so is unclear, but Childers seems to have had an extraordinary grip on de Valera's thinking, and he fed de Valera's paranoia about British power. Childers argued that Canada had de facto sovereignty because it was large and far away from England, which was, after all, the superpower of the period. Ireland, being small and near England, would not be able to emulate Canada as far as sovereignty was concerned.

De Valera's own formula of 'external association' would not be easier to maintain than the Treaty settlement, Kennedy argued. An isolated Ireland, with no obvious allies other than, possibly, Soviet and German mischief-makers and embittered Irish-Americans, would quickly become a de facto British dependency. Collins grasped this point early on; de Valera took at least a decade to understand it, although it took until 1949 for him to use Collins's own argument, with fantastic chutzpah, as a whip with which to beat the Inter-Party Government's declaration of the Republic of Ireland and consequent leaving of the British Commonwealth.

However, this elementary point about the importance of dominion support was rarely made in public at the time; under the Treaty, after all, the Free State, puny though it might be in itself, would have the backing of Canada, Australia and the other old dominions in preserving and extending its sovereignty. By way of contrast to his paranoid misunderstanding of the actual sovereign status of the Free State, de Valera saw through the partition and Boundary Commission provisions immediately. The Treaty was to safeguard Northern Ireland within its 1920 boundaries. He had, significantly, nothing new to offer in the place of the Treaty provisions. Kennedy wrote privately in early 1922, suggesting a formula to be inserted in the Free State Constitution to placate Republicans:

> Crude suggestion of words to meet *one* cry of de V.
>
> From and after the adoption of this constitution by the people of the Irish Free State, neither the British Parliament or the British Government shall have or exercise any authority or control of any kind whatsoever in the Irish Free State, except in accordance with the schedule hereto [the Treaty] nor shall any action, whether of peace or war, taken by the said Parliament or Government bind the legislature of the Irish Free State unless, and until freely adopted by them and no forces, military or naval, in the service of the Irish Free State shall be subject to any other authority than that of the Irish Free State.

At about the same time, Kennedy echoed de Valera in pleading for a non-doctrinaire interpretation of the 1919 declaration and oath. What is really startling is how little divided them; they resemble, to this writer writing two generations later, the Big-Endians and Little-Endians of Jonathan Swift's strangely prophetic satire *Gulliver's Travels*, written, very properly, in Dublin. Even at the time, many saw it that way.

THE FEAR OF DISORDER

A clinging to legal forms in the shape of defending the voters' decision to accept the Treaty steeled the Free State government to its determined and occasionally bloody defence of the new electoral democracy. Kennedy wrote in August 1922 that disorder was the greatest menace to democracy in the twenty-six counties. The government would have to 'at least get a grip' on this disorder. The Free State would have to learn rapidly from history two lessons:

> The first is that practically every serious challenge in history against the constituted authority of a Nation which has been overcome, has been so overcome by prompt, effective, vigorous and utterly ruthless action.[4]

The main, not very reassuring, example he offered of this generalisation was the recent crushing, by joint action of the Reichswehr and the paramilitary Freikorps, of the Spartakus pro-Soviet uprising in Weimar Germany, which featured, among other delights, the murder by paramilitaries of Karl Liebknecht and Rosa Luxemburg and the dumping of their bodies in the Landswehrkanal in Berlin. Kennedy continued:

> The second [example] is that wherever that challenge to Authority from within the Nation was not encountered, whenever there was delay in dealing with it—due to a mistaken idea of humanity or any other reason, the invariable tendency was for the distemper to prosper and grow and eventually to overwhelm the National Government.[5]

Here his comparative parallels were King Charles I and the Cromwellians, King Louis XVIII and the French Revolution of 1830, King Carlos of Portugal, and Kerensky. In general, Kennedy concluded, the disaster of total revolution occurred in countries where the hand of the ruler was unwilling or unable to strike at a challenge to its power. Kennedy was not alone in thinking like this, as we have seen, and by January 1923 Kevin O'Higgins, arguing in a similar vein, was urging executions in every county *pour encourager les autres*. By then, of course, life had become cheap; O'Higgins's father had been murdered, and most of the Free State government had had relatives or friends threatened, burned out, beaten up, or killed.

As law and force took over from comradeship as a binding principle, lawyers became increasingly important ideologues on the Free State side. Legal and pseudo-legal argument was used to offer rationales for policy. However, an increasing determination to repress rebellion, if necessary by illegal means, also gripped their minds. The executions of Barrett, McKelvey, Mellows and O'Connor were certainly illegal, whatever the *Realpolitik* reasoning of the government; they were executed without trial, for no particular crime other than being on the wrong political side; as jailbirds, they were notionally held guilty for crimes they could not possibly have committed. Blythe, honestly enough, described these particular executions as acts of war and so, apparently, extra-legal if not illegal.

The determination of the government to stop the murder, vandalism and pillage grew as the Civil War went on. On 27 February 1923, W. T. Cosgrave, now President of the Executive Council, met a group of well-intentioned IRA veterans headed by Donal Hannigan and M. J. Burke. This group described itself rather innocently or naïvely as neutral and as being neither pro nor anti-Treaty. They pleaded with Cosgrave for a ceasefire and a return to the 'Pact' arrangements of mid-1922, some anti-Treaty participation in government to be permitted. Cosgrave cut them short. The republicans were virtually beaten, he pointed out; people were now giving the Free State information willingly.

> There was a lull after the first executions but once the people saw we were in earnest they came along. We never got so much information as we are getting now. The executions have had a remarkable effect. It is a sad thing to say, but it is nevertheless the case. The unfortunate thing about them is you have to execute the unfortunate dupes, and the responsible people were not got.

Cosgrave urged upon them his own understanding of the situation. It was not for any self-appointed elite to decide who was to rule the country; neither the republicans nor the Free State leaders had that right, and only the people had the right to decide it by secret ballot. The elitism of 'republicanism' was going to be stopped. In a chilling sentence, he expressed his determination to defend the infant democracy by mass killing if necessary:

> I am not going to hesitate and if the country is to live and if we have to exterminate ten thousand Republicans, the three millions of our people are bigger than this ten thousand.

Cosgrave also observed that because of the Civil War, provoked, in his view, by de Valera and O'Connor, there was now relatively little hope of the North 'coming in' to the Free State. The fighting in the south had made partition deeper than it might otherwise have been. He said that he was going to try again for an all-Ireland parliament, but it would never happen until 'these fellows down South [in Munster] accept fully our present position.' In a more formal statement, he informed the neutral IRA group:

You must know there is a fundamental difference between the vast majority of the Nation and those in armed hostility to the people. On behalf of the majority we accept a free exercise of the ballot box. The people must be free to exercise judgement in elections and armed interference with the public will not be permitted. If there is to be peace on these terms then the armed opposition to peace must be crushed. And it is nearly crushed and will shortly be entirely crushed. Irish democracy is too well-founded to tolerate the imposition of a new political aristocracy. The people must be free to dispense with politicians who may have rendered good service but whose period of usefulness has for some time been eclipsed.

A final ceasefire came on 24 May 1923. Several thousand people were dead, much property had been looted, and many forced transfers of property, much of it sectarian in nature, had occurred. The extent of the disaster perpetrated by the IRA has never been quantified and rapidly became part of Ireland's extensive secret history, not least because a large chunk of the IRA ended up as the government ten years later. Early Free State estimates of the cost of the Civil War put it at £50 million, a vast sum by the standards of the day: in 1996 money that would be the equivalent in purchasing power of perhaps £1,750 million. As the gross national product of the twenty-six counties was probably less than a third of that of 1996, it possibly represents the sociological equivalent of about £6,000 million, all taken out of the economy in eight months—possibly a quarter of a year's GNP, or the equivalent of the entire EU tranche for Ireland in the 1990s.

The cost was disproportionately borne by the Protestant minority in country areas, who were sometimes murdered, commonly physically threatened and often hounded out of Ireland by the republicans or by local agrarian opportunists. The main reason for the parsimony of governments in the 1920s, later used by de Valera's party as a stick to beat the governments with, was the necessity of whittling down this enormous debt, which was actually done with impressive speed. The expense of the Civil War, caused by the republicans, was then naturally used by the republicans, temporarily cowed, to win elections at the hands of an either forgetful or opportunistic electorate.

At the end of April 1923 de Valera, after much ideological prevarication, sent a message via senators Andrew Jameson and James Douglas to Cosgrave, suggesting an amnesty for prisoners and a renegotiated oath. He suggested that IRA arms not be handed over to the Free State government but stored in 'neutral' arsenals. Cosgrave sent back a moderate but very cold set of conditions of surrender, as cited in chapter 4.

The acceptance of this rather mild set of conditions was, he continued, a preliminary condition for the release of prisoners. When arms were surrendered by the IRA, the Free State army would cease hostilities. Interestingly, Cosgrave displayed considerable psychological empathy with the humiliated IRA soldiers; the surrender of arms 'would be made with as much consideration as possible for those concerned.' Weapons could, for instance, be given into the care of local clergy rather than being surrendered directly to Free State army personnel or to the Civic Guards. Young men of the Public Band, government officials felt, had a strong sense of the ridiculous and a good deal of personal pride. The Free State also declared that prisoners who signed the simple promise not to take up arms against the elected government of the country would be released. De Valera's people would be allowed full rights to campaign politically and to canvass for the forthcoming election. De Valera replied to the effect that the oath of 'allegiance' was the real sticking point.[6]

From early on, the Free State was clearly thinking of breaking the IRA 'irregulars' while diverting as many of them as possible into legal and unarmed political activity within the structures offered by the new constitution. In a strange and ironic sense, the true founder of Fianna Fáil was William T. Cosgrave, because he clearly offered de Valera a 'middle way' between an outright acceptance of the 1922 settlement and armed insurrection against it. He deliberately made possible a separation between de Valera and the extremists of the IRA. Possibly on the advice of the Catholic bishops, he had already apparently begun to hope that de Valera was not politically irredeemable.

As early as May 1922 the Free State government had seen clearly that civil war would probably entail a permanent partition of the country; the unionists would finally have got away with the rebellion of 1912, courtesy of the Conservative Party, the German imperial government, their own military prowess, and, of course,

Rory O'Connor and company, who had undermined Collins. During and after the Civil War the Free State consistently encouraged dissident republicans and socialists to enter civic political life. The Free State government realised rapidly during the later phase of the conflict that the young men of the IRA, after several years of fighting and a thorough beating by the Free State army, wanted by and large simply to go home and be left in peace. However, they feared ridicule and being laughed at or hissed at by young women. Pride was a large consideration, as it is so often in Ireland. In some cases the young IRA men feared being shot as 'deserters' by the die-hards on their own side.[7]

A covert decision seems to have been made by the Free State government, possibly communicated informally to the anti-Treatyites, that the courts would not pursue acts of theft and murder that had occurred during the period between 6 December 1921 and 27 April 1923.[8] In essence this meant that property stolen or 'commandeered' during that period would remain in republican or private hands. Richard O'Kennedy, writing half a century later, recalled that during that year and a half

> these vultures flocked from far and wide ready and able to make money out of the agony of the country. They robbed banks and their agents bought houses in Dublin on their behalf. When the Civil War ended, those new rich moved with impunity into their new shops and undoubtedly enjoyed the fruits of their acumen.[9]

Even Liam Lynch, a guerrilla leader of some charisma, great bravery, and considerable implacability, actually conceded the generosity of the earlier offers from the Free State during the civil war that he himself was waging. He circularised IRA commanders in February 1923 to the effect that the republicans had received numerous offers and that the Free State had granted 'practically everything except recognising the independence of the country.' Needless to say, however, he was going to fight on, although he had not long to live.

After the war the Free State army was rapidly demobilised. The psychological problems faced by many of the Free State veterans resembled those of their republican counterparts, and some limited interaction between the unemployed men of both sides did occur. However, the Free State veterans were given job preference and, in many cases, pensions. The IRA veterans usually had nothing. This statement must, however, be qualified by the observation that many of them had jobs with the Post Office, in educational establishments or with local authorities and often seem to have been on half-pay and leave of absence while taking up arms against the government that was paying them, a rather Irish situation.

A year after hostilities ended and, significantly, shortly after the Army Mutiny, James Kennedy wrote to Mulcahy from Thurles, close to the area where the entire Anglo-Irish War and, afterwards, resistance to the Free State, had begun. Tipperary was a county in which particular bitterness had been caused by the fighting in the Civil War. Many of the soldiers from both sides, but perhaps particularly from the anti-Treaty side, found it extremely difficult to go back into civilian life in their own areas.

> They lorded it too much and after big money, position of authority and a feeling very pronounced of being somebodies it was too much to expect them to go back easily and besides the Irish have a keen sense of the ridiculous and these men being most ignorant had missed their power and made many enemies outside of Republicans. Again a great number can never live in their own districts with any sense of security. They know this. Then to keep themselves in they pretended an anxiety about the Republic. The people realise that the men are not wanted, that the country can't afford to keep them, and that in a reduced army there will be fewer officers and if there is to be an army worthy of being so called the officers must be men of some education, some decency, some manners and men whom public and privates can respect. Others than the existing [officers] would be required for this and it was all fake that the men who 'saved the country' were being scrapped for ex-Black and Tans, English Soldiers etc. The public are not deceived by this and the propaganda is a failure.[10]

Employment for veterans of the military conflict became an obsession. As mentioned above, favour was given to veterans of the Free State army, while anti-Treaty veterans remained out in the cold. However, many of the latter who had had employment in public sector positions in the local authorities or in teaching commonly managed to hold on to these jobs, or got them back after some time. Many republican teachers seem to have enjoyed clerical protection, of a kind that the Free State authorities feared to defy, or at least felt it unwise to defy for prudential reasons. The authorities commonly hoped that secure employment would keep these people out of mischief. There was, for whatever reason, relatively little victimisation, apparently as a settled, if unspoken, policy of reintegrating anti-Treatyites into the polity.

On the other side, so to speak, Mulcahy resisted Free State army veterans' suggestions that British army veterans in public employment be dismissed to give jobs to Free Staters.[11] A very large proportion of the new civil servants had served under the British and continued, in many ways, to work as they had worked before 1922. Quite commonly, officials found themselves working under men whom they had had locked up some years previously. Similarly, after 1932 the same pattern was to repeat itself: tempers had to be kept, and generally were, possibly because they had to be.

After 1921, new departments were inserted among the old ones, in particular a Department of Finance, built up from the Revenue and Customs and Excise, and a completely new Department of External Affairs, later to be renamed Department of Foreign Affairs. The latter department was unusual in that it managed to keep its recruitment system separate from that of the main civil service.

BUILDING A NEW STATE

The civil service had long been a stable source of employment for young men with some education. However, large portions of it had been sequestered for political patronage by both the Irish Party and the Unionist Party. This was particularly the case at local government level. Under the new regime the whole issue of local government appointments was tackled by the Local Appointments Commission, set up in 1926, detached from the control of local politicians and ecclesiastics. The appointment of local dispensary doctors tended to be a particularly conspicuous bone of contention, involving as it did not only local politics but also the religious orders involved in medical care and the traditional Catholic-Protestant religious tension. However, it took time for the change in the rules to sink in generally. As Minister for Local Government and Public Health after the August 1927 general election, Richard Mulcahy was inundated with the usual flood of requests, often from nuns, to 'fix' local appointments over the heads of the new Local Appointments Commission. In a letter of August 1927 in response to one such request he wrote proudly that the old British patronage system was being abolished, that he had now no power to grant the request and that

> outside persons, including Ministers, have as little influence or right to influence appointments to the Civil Service, where candidates are appointed as a result of definite examination.[12]

In fact a Civil Service Commission had been set up in 1923 during the Civil War as one of the first major policy acts of the new government. Competitive examination systems were set up for the general civil service, army, and Civic Guard. Impersonal recruitment of civil servants at both local and national level was institutionalised on an impressive scale. Such examinations discomfited those who liked to characterise the new regime as corrupt, snobbish, undemocratic, and gombeen, and, as we have seen, these academic requirements enraged many IRA hopefuls. The effect of the new merit system was to make the service more professional, probably more intelligent, more honest, but perhaps also more rule-bound, cautious, and divorced from local and national political life.[13]

COURTS, LAWYERS, AND WIGS

The courts system was an early object of Free State leaders' reformist energies. For obvious reasons, the Free State had huge problems with the enforcement of ordinary law, quite apart from having to deal with an active political rebellion against its authority. Nonetheless, the courts system was overhauled with great rapidity in the first year of the Free State. Under the Dáil government, Republican courts had succeeded in replacing the British system in large parts of the country, particularly in the west and the south. The takeover was not as complete as was that of the local authorities but made a greater public and international impression, as the new courts often did administer an inexpensive, even-handed and sensible arbitration in everyday civilian disputes. Even those unsympathetic to the revolution commonly resorted to the 'Sinn Féin courts', and the British authorities sometimes, in one of their rare fits of common sense, treated them as extra-legal arbitration councils and left them alone. In many places the Republican courts picked up on the tradition of Land League tribunals and on even older traditions of local non-legal 'midnight courts' of arbitration over landholding, religious dues, and breach of promise cases. The decisions of the Dáil courts were theoretically enforced by the local IRA and Republican Police, echoing both the old Whiteboy or Public Band tradition of local arbitration and the aspired-to republican civic order of the imagined future.[14]

In early 1922 the Dáil and Provisional Governments found themselves in charge of two mutually exclusive court systems, the British and the Dáil courts. The latter were more of a liability, because many of the Dáil justices were anti-Treaty, and attempts were made by republicans to use the Dáil Supreme Court to declare the Third Dáil illegal and to declare the Second Dáil to be still in existence; Eoin MacNeill, as Chairman of the Second Dáil, was issued a writ of *mandamus* by the Republic's Supreme Court ordering him to summon the Second Dáil after the general election of 16 June 1922 so that, apparently, it could decide whether or not to dissolve itself in favour of the Third Dáil. The Supreme Court and the Dublin area Dáil Courts were hurriedly closed down by the Dáil-cum-Provisional Government in early July, and the remainder of the Dáil courts were shut down at the end of August.

Another, very practical and non-political reason for closing down the Dáil courts was that even under Dáil 'law' the courts had very limited areas of jurisdiction. Furthermore, the very local parish courts seem to have been unpopular and were sometimes used by local factions as weapons against local rivals: Judge Hatfield got to sentence defendant McCoy.[15] At the same time, the British resident magistrate system was closed down, as were grand juries and parish courts. However, the new regime had a serious problem; the traditionally unpopular British petty sessions courts were going to have to continue in being until a new Free State courts system was operating, which was going to take a year or so.

The abrupt abolition of the Dáil courts gave rise to a good deal of popular suspicion that the British courts were being brought back by a reactionary and pro-British clique. The Dáil county-level courts had apparently been rather popular and had generally been staffed by local people, sociologically not very different from the bulk of the local population and sympathetic to the mentality of the local community. The British courts, on the other hand, had been staffed by people seen as alien, of the wrong class and hostile to, or uncomprehending of, the sentiments of the locals. However, the new government was clearly determined to avoid continuity either with the British system or with the Dáil system. British lower-court judges were to be pensioned off as soon as practicable and replaced rapidly with new ones with a 'national' background. A new, simplified District (county) Court system, presided over by 'district justices' with powers of summary jurisdiction, was decided upon and announced on 31 August. District justices were not to wear wigs. No effort was made to resuscitate the Dáil parish court system; the stated ground given by the Free State government was that it was ineffective and corrupt.[16]

A general thrust of the reforms, as in the case of local admin-istrative reform, was a wish to have a simple, inexpensive and streamlined system that was also insulated against local pressure and local vested interests. A deep understanding of local gombeen, farmer and clerical power to subvert the course of jus-tice lay behind the Free State's reforms. The new courts, in line with 'republican' puritanism, would not, it was envisaged, stand on ceremony. A dislike of imperial splendour was evident. Serjeant MacSwiney, one of the architects of the new system, reminisced scornfully about the old British circuit court's elabo-rate ceremonies, including a 'quaint and archaic oath'.

> The opening of a Commission of Assize is in the nature of a grand ceremony. The judges are escorted to the Court by cavalry. The trumpet announces their arrival. Sometimes there is the music of a full band, which reminds one of the Duke of Plaza-Toro.[17]

It was suggested by several government members that the distinction between barrister and solicitor be abolished. This suggestion has yet to be acted upon seventy years later, a telling sign of the formidable lobbying power of lawyers, rivalled only by that of the publicans and the bishops in the new Irish polity. Republican puritanism and dislike of hierarchical symbolism also was evident in the campaign inside the Free State government against the lawyer's wig. Wigs were held to be archaic, unhygienic, uncomfortable, and, above all, a relic of English rule. Furthermore, wigs were made in England. This campaign was successfully fought off by the legal establishment and its allies in the Senate, led ably by Lord Glenavy. The result was a situation whereby lower courts did without the wig while higher courts required it: a classic Irish post-revolutionary hybrid solution.

Hugh Kennedy wrote ruefully to Louis Walsh, one of the first district justices, in late 1923 that ordinary politics was rapidly getting the better of his highly imaginative efforts at reform of the costume of the legal profession. This included a neo-mediaeval cowl, designed by the Dun Emer Guild of Bray, to replace the wig, and a cloak of many colours, echoing Brehon tradition, to replace the usual lawyer's gown.

> The Bar is hostile to any change and, I fear, rather obstinately hostile. Some designs were being made for me—quite privately —but the designer unfortunately showed them to a member of the Bar none too friendly, with the result I had to scrap the thing and leave it so for the time being. It occurs to me that if we could get some definite information on colour under the Brehon tradition, it would be useful. It is a funny thing that the Bar clings to the wig with the greatest intensity, even to the extent of sending a lot of money out of the country to replace those burnt in the Four Courts.[18]

Kennedy admitted that one of his problems was that there were no pictorial representations of what a 'brehon' or traditional judge's ceremonial costume might have looked like, five hundred or a thousand years previously. The experiment with the cowl was actually carried out in the mid-1920s but did not last very long, possibly because of unseemly public amusement; as already noted, the Irish had, and still have, a strong sense of the ridiculous.[19] Since then district justices have sat bare-headed and wear a simple short robe. Salaries of district justices were to be substantial so as to give the holder of the office local status and immunity to financial pressures. Judicial appointments were to be promotional and bureaucratised so as to get away from the pervasive patronage system of the British regime.

The new court system was indeed more simplified than its predecessor had been and, rather like the civil service reforms, more biased in favour of impersonal and rule-bound action and more proof against political interference. Like the Local Appointments Commission and the Civil Service Commission, the new courts were an example of the opportunity a post-revolutionary government has to instigate reforms, as long as it moves rapidly and before new veto groups establish themselves and clog up the policy process. The Free State elites took impressive advantage of this window of opportunity between 1922 and about 1926.

ELECTORAL LAW

In a similar vein, the law on elections was overhauled and the system put under the appellate control of the judges. Traditionally, the voters' register had been made up by a do-it-yourself system under which the political parties proposed additions to the register and challenged them in a beggar-my-neighbour fashion. In a pattern characteristic of Free State reforms in general, parties were divested of the power of appeal, and voters became automatically registered through the sheriff's office. The right of party challenge remained.[20] Unfortunately, the system has not stopped personation, which seems always to have been rather common in Irish elections but which very certainly was reduced by the Free State reforms. One of the main impulses towards impersonation after 1922 was, naturally, the newly competitive party system inaugurated by independence. One of the reasons for the apparent commonness of personation is the absence of a national identity card and the lack of any real tradition of insisting that citizens be able, at all times, to prove who they are, a traditional lack shared, of course, with Britain.

The suffrage reform was substantially complete by mid-November 1922, in anticipation of an early republican capitula-

tion and an early general election, the 1922 verdict being rightly seen as tainted to some extent by the near-war circumstances
in which it had taken place. The *Freeman's Journal* trumpeted the
new electoral bill loudly.

> The Bill is the fulfilment of the pledge of the supporters of
> the Treaty to submit the settlement to a full plebiscite of the
> people at the earliest possible moment.
>
> Objection was taken to the last election because the regis-
> ter was old and the franchise was not wide enough.
>
> Women under thirty were excluded, an exclusion alleged
> to be prejudicial to Mr. de Valera's propaganda.
>
> These objections will now disappear.
>
> Will the opponents of the Free State accept this tribunal?
>
> If words could bind Mr. de Valera he is doubly and trebly
> bound to accept the verdict . . . [21]

CONSTITUTION-MAKING

At the pinnacle of the new structures was the Constitution of the
Irish Free State, to which the text of the Treaty was annexed.
Formally quasi-monarchical, the document actually had as its
central principle the sovereignty of the people. Every effort was
made to sideline the King's representative and to water down
the oath. The creation of the Constitution occurred during the
run-up to the Civil War, between January and June 1922. The
drafting committee was chaired by Collins, who worked particularly through James Douglas, a Dublin Quaker businessman. An
American lawyer, C. P. France, was legal adviser. Darrell Figgis
was vice-chairman, and other significant figures included Hugh
Kennedy, Kevin O'Sheil, a barrister of Dáil courts fame, John
O'Byrne, also a barrister, James MacNeill, brother of Eoin
MacNeill, James Murnaghan, a law professor and a well-known
nationalist, and Alfred O'Rahilly, a Cork scientist who was a well-
known, colourful and rather original Catholic ideologue.[22]

Essentially the committee faced an impossible task. They had
to satisfy the pro-Treaty government, the republican opposition
and the British government. The monarchist-democratic hybrid
they came up with would never wholly satisfy any party, and they
knew it. Various devices were used to highlight the conciliatory

character of the finished document. For instance, the device of the 'extern minister', who would be responsible individually to the Dáil rather than to the government and who could in theory be a member of an opposition party, was provided, in the faint hope of inducing participation in government by moderate anti-Treatyites of the Gavan Duffy type. The doctrine that sovereignty actually rested with the people of Ireland rather than with the British monarch was clearly stated. The hope was that de Valera could at the last moment be separated from the anti-Treatyites and would accept some softened version of the Free State formula. It was a forlorn hope.[23]

The ideological susceptibilities of British politicians, in particular their adulation of the symbols of monarchy, also had to be taken into account. Rather cleverly, Collins used the threat of a possible collapse of the Provisional Government and its probable replacement by an anti-Treaty regime under de Valera and Lynch as a device to inveigle the British into accepting a much watered-down version of the oath.[24] The Treaty was finally ratified by the British on 31 March 1922.

The constitutional committee gave the Provisional Government three draft constitutions to choose from on 8 March. However, no final draft was published until the morning of the 'Pact Election' on 16 June. The British had been horrified by the crypto-republicanism of the draft submitted to them and forced the Irish to rewrite it in late May. They were particularly galled by the apparent slighting of the Crown but did accept with bad grace the watered-down version of the oath. They were furthermore dismayed by the absence of final judicial appeal to the British Privy Council and the downgrading of the Governor-General to the status of a rubber stamp. On 1 June the British gave the Irish what amounted to an ultimatum, demanding that the position of the Crown be identical to that which it had in the other dominions, that the Treaty oath in its weakened form be included in the Constitution, that Privy Council appeal be included, and that the Free State be clearly declared to be within the British Empire and not in any relationship of 'association', evidently an echo of de Valera's document no. 2.[25] On 2 June the Irish gave in completely, but by this time civil war was inevitable; no concession by the British short of outright 'republican' independence could have altered that fact.

The events of 1921–22 did not settle the issue of constitutional legitimacy, and Irish politics was bedevilled for a generation afterwards by the issue of whether or not the Leinster House parliament had the right to rule. The fact that the pro-Treaty side won the elections of 1922 and 1923 cut little ice, naturally enough, with mainstream republicans. Soon after the 1922 election, for example, Count Plunkett summarised republican views, using a pseudo-legal style of argument that strangely echoed that of Hugh Kennedy on the other side.

The Second Dáil, he argued, at its last sitting had adjourned its further sittings to 30 June, two weeks after the election. Eoin MacNeill, as Chairman of the Dáil, had the duty to summon its members, and a *mandamus* had been given by the Republic's Supreme Court to compel him to summon the Second Dáil. The Second Dáil was therefore still in existence, and no Third Dáil existed, notwithstanding the election of 16 June 1922. The Second Dáil when it met would have the right to pass any enactment it wanted and would have the power to declare the 1922 election valid or invalid; if it did the former it could then dissolve itself. 'If the so-called "Third Dáil" met now it would be merely a political gathering without any authority to legislate.'

Even then, he claimed, were the Third Dáil to assemble it would first have to take the oath of allegiance to the Republic, as provided for by decree no. 13, passed in 1919. The Provisional Government was unknown to the Constitution of the Irish Republic and had been tolerated only as a device to placate the power of Britain. The Treaty was no treaty in the eyes of the British, and neither state had really ratified the document. Furthermore, the Treaty 'is invalid because it surrenders the independence of Ireland . . . According to international law, any Treaty that destroys the Independence of one of the contracting States is not binding on that State.'

British troops had not been withdrawn, Plunkett alleged inaccurately, and the Westminster Parliament had continued to legislate for the twenty-six counties. The Republic therefore still existed and it was the obligation of all Irish representatives to give it allegiance. 'To take part in the proceedings of any body calling itself a legislature, which is not the lawful legislature, is an act of rebellion against the law of the state.'[26]

It was against this kind of argument, an extraordinary mixture of logic, illogic, and pure fantasy, that Hugh Kennedy was vainly pleading in early 1922 when he argued privately:

There are two forms of states. In one form, all Legislative, Executive and Judicial authority is derived from the people who compose the State and who give the State its legal existence. In the other the legislative, executive and judicial authority is not derived solely from the people who compose it, but such powers are derived from another power external to them. In this latter form the people who compose the State do not give the State its legal existence. Its legal existence rests upon and flows from the external authority. A conflict exists in Ireland as to whether the people of Ireland can establish a State—i.e. give legal birth to a State of their own creation—a State in which all the legislative, executive and judicial authority is derived solely from the people of Ireland in the exercise of their sovereign rights as a free people. The answer to this question which agitates the people of Ireland rests upon the answer to another question, viz.—

Was the Document signed December 5, 1921, and designated 'A Treaty Between Great Britain and Ireland' in reality a Treaty? [Emphasis in original.]

Reasoning that a treaty can only be signed between two sovereign states, Kennedy argued that its very title demonstrated Irish sovereign statehood. It followed that a sovereign Irish state had agreed to place certain symbolic restrictions on its sovereignty for the sake of real political gains.[27] In effect, Kennedy was right: what the Treaty represented was the beginning of a huge international constitutional revolution that would eventually dismember the entire British Commonwealth and Empire peacefully and in accordance with the legal forms of both the United Kingdom and the successor states to the colonies that had once formed the empire. Republicans in particular had no idea how revolutionary the British concessions actually were. Ironically, one of the reasons for their myopia was the necessity faced by the British government of hiding the significance of the concessions from their own parliamentary colleagues.

Under Plunkett's rather tedious jargon there lay a justification for political assassination, although quite unintended as such by Plunkett. The IRA could see itself as the lawful army of an existing state and see the representatives of the Free State as usurpers, as collaborators, and puppets of the British. The fulcrum of his argument was the fact that the Second Dáil had indeed never dissolved itself. However, neither had the First Dáil; it was assumed to have been dissolved when the 1921 elections occurred. The reason the First Dáil never dissolved itself was that it was feared that the British would cancel the 1921 elections, and the Republic would then have had no Dáil at all. Similar reasoning perhaps lay behind the pro-Treatyites' decision not to dissolve the Second Dáil; however, in their case the fear was of a republican *coup*, not a British take-over.

Furthermore, going by Plunkett's logic, Ireland perhaps possessed two legitimate Dáils as well as an impostor in the form of the Third or Free State Dáil. The membership of all three presumably overlapped considerably. The Free State people seem to have taken the simpler view that the vote on the Treaty, together with the June election, disestablished the Republic decisively and that there was a satisfactory constitutional continuity between the Republic and the Free State. Unfortunately, some denied that such a continuity existed. This denial of continuity, much encouraged by de Valera, did immeasurable damage.

Despite such exotic features as extern ministers, the referendum, the initiative, and proportional representation, the new constitution echoed faithfully the Westminster model of parliamentary democracy. The Executive Council was responsible to the Dáil and rapidly became dependent on the steady support of one or other alliance of parties in the Dáil. Eventually the new state was to evolve one of the most regimented party systems in Europe, the Senate was to wither away, and the extern minister idea was to be discarded. The original crypto-republicanism of 1922 was to become more open, and finally, in 1949, a republic was to be declared. The 1922 Constitution was to be replaced by a new, more populist and more republican constitution in 1937 under the aegis of de Valera, but the essential structures devised by Collins's 1922 constitutional committee persisted. Behind Bunreacht na hÉireann of 1937 lurks the unacknowledged ghost of the Constitution of the Irish Free State. De Valera's constitution was, however, to achieve a life of its own in a way that the previous document never quite succeeded in doing.

An unwritten but central feature of the 1922 constitution was the relationship created between the government and the civil service. An early act of the Oireachtas, the Ministers and Secretaries Act, 1924, governed this relationship, and still does, two generations later, despite massive constitutional evolution in other areas. This Act provided for the first eleven departments of state: President of the Executive Council, Finance, Justice, Local Government and Public Health, Education, Lands and Agriculture, Industry and Commerce, Fisheries, Posts and Telegraphs, Defence, and Foreign Affairs.

More permanently, however, the Act enunciated the doctrine that the minister of each department was a 'corporation sole' and was in theory responsible for the actions of every administrative or executive officer in the department, even if the minister was unaware of these actions and even though it was physically impossible for a minister to be aware of the thousands of instructions issued in his name.[28] One effect of this unrealistic theory of responsibility was that civil servants were enabled to hide behind the authority of the minister and disguise as his the decisions that they, rather than he, were actually making. The Act essentially reinforced the centrality of the British-created bureaucracy to the new state. As already related, unlike the Russia of 1918 or the Germany of 1933, there was no wholesale purge of civil servants. Some indeed chose to go to Britain or Belfast; most, however, elected to stay on, including many Protestants who preferred Dublin to either London or Belfast. For a generation after independence their traditions informed the practice of government at least as much as did the ideas of either the Gaelic League or the Catholic Church.

The overall outcome was the creation of a democratic, crypto-republican and markedly centralised state, rather authoritarian and secretive in its political style and sceptical of the public-spiritedness of the population to which it owed its right to rule. Even the transfer of power to de Valera in 1932 was not to undo the psychological damage the Civil War did to relationships between elites and population, which remained manipulative and insufficiently civic in character. The fact that democracy remained rooted in Ireland was indeed no mean achievement, but it was damaged by post-revolutionary disillusion, by the brutality of the violence, and by the sense of mutual betrayal that filled the minds of the leaders on both sides. Irish democracy, a very great achievement, was a disappointment; the post-revolutionary hangover was a large one.

The crisis of 1922–23 also had the effect of imbuing independent Ireland's new rulers with a distrust for popular consultation. The referendum and the initiative, included with such high hopes in the Constitution in 1922, were abolished in 1928, and the Free State Constitution was amended during its lifetime only by Act of the Oireachtas and never by popular referendum, as originally envisaged. The referendum was restored in the 1937 Constitution but was, significantly, not used for over twenty years after its enactment. The first popular referendum on the Constitution took place on the same day that de Valera was elevated to the Presidency and in effect retired from active politics. The referendum did not begin to feature as a major institution in political life until the 1960s. Since then it has finally become what it was presumably originally intended to be, the routine way in which the people change their Constitution or decide not to change it. In the perspective of a future generation, the achievement of a remarkably lively constitutional life for the majority of the people may be seen as Eamon de Valera's greatest achievement and, perhaps, as his unadmitted but real atonement for his behaviour in 1922.

A penchant for emergency legislation and the substitution of administrative fiat for court decision also characterised Irish government for a considerable time after independence, and to an extent this tendency still exists, although increasingly trammelled by the willingness of the judges to assert themselves against the will of the state authorities. Much of this tendency towards arbitrary state action was an echo of British traditions of government in Ireland and has shown distinct signs of withering away as the process of cultural decolonisation has proceeded.[29]

The legitimacy of the state remained uncertain for a considerable time. The Free State dealt with this in several ways. Firstly, it drew on the superabundant reserves of political legitimacy enjoyed by the Catholic Church at that period. The new politicians lost no time in making their personal piety publicly known, in enacting laws enforcing public morality along lines pleasing to the church, and in associating themselves as representatives of a Catholic state for a Catholic people. Cosgrave made highly publicised visits to the Papal Nuncio and, on one occasion, paid a visit to the Pope. This public piety was as true of the pro-Treaty governments of 1922–32 as it was to be of the Fianna Fáil governments after 1932. The loss of the mainly Protestant north-east made this process easier and probably permitted it to go much further than it otherwise would have.

The alliance between the authoritarian, Counter-Reformation Catholic Church with the populist and egalitarian traditions of Irish nationalist democracy might seem paradoxical at first glance but was actually a new expression of an old alliance, originally devised by Daniel O'Connell and exported to continental Europe in the nineteenth century as one of the central ideas of the tradition of Christian Democracy. As I have argued elsewhere, Ireland had little of a Great Tradition that the common man could call his; what he had was a Little Tradition, based on kin, local solidarity, folklore, and Whiteboy political action: the Public Band. O'Connell was the man who tried to give Ireland a combination of liberalism, democracy, and popular Catholicism. Irish democracy, a century and a half after O'Connell, still bears the birthmark, in the form of a strong general understanding of the mechanisms of representative democracy combined ultimately with a dislike for, or unawareness of, some of the liberal and individualistic ethical implications that inform those mechanics.

An exaggerated popular nationalism, common to many new states, was also pushed forward. Irish dancing, music, costume and language received official encouragement and subsidy. Cultural phenomena such as soccer, Protestant opinions, jazz, British newspapers and dislike of either Gaelic revivalism or Catholic triumphalism came to be declared anti-national. A systematic attempt to eradicate from the culture ideas that did not tally with the neo-Gaelic nationalist orthodoxy was mounted. The intellectuals and the artists were to have a thin time of it for thirty years, theatre being a strange and possibly accidental exception.

The new state was, however, also to be a pioneering experiment in Catholic democracy and was, for a long time, to be the only stable Catholic democracy in the world; other Catholic countries had a painful encounter with the ideas of liberal democracy and commonly succumbed to one or other kind of authoritarianism in the early twentieth century, usually because of the Catholic Church's terror of secular and popular rule. Despite Ireland's brush with Rory O'Connor and company in 1922, this was not an outcome of the Irish revolution; the Catholic Church backed up the democratic solution, despite its own philosophical detachment from the ideology of democracy.

The greatest advantage the Free State had was the utter incoherence of the republican opposition, an unlikely collection of ultra-Catholics, socialists, Bolshevists, agrarians, and gunmen, leavened by a modicum of rather able people who had not yet found their feet in what was still to some extent a pre-political popular culture. An Irish correspondent for *La Vie des Peuples* observed in November 1923 that the real advantage the Free State government had was the apathy of large numbers of people, as demonstrated by their abstention from the August 1923 election. As rendered for ministerial consumption by a civil servant, the argument ran:

> The problem of reconstruction is also dealt with, and the Writer expresses the opinion that the Government will be able to find all the money necessary within its own borders and that a good constructive policy will tend to bring the Republicans down from the sky. The Republican Party is described as a combination of unstable elements held together more by their opposition to the personnel of the present Government than to their dislike of the Treaty itself.[30]

Prophetically, it was predicted that de Valera would eventually swallow the oath. The fragility of the republican movement struck several observers. As early as May 1923 the break-up of the republican movement was described as 'astonishing'. Ireland was already 'virtually normal'.

> It would appear that Dev is taking the advice so often offered him—to create a powerful political party out of the Republican element in the country and make a bid for power through the ballot.

Defeated republicans under escort in Dublin in May 1923 were described as singing the new national anthem, 'The Soldier's Song', with its opening line 'Soldiers are we.' A Free State soldier escorting them was heard to mutter, 'So are we, bad cess to it.' A general 'indescribable' atmosphere of 'peaceful mediocrity' was 'settling on Ireland,' announced the *Morning Post* of 18 May 1923.[31] The twenty-six counties, it declared pontifically, was about to start recovering from the murder, looting and destruction of the previous few years. It was to take a generation, however, for the psychological, as distinct from the material, destruction to be made good. The constitutional evolution that the creation of the Constitution of the Irish Free State initiated was greatly to facilitate this process of recovery.

THE NORTHERN NIGHTMARE

Northern Ireland had already been functioning for over two years before the Free State came into legal existence in December 1922. On 6 December, Cosgrave announced in the Dáil the coming into existence of the Free State, one year after the signing of the Treaty. Under the terms of the Treaty, the six counties had a month (the 'Ulster Month') to opt out, if they so wished, from a notionally 32-county Free State. Cosgrave, as related below, publicly invited the North to stay in the Free State.[32] This explicit recognition of a unionist veto on the reunification of Ireland was to be withdrawn by de Valera in 1937 and not restored again by an Irish government until 1985 in the form of the Anglo-Irish Agreement.

Strangely, as has often been noted, little was said about Northern Ireland during the debate on the Treaty. Why this was so is unclear. In part the pronouncedly southern and often localist character of the Dáil deputies themselves had something to do with it. Also, a strange trust seems to have been placed in Collins's assurances about the Boundary Commission's efficacy; Collins seemed to many to be the man who could do almost anything. Essentially Collins argued that the commission would award so much of the North (Derry city, Fermanagh, Tyrone, south Armagh and south Down) to the Free State that the Northern polity would become non-viable and sue for admission to the Dublin state. As we now know, the commission did no such thing, and its tiny awards, favouring Northern Ireland somewhat more than it did the Free State, caused Dublin and London to bury it in 1925 in return for a financial settlement that benefited the still rather strapped Free State and left the boundary as it was. Ironically, a smaller, more solidly unionist Northern Ireland as imagined by Collins in 1921 would have been more rather than less viable; a prejudice against microstates rather understandably gripped their minds, as they lived in a world of mighty empires. As already observed, one of the few to be sceptical about the commission was de Valera, who assessed its limited potential immediately and accurately. Collins also apparently wanted to destabilise Northern Ireland militarily and sent 'laundered' IRA rifles north in early 1922. This may, however, have been a combination of an attempt to provide defence for northern Catholics and an attempt to keep the Munster IRA, the Men of the South, on his side.

Any possible military attempt on the part of the Free State to attack Northern Ireland was immediately stymied by the outbreak of the Civil War. Perhaps one of the few good results of the Civil War was that it rendered a more ferocious all-Ireland sectarian bloodbath less rather than more likely. The death of Collins in August 1922 visibly changed Free State policy towards Northern Ireland, and Cosgrave repeatedly accepted Northern Ireland's constitutional right under the Treaty to opt out of the Free State, which of course it did. On the day the Free State came into existence, 6 December 1922, Cosgrave, as President of the Executive Council, proudly announced the legal formation of an Irish state and acknowledged the honourable manner in which the British had treated the Provisional Government since the Treaty. However, the real core of his message appears to have been addressed to Ulster. The Northern parliament was to meet shortly to decide whether or not to 'join us on the terms of the Treaty.' He expressed his hope that they would so do, and promised generous representation in an all-Ireland Free State. However, he also said:

> On the other hand, should they decide to cut themselves off from all contact with us, we will regret very much such a decision. We will consider it both inopportune and unwise,

believing, as we do, that it is bound to have disastrous reactions on Northern enterprise. Nevertheless, as they are perfectly entitled to take this course under the Treaty, we are bound to respect such a decision in the event of its coming to pass.

It seems to have been tacitly accepted by Dublin that Northern Ireland was too big for them to handle, particularly because the pacification of Munster and Connacht was incomplete. Louis Walsh, a 1916 veteran and a six-county man himself, wrote to Hugh Kennedy in September 1923:

> The whole Ulster Problem has been grievously mishandled and people will not face the fact that there is here in the North a solid population alien from us in thought and look, distrustful of our character and capacity, and with a big Empire standing behind them.[33]

Kennedy had come to similar conclusions much earlier. In late August 1922, significantly after the death of Collins, he wrote that there was no point in trying a military attack on the 'North East'. Guerrilla tactics were hopeless, because the majority supported the government in Belfast. Furthermore, the boycott of Northern trade in the South had no effect; 'our boycott would threaten the Northern shipbuilding no more than a summer shower would threaten Cave Hill.' Virtually the same could be said of the linen industry. The Free State would have to behave constitutionally, he argued; the use of arms was out of the question. Later, in December 1922, Kevin O'Sheil expressed secret fears to Kennedy that the Boundary Commission would favour the North and enrage the Free State's allies in the North, forcing them, by implication, into the arms of the IRA.

> The Northern indignation will penetrate far into the Free State and greatly add to our difficulties. It may be a cause that will turn the Government out at the next election and replace it with a strong Die-Hard Government, which would be bitterly opposed to peaceful arrangement of any sort with the North . . . it will give a new lease of life to Irregularism, which is now practically on its last legs.[34]

A Captain E. L. MacNaughton wrote to Kennedy emphasising the overwhelming power of the Orange Order in the North.

> It practically amounts to this that the Protestant mob, noisy, ignorant, bigoted almost beyond belief, rule and hold sway in the 'Northern' area. They are the real masters. There is no genuine leadership. The leaders do not lead; they merely follow. They fear the machine; they cannot control it; they give utterance to those sentiments which will please this gang; to breathe a word about rapprochement would be for them political suicide.[35]

Militarily, it was scarcely ever on, for the reasons given by Kennedy and his colleagues and for other reasons as well. Firstly and most obviously, the Free State had its hands full with the rebellious IRA. Secondly, the strategic position of Ulster unionism was excellent, and Ulster unionist men had a considerable military tradition; furthermore, they had firm British support. However, there is another reason why the Dublin leaders, with the possible exception of Collins, never seriously contemplated military action against the North. The underlying cause of Dublin's unaggressive posture was simply democracy; a Northern war would have been deeply unpopular, and any government embarking on such an adventure would find itself out of office very rapidly. One of the few absolutely valid generalisations comparative politics has come up with is the proposition that stable and established democracies do not make war on each other; wars directed by governments occur between non-democracies or between democracies and non-democracies. By late 1922, despite the fighting in Munster, the Free State had already made the structural transition from revolution to democratic order, and attacking one's neighbour is very unpopular in a democracy, even if you have what seems to be a legitimate grudge against them. Democracies are unheroic, unless attacked from outside; they can then become implacable in their own defence, as war becomes genuinely popular in a democracy that has been attacked; the examples of France in 1914, Britain in 1940 and the United States in 1941 come to mind.

EXPECTATIONS OF CONSTITUTIONAL CHANGE

Michael Collins repeatedly said that the Treaty was a stepping-stone to untrammelled independence and that more would come, and come quickly, to the new state. P. S. O'Hegarty prophesied the dismantling of the Treaty settlement and the end of the ports agreement quite accurately in his influential 1924 book. He also prophesied the end of partition, something that still looks rather unlikely seventy years later.[36]

The evolution of the independent state, theoretically through the Irish language but actually through the English language, can conveniently be summarised as in table 2. It is now difficult to realise what a wealth of sterile argument centred around these words. Also, it is ironic to observe how dominant the English version of this terminology was over the Irish version, despite the tenets of the nationalist ideology, in particular de Valera's version of it. For example, his constitution of 1937 was drafted in English, translated into Irish, and *enacted in Irish*, so that the interpretation of the Constitution depends on the existence of legal experts whose Irish is perfect. This is despite the fact that the Irish version was, even at the time, less understood by legal authorities than was the English version. The two versions conflict

TABLE 2

Variations on a theme: constitutional nomenclature, 1916–49

Document	English	Irish
1916 Proclamation	Irish Republic	Poblacht na hÉireann
Independence Declaration, 1919	Republic of Ireland	Saorstát Éireann
Constitution of Irish Free State, 1922	Irish Free State	Saorstát Éireann
Bunreacht na hÉireann, 1937	Éire/Ireland	Éire/Ireland
Republic of Ireland Act, 1949	Republic of Ireland	Poblacht na hÉireann

sharply, more perhaps than most Irish citizens would like to be generally known. As a monument to a marriage between Anglo-American pragmatism and Irish philosophical fanaticism, the Constitution of 1937 takes some beating. The *Saorstát* versus *Poblacht* argument was commonly carried on between parties who knew little or no Irish.

Michael Collins's 'stepping-stone' theory was to be vindicated. Private recognition of the achievements of Cosgrave's government came also from an unexpected quarter: Eamon de Valera. In 1932 he admitted in the Senate, soon after taking power, that the Free State had achieved a level of practical independence that he had not believed possible in 1922. Tim Pat Coogan relates a revealing anecdote that is terrifying:

> De Valera himself once, privately, passed a notable judgement on the general performance of the Cosgrave administration. [His son Vivion, in the mid-1930s after de Valera's victory,] had been waxing eloquent on the iniquities of the 'Free Staters' in the approved Fianna Fáil fashion of the time when, to his great surprise, his father stopped him frowningly. 'Yes, yes, yes,' de Valera said testily, waving a forefinger, 'we said all that, I know. But when we got in and saw the files . . . they did a magnificent job, Viv. They did a magnificent job.' De Valera was too intelligent a man to allow his intellect to be clouded by his own rhetoric.[37]

The trouble was that he kept his intellect private and his rhetoric public. Ireland has paid dearly for this particular spiritual partition.

7

The Prospects for Democracy and the Irish Experience

Electoral democracy has become, as Robert Dahl and Francis Fukuyama, among others, have argued, the standard form of human government in the late twentieth century. Even obvious dictatorships tend to describe themselves as 'democratic', 'popular', or 'national', words that in many languages overlap with the word for 'people'. The intellectual and emotional appeals of classic, Italianate, fascism (as distinct from its first cousin, German Nazism) and of state communism have faded; in the former case, military and moral defeat did for it; in the latter case the both horrifying and ludicrous historical exhibits of the Soviet Union and the People's Republic of China have given us stark reminders of the consequences of heavily organised human bossiness backed up intellectually by romantic and historicist ideas. The claims of both left-wing and right-wing sets of totalitarianism to efficiency, moral superiority and aesthetic merit are now profoundly disbelieved and are deeply unfashionable, even in Paris. Extreme rightists and extreme leftists around the world now disguise their arguments under layer after layer of pseudo-democratic rhetoric, with less and less success.[1] The most successful criticism of Western democracy has been derived from the effects of its success: the accumulation of riches, often in the hands of relatively few people, and the consequent undemocratic concentration of social, cultural and political power in the hands of a minority.

An inchoate form of national socialism, for want of a better phrase, is perhaps now the major rival to electoral liberal democracy, but this form of government has no intellectual roots to compare with those of electoral democracy. National socialist political systems, as exemplified by the Ba'athist regimes of Syria and Iraq or the communist party-states of China and Viet Nam, are modelled on the European party-states of the 1930s and consist of authoritarian oligarchies driven commonly by militarism and the wish to emulate, or simply copy by authoritarian means in a definitely second-hand way, the democratic West. Inequality in such states is far greater than it is in liberal democracies, as there is rarely a large middle class and skilled working class that are permitted to enjoy the fruits of their labour unfettered by taxes and, commonly, the taxes on human beings known as forced labour and compulsory military service.

In a more easy-going form, some national socialist regimes consist of oligarchies that control the party apparatus and have quasi-democratic links with the population; Mexico, Iran or Egypt would offer 'populist' examples of this major modern alternative form of government. Resistance to electoral democracy is particularly consistent in two of the world's great culture areas: the countries influenced by Chinese civilisation and the Muslim world, between them embracing about half of humanity. Democracy, as argued earlier in chapter 1, has also generally had difficulty in establishing itself in poor or badly educated countries.

A last type of government, perhaps no more common in this century than before, is 'kleptocracy' or rule by thieves, lightly veiled by democratic, communist or national socialist forms. Haïti is a well-known example, as are Zaïre, Guinea-Bissau, and Burma. Commonly, outright kleptocracy coincides where allegiances of a blood or tribal type far outweigh any abstract loyalty to state, nation, common interest, or law. Kleptocratic tendencies exist in all forms of modern government, but usually there are restraints to its growth that assert themselves.

UNDERDEVELOPMENT AND IRISH DEMOCRACY

The Irish experience can offer many insights into the prospects for electoral democracy in the modern world. The Irish achievement of stable democracy in a context of alleged relative poverty and underdevelopment has been an intellectual chestnut of political science for a considerable time. As we have seen, the argument centres on Lipset's well-known and by now well-worn arguments concerning the correlation that has been seen to exist between sustained democratic life and material well-being.[2]

Since the publication of the original arguments in 1959–60 the argument has been much refined, but the central hypothesis, that there is a broad relationship between economic development and democracy, has never been frontally challenged with any great success.

A corollary of Lipset's thesis is that Ireland, along with Costa Rica, India and a few other actually or notionally poor countries, is a deviant case: it has been consistently 'too democratic' to fit the regression line linking economic indicators with indicators of the presence of democracy. Munger, for example, points out that Ireland scored lowest in material well-being in 1960 on a standard list of about twenty stable democracies and had a general developmental profile more consistent with the politics of instability or left or right-wing authoritarianism. Intriguingly, the only developmental indicator Ireland scored well on was the provision of mass education for younger people. However, relative equality of agrarian landholding, or the existence of something approximating a free-farmer, owner-occupier democracy, has also been a characteristic both of Ireland and of a number of other Western stable democracies, as suggested in chapter 1.

Reacting to this literature, the Canadian political scientist R. K. Carty declared the Republic to be 'among the most politically overdeveloped countries in the world' and attempted to explain this apparent anomaly by appealing to the long Irish tradition of party-building and the country's idiosyncratic experience of mass politics during the century before independence. I have offered a more extensive and somewhat more tentative version of more or less the same argument in *The Evolution of Irish Nationalist Politics* (1981).[3] All writers concerned, including myself, accepted Ireland's alleged exceptionalism.

The main problems with the Lipset approach are threefold. Firstly and most obviously there is a serious danger of economic determinism. Tacitly or otherwise, it is assumed that economic performance is the causal or independent variable and that political phenomena such as democratic elections, political parties, the rule of law and political beliefs of elites and masses are 'superstructural', are epiphenomenal, or are best looked at as dependent variables. Since Marx, the entire vexed relationship between economic activity and so-called 'superstructural' entities such as political culture and those listed above has been unresolved.

However, any discussion of the relationship between economic development and democracy should at the very least be open to the possibility of the relationship between political life and economic life being reciprocal or even the reverse of that posited by the Marxist tradition.

Brendan O'Leary, for example, has suggested that it could be argued that capitalist economic development is the historical fruit of the establishment, as a unique phenomenon, of a rule-bound and pluralist political order, whose rules bind the rulers as well as the ruled.[4] This phenomenon of the law-bound state first occurred in the classical world, in embryo and crippled form, but blossomed fully in early modern Europe and North America. Interestingly, O'Leary, in preparing his thesis, started by arguing for the existence of something like the Asiatic mode of production as suggested by traditional Marxist theorists and then found such a mode of production to be non-existent in the case he selected, historical India. Rather reluctantly, I suspect, but certainly very honestly, he finally came to the conclusion that, *pace* Marx and a cloud of scribblers, non-arbitrary and predictable government is the first essential for capitalist economic activity or any other activity to prosper; the businessman, the artisan, the inventor and the writer must be individually sure that they will not be persecuted by a predatory state, workers must be sure that taxes will not suddenly become confiscatory in some anomic way, and people must be reasonably sure that they will be permitted to enjoy the fruits of economic labour in peace. Not only must government be law-bound and property rights guaranteed but the state must also be able to enforce these rules on other people as well; the most historically radical right is the right to be left alone. Order, in the crucial sense of predictability, comes first, this argument would have it, then comes rule-bound order, and only then comes economic development.

A second, more central and perhaps less obvious objection to the Lipset argument and procedure is its methodological holism. Holism in the social sciences consists of a tendency to regard the collectivity as the main object of analysis rather than the individuals, families, classes and organisations that make it up; it is essentially the philosophical equivalent of failing to see the trees because one is too conscious of the forest. Holism also makes one insensitive to the often crucial issue of the nature of the relationships between the entities that make up the collectivity. A thousand football supporters form a very different collectivity from, for example, a thousand soldiers under discipline, a thousand citizens at a party rally, or a thousand people at a garden party.[5]

Similarly, relationships between the citizens of a Western democracy are different from those existing among citizens of a communist totalitarian state or a feudal kingdom. Even within the family of Western democracies, interpersonal relationships vary astonishingly: the relationship between the police and the citizen is very different in France from those existing in Ireland or Spain, for example. Karl Popper's well-known strictures on holistic approaches are well taken.[6] Holistic approaches tend, deliberately or otherwise, to disregard the fact that social groups such as classes, armies, bureaucracies, electorates and nation-states are aggregates of individuals, each of whom has purposes, relationships, consciousness, a store of information and abilities that are unique. Furthermore, these are institutionalised groups, forming more or less rule-driven aggregates. The cultures these individuals are formed by give them very different accounts of the world in which they live.

Also, in any collectivity, some individuals will be more energetic, effective, active, experienced and important to the life of the collectivity than are others; elites have, almost by definition, more say about the future of the group, including its organisation and basic rules, than have others; this is true even in heavily democratised societies. Elites are often in effect self-selected, unusual in personal character and ability, and deeply atypical in abilities, motivations, and opinions. This is generally more likely to be true at a time of revolutionary crisis or regime change than in 'normal' times of relative stability, when impersonal and conformist mechanisms tend to assert themselves in the process of elite selection. Therefore, 'collectivist' theories, pointing to impersonal 'law-like' processes deriving from structural factors, tend to rule in intellectual life in peacetime; in time of crisis the romantic, psychologistic Great Man theories of history have their day.

The founders of a political system, commonly a relatively small group of people, tend, then, to have a huge responsibility for setting the system up one way rather than another, for when the time of change, usually less than ten years, has passed, the structures the elites have devised tend to crystallise and become relatively immutable. Peter's legacy and Stalin's mark lie heavily all over the modern Russian state, and it will certainly take decades, perhaps centuries, for Russia to recover from leftist totalitarianism, if it ever does. Similarly, James Madison's constitutional handiwork of 1787–88 still guides the actions of modern American presidents in situations that Madison could not possibly have imagined. Again, modern Federal Germany was in considerable part the creation of a brilliant German-American constitution-writer, Karl Friedrich. Charles de Gaulle did much to create modern France; his constitution of the Fifth Republic was designed to fit himself at a time of great crisis, but it has also fitted France in the years since 1958. However, behind de Gaulle lies, as Alexis de Tocqueville so convincingly argued, a French political tradition of centralism that long antedated the French Revolution.

Similarly, in the Ireland of the 1920s a key group of almost forgotten but brilliant people, principal among them William Cosgrave, Hugh Kennedy, Kevin O'Higgins, and Kevin O'Sheil, created the polity that de Valera inherited and tried desperately and unsuccessfully to refashion after his own ideas and, in a way, after himself. De Valera was, strangely, the ultimate Free Stater: he legitimised the polity he did so much and so energetically to delegitimise ten years earlier. Furthermore, the electorate permitted its reluctant servant to get away with this rebaptism and become its leader and, eventually, obedient servant.

Holism invites you to underestimate the crucial importance of a few individuals in strategic institutional positions at the time of change, to see human history as the outcome of large, unreasoning and impersonal forces, sometimes conceived as being almost mystical in nature, and to underrate the capacity of human beings to create, make choices and steer the collectivity onto one course rather than another. Also, holism encourages you to underrate the importance of ideas and information. It also encourages passivity, irresponsibility, and fatalism: a general intellectual shrugging of the shoulders on the part of certain kinds of intellectuals.

A third and closely related difficulty is provided by the 'unit of analysis' problem. Independent Ireland, like postwar West Germany, newly independent India, and nineteenth-century

Canada, was as much the creation of forces originating in a political system external to itself as it was that of internal social forces, agencies, or individuals. Firstly and most obviously, Ireland had been re-created as an English-speaking country, subject to laws modelled substantially on those of England, in the seventeenth and eighteenth centuries.

Despite the claims of certain kinds of Gaelic revivalists, this transformation was, and is, irreversible. An Ireland left to itself by the English and Scots in the seventeenth century would certainly have evolved in a different way; whether for better or worse is, of course utterly impossible to say. Perhaps the potato would never have been introduced, for example, and perhaps there would have been no Great Famine, no wrecking of a country and, perhaps, no extinction of an entire culture. Perhaps Irish would have remained the main vernacular and provided a serious competitor for English, much as Welsh has in Wales or as Catalan has in eastern Spain. Perhaps Irish would have established itself as a genuine commercial and state vernacular, as some of the original Gaelic Leaguers and Sinn Féiners dreamed. Certainly ecclesiastical architecture, spared Cromwellian devastation, would probably have constituted an improvement on the nineteenth-century Catholic triumphalist and twentieth-century brutalist churches that Ireland possesses in abundance.

Alternatively, the country's history might have been as catastrophic as it actually has been but in different ways. For example, a potato famine might have occurred under a post-1798 Irish government and the country might have ended up in producing a cold and wet version of Haïti. No-one can know.

Again, an unpartitioned independent Ireland in 1922 might have had a very different history from that the actual partitioned country has had; it might have collapsed in civil war, or it might have engineered a tolerable collective life for itself; republicans of a certain type claim that a liberal or socialist state, based on the poorer classes, would have emerged. They have, however, offered no coherent or convincing arguments for their view. Generally, their more effective arguments in their own favour have been expressed less in the words of Marx and Lenin than in the bullets of Kalashnikov.

Furthermore, as this book has suggested, partition changed the actual boundaries of the political system in a way that was specifically intended to render each part of Ireland more amenable to self-government than an independent all-Ireland polity was envisaged, rightly or wrongly, to be likely to have been. It was calculated, correctly for the South and incorrectly for the North, that giving each ethnic group its own polity or sub-polity would bring peace.[7] It was hoped that these two entities would make some kind of deal with each other that would render Ireland generally politically content, whether as a united commonwealth or as two friendly but separate entities. Certainly a 32-county Dublin-ruled polity, if set up in 1922 as a Free State with what I would like to term the oath of allegiance and fidelity, might have found itself facing not one but two civil wars, one in Munster and another in Ulster. It seems unlikely that the polity would have survived as a democracy, or even as a single entity.

Political systems therefore are not simply emanations of economic life but rather devices, or constitutional machines, designed by human beings for human beings to live in; they are also normally designed to suit some human beings more than others. Furthermore, they are often designed to realise some general ideological purpose. They are artificial, not natural, entities and are well or badly designed. They are often also *differently* designed; federal institutions fit Germany very well, as Germany is a 'city-state' country or set of countries (*Länder*) with no obvious core, whereas it is not immediately obvious that Denmark, Finland or even France would be any better governed as federal states.

Lastly, political systems may be designed for different philosophical or cultural purposes. They may, for example, be constructed to protect a particular religious community, as in the case of Israel and, to a considerable extent, Ireland, Poland, and Pakistan. By way of contrast, they may be constructed to bring together many different people of different religion and even language, as in the case of the United States, Switzerland, India, the Soviet Union as was, or post-1918 Czechoslovakia. Political systems may be designed as democracies, national socialist party-states, predatory garrison states, or kleptocracies. They may be designed as one system and subsequently shift into another, notionally degenerate form or ascend into a more advanced form. Some may have laws that protect private property and even private sector greed, whereas others may have laws that promote the material protection of the common people but also the political and material interests and even greed of public sector elites.

Some radical and authoritarian political systems, such as 1930s Nazi Germany or 1980s Ba'athist Iraq, were designed deliberately as allegedly 'advanced' political machines to conquer the territory of neighbours, often in the name of some religion, nationalist programme, or socialist political prescription. The variety of human government is immense, and Aristotle's intellectual ghost is alive and well in the late twentieth century.

The political ideas, emotions and mutual expectations of powerful people at the time of national independence tend, then, to be crucial to any understanding of the political system that is the outcome of the regime change, just as much as is the pre-change collective experience of the masses. The character of elite political culture is central to any estimate of the prospects for democracy in any nascent polity, quite apart from economic conditions or even traditions of civil strife. Yugoslavia might have worked out some kind of democratic stability or peaceful divorce but lost that chance a very long time ago, as it had not got the elites with the appropriate pluralist ideas.

Even if Yugoslavia had had true world-class politicians of the stature of de Gaulle, Adenauer or Roosevelt it might have disintegrated. As it was, only politicians who wished to deny and repress Yugoslavia's extraordinary internal tensions were in power; they sat, Soviet-style, on the Balkan pressure cooker for a generation. Similarly, Irish unionist and nationalist leaders between 1912 and 1923 did not, between them, have the ideas, power or will to create an all-Ireland polity; they might have succeeded in creating one had they truly wished to. The point is that they did not possess any consensus on the desirability of any such polity; despite the ranting of many ideologues, it was clear at the time that the British would have liked a united Ireland, subject to their (mainly strategic) conditions. It was also evident that unionists were utterly against the idea and were politically and militarily well organised. The more realistically minded of the nationalists preferred a bird in the hand to two in the bush: twenty-six controllable counties versus thirty-two pretty uncontrollable counties.

John Coakley, in his study of political succession and regime change in Ireland, Finland, Czechoslovakia and the Baltic republics after 1918, argues ultimately that Lipsetian economic determinism cannot explain why it was that Finland, Ireland and Czechoslovakia evolved into stable democracies whereas the Baltic states experienced early authoritarian takeovers; elite political culture, he argues, was a major determinant, and the extent to which the leaders had absorbed democratic ideology was crucial.[8] The elementary conclusion follows that the perceptions and beliefs of leaders and followers count for as much as the class backgrounds of political elites and their followers.

As table 3 illustrates, there were no gross developmental contrasts between the three states that created stable democratic orders during the inter-war period and those that divested themselves of representative governments. The true contrast is between the three Baltic states, which had a long experience of Tsarist authoritarianism and little experience of even local self-government, and the others, which, in different ways, had experienced domination of a more lightly administered type. The latter had also had as their metropolitan powers states that had considerable stocks of democratic values themselves. Finland's mentor was Sweden and its other brother-Scandinavian democracies; Ireland's models were Britain, the old dominions, the United States, and, to an extent, France and other European democracies and near-democracies of the period. Similarly, Czechoslovakia, dominated politically by the Czechs, had elites who had internalised Austro-German traditions of local self-government and nationalist democracy. Czechoslovakia's problem was its German minority, locally concentrated and contiguous to mother Germany, and also the fractious Slovaks, long submerged under Hungarian domination. The Slovaks—Catholic, more rural, more 'eastern', and less experienced in quasi-democratic politics—turned easily to an authoritarian and Catholic clerical fascism under Nazi domination between 1939 and 1945. Two generations later they were, of course, to complete a divorce from their Bohemian cousins. These cousins were to be silent but evidently very willing consenters to this parting of the ways.

This neo-elitist argument perhaps needs some further emphasising. The intellectual history of countries' elites has tended to be disregarded in favour of the examination of class structures, levels of economic activity, proportions adhering to one religious faith or another, proportions speaking different

TABLE 3

New electoral democracies in northern Europe, 1918–1939

	Significant dissident minorities	Proportion agrarian	Proportion Catholic
1. Successful			
Czechoslovakia	24% German	40%	76%
Finland	11% Swedish	65%	—
Ireland	7% Protestant	53%	93%
Mean	14%	53%	56%
2. Unsuccessful			
Estonia	8% Russian	59%	—
Latvia	11% Russian	61%	23%
Lithuania	—	77%	81%
Mean	6%	66%	35%

Source: Coakley, 'Independence movements and national minorities', 215–48.

languages, popular cultural traditions, etc. Certainly these variables are important, but one cannot 'read out' the political outcome from a combination of these variables. The ability of elites to work together, their readiness to trust each other, their intellectual stock in trade, their role models at home and abroad and the nature of their familial and scholarly formation are all crucial, particularly at the critical juncture of the regime change; in effect, I am arguing for a cultural and 'structural history' approach as against standard social science psychologistic or anthropological styles of analysis. The latter styles certainly have their uses but must ultimately be subordinated to the former.

So, for example, Finland had, as already suggested, at its back one of the oldest democratic traditions in Europe, in the shape of Sweden. Sweden's post-imperial tradition of pluralism and representation is rivalled in longevity only by those of Denmark, England, Scotland, the Netherlands, and Switzerland. Furthermore, Sweden had been the ruling power in Finland before 1815, and the Swedish language and Swedish elites dominated Finnish domestic government for a long time even under Tsarist Russia. Sweden was a good exemplar for the Finns: it had experienced an extraordinarily tranquil transition from aristocratic to democratic rule, partly because of the unusually egalitarian structure of its rural society and partly because a popular monarchy checked the power of the aristocracy; Sweden invented the alliance between king and yeoman-farmer. Finally, Finland's native Swedish-speakers were allied with the Finnish cause against the Soviet menace; the Finns could easily accept Swedish culture and tutelage. The Swedes, after all, represented the West, as against the Eastern totalitarianism of Russia, whether in its Orthodox Christian or atheistic communist guise. Finnish elites internalised a version of Scandinavian political culture. The leaders of the Baltic states, by way of contrast, seem to have internalised versions of Russian and German authoritarianisms.

Rather similarly, Ireland aspired to recognition as an old European nation rather than as a British province, but the Irish elites wanted very much also to be seen as modern democratic leaders who could meet the leaders of the nations of the white English-speaking world of that period on terms of equality; they looked up, somewhat shamefacedly, to a version of English constitutionalism and law-giving, even if they could not quite admit this and, sometimes, pretended to possess an alternative loyalty to an essentially uncomprehended Gaelic past. Their most uninhibited political loyalty was to a Catholic democratic political idea, one that was theoretically pluralist and invented by Daniel O'Connell rather than by Theobald Wolfe Tone or Patrick Pearse.

It certainly helped these nationalist constitutionalists that an analogue of the Swedish Finns existed in the form of a small but very significant Protestant nationalist tradition in the form of figures such as Tone, Thomas Davis, John Mitchel, and Charles Stewart Parnell. These names could be used to present Irish nationalism as not just a veneer for Catholic triumphalism, which in practice it admittedly often was. However, Catholic integralism had to fight with 'Anglo-American' traditions of liberalism and pluralism, and had no total victory. In fact, in the long run the Catholic integralists were to lose. One of the reasons for this defeat was the closed and non-arguable set of theses that the Catholics enshrined in Irish law. Once these became questionable, they were ignored or openly defied.

Czechoslovakia presents us with a more difficult case. Democratic values were indeed strong among the Czech elites, but majoritarianism had an obvious appeal to the small Czech majority, beset as it was by German, Slovak, Hungarian and Ruthenian minorities who could not unite against the Czechs. The Czechs tended to monopolise power, although their rule was relatively tolerant. The Baltic states, with, if anything, more favourable 'objective' circumstances surrounding their independence, succumbed rapidly to authoritarianism, indicating an internalising of some Russian and German right-wing authoritarian values. Political culture, particularly the subculture of the elites, must bear more of the weight of explanation than it is commonly asked to do.

> The failure of the leadership of the major political forces in the new [Baltic] states to coalesce diminished the legitimacy of some of the liberal democratic regimes of the inter-war period. The extent to which the authoritarian coups may have been related to inadequacies in political structures or to strains associated with the economic recession has been discussed [here] . . . with inconclusive results. A further consideration should be added: that of political culture. The Irish, Finnish and Czech elites and a section of the population had been involved in a form of limited democratic politics since about 1830, 1863 and 1861, respectively, while a much larger share of the population became involved in mass politics after 1885, 1906 and 1907. The Estonians, Latvians and Lithuanians lacked this training; they had no experience of parliamentary politics before 1906, an insignificant number were members of the four Dumas and the electorate could vote only indirectly in Duma elections.[9]

However, Finland, Ireland and Czechoslovakia do not offer a stark contrast. All three showed marked signs of instability at different times. Finland, most obviously, fought a short but bloody Red versus White civil war in 1918 over the issue of whether Finland should become part of the Soviet Union: capitalist independence versus communist union. The Finns also had a brief flirtation with fascism in the form of the Lapua movement of central Finland in the early 1930s. Ireland, as we have seen, fought a short 'intra-Catholic' civil war on the linked issues of majoritarianism and membership of the British Commonwealth or Empire as against an incoherently held vision of an isolated, pure and virtuous republic. Czechoslovakia found its German minority to be of uncertain loyalty and easy meat for the seductions of Nazi pan-Germanism in the 1930s; the Sudetendeutschen were fundamentally indigestible, had no loyalty to the hybrid and Slavic state of Czechoslovakia, and, at the urging of the Reich, wrecked it, to their own eventual complete undoing. Overall, comparative analysis suggests that the Irish and the Finns were rather lucky, clever, or crafty.

DEMOCRACY AND SOLDIERS

A key variable in each of the national cases we have being discussing was the ideological values entertained by the *military* elites in the new states. Finland very obviously had an army imbued with Finnish nationalism and an anti-Russian feeling partly derived from nationalism and partly from the experiences many elite formations had had in fighting for Germany on the eastern front during the First World War. Finland's war with Russia was a popular war, and its army could, and did, easily slip into the role of Defender of the People. In Czechoslovakia, similarly, a new country, under threat of dismemberment by embittered and truncated neighbours, had an army loyal to the nation and its institutions, so much so that its most likely time of mutiny was during the crisis of 1938, when the government decided not to use the army to resist the Munich settlement. In a sense, Czechoslovakia's founding myth was the epic of the Czech Legion, which Lenin eventually had to bribe to leave the Trans-Siberian Railway and go home by America and Europe after the Russian Civil War.

In Ireland, the army of 1922 was from the very beginning an army defending the state against internal enemies, and arguably still is, seventy-odd years later; the army of the Free State was raised specifically to prevent a *coup d'état*, as distinct from perpetrating such a coup, as alleged by de Valera at the time and for years afterwards. His allegations, persistently reiterated, had enormously damaging and demoralising consequences. As Eunan O'Halpin has put it, the greatest threat to the Irish state since independence has been an internal one, whereas the conventions of democratic politics and of military professionalism suggest that armies exist to defend countries from external attack, to project national power externally, and to contribute in some way to the maintenance of international order. In terms of any of these criteria the Irish army has never been much more than a simulacrum. However, it has been highly effective in defending the state from within. *Simply by its existence the army has been a bulwark against a republican seizure of power.*[10] [Emphasis added.]

Despite some talk of a coup in 1924 and 1932 and some murmurings of an attack on the North in the mid-thirties and in 1969–70, the army has always accepted its role as the defender of the Irish democracy; this in turn is a result of its role at the time of state-formation in 1922: an army specifically created to defend a civilian civil order is psychologically unlikely to evolve an ideology of the army as *poder moderador*, as the guardian of the nation and possessing the bounden duty to intervene in political life when things are not going as the officers would wish. Another explanation would refer again to elite subculture; the leaders of the state and the leaders of the army had been comrades-in-arms before 1922, and even de Valera's coming to power in 1932 was safeguarded by the wish of the army officers to bind up the wounds of the Civil War and to forgive and forget. Army folklore's famous senior officer's question, 'Do we salute him or shoot him?'—concerning a Fianna Fáil minister's arrival at Army Headquarters in 1932—was given a tacitly democratic answer in the form of obedience to the new government.

ECONOMICS AND DEMOCRACY

To return to the Munger and Carty analyses, both of which assume Irish political overdevelopment relative to its economic performance, it is not even clear that Ireland was so poor a country at the time of independence. Certainly it was not a rich country, but it had enjoyed a considerable, mainly rural, boom in the years before 1921. Table 4 presents some estimates of real economic product per head for European countries relative to the United Kingdom, culled from the work of Kennedy, Giblin, and McHugh.[11] The authors themselves remark that the figures indicate that the twenty-six counties' 'relative standing was surprisingly high for a country commonly thought of as very poor and undeveloped.'[12] In Table 4 I have rearranged the economic data to segregate the countries into those that succeeded in establishing stable electoral democracy in the inter-war years from those that either did not attempt to establish democracy or abolished democratic institutions. I have omitted Germany and the Soviet Union, both very large countries, in an attempt to control for the grosser effects of holism. Comparable figures for the Baltic states were not available.

TABLE 4

Selected successful and unsuccessful democracies and non-democracies in Europe, 1918–38, and estimated real product per head, 1913 (UK = 100)

Successful democracies		Unsuccessful democracies and non-democracies	
United Kingdom	100	Austria	65
Switzerland	84	Italy	43
Denmark	83	Spain	37
Belgium	76	Poland	36
Netherlands	69	Hungary	35
Sweden	66	Romania	35
France	63	Greece	31
Ireland	61	Portugal	31
Norway	57	Yugoslavia	28
Finland	49	Bulgaria	23
Czechoslovakia	47	*Mean*	37
Mean	76		

Source: Kennedy, Giblin, and McHugh, *The Economic Development of Ireland in the Twentieth Century*, 14–15.

However, the data in table 4 also indicate that *around the time of Irish independence*, during the crucial period of regime change and institutional formation, the Munger-Carty problem did not in fact exist. Ireland, admittedly poorish by the standards of European democracies of the period, was possibly nearly twice as prosperous as the average of the non-democracies on the Continent. Like Britain, Ireland did well in the late nineteenth century, particularly when compared with its disastrous early nineteenth-century experience. Ireland was to become relatively poor after independence, and some at least of the political tribulation of the 1930s and 1950s can be attributed to economic travails. Also, the figures in table 4 possibly underestimate Irish wealth at that time. Coakley's argument, therefore, is valid in an other-things-being-equal context. Democracy's chances depend on elites in relatively rich countries; in poor countries the dice are loaded against it, usually, but not always, decisively. The real political achievement in pre-war Europe was that of Czechoslovakia; a totally artificial state, with poor infrastructure in the east and a wildly disparate ethnic make-up, it managed to hold itself together remarkably well until destroyed by outside forces, deserted by Britain and France in the face of Nazi Germany.

Admittedly, figures of this kind are, to say the least of it, fuzzy; the overall impression is, however, not counter-intuitive. Perhaps the real question that should be asked is the *reverse* of that asked by Munger and Carty: why did Ireland experience so much violence, much of it anti-democratic, between 1913 and 1923, when economic life was actually going quite well? Here I would appeal to the idea of the relative autonomy of elite subculture and suggest again, as I did in chapter 2, that Irish leaders were at best 'unenthusiastic democrats' and ambiguous, as many Catholics of the period were, in their attitudes to democracy, commercial civilisation, philosophical relativism, and the rule of law. Cosgrave, O'Higgins and Mulcahy were unusual in being unconditional democrats, and they killed people for the nascent Irish democracy that they saw as menaced by the anti-Treatyites.

The objection of so many anti-Treaty leaders to the lack of 'spirituality' of the Treatyites may in fact have been central to the quarrel; democracy and prosperity, a secular society and commercialism, were emotionally unsatisfying. Fukuyama has made a similar comment about the central problem of secular democracy: its inability to satisfy spiritual yearnings, the wish to be heroic and a wish to serve the community in a self-sacrificing way. A true community, Mary MacSwiney and others claimed, was united by more than material interest; man does not live by bread alone. These ideas about the right relationship between the individual and the community are by no means despicable and are still being argued about in independent Ireland two generations later.

Another reason for the violence was the relative prosperity of the period, which gave people ambitions of a kind that previously could only be realised in the fabled post-European land of the United States; furthermore, the First World War had inured one section of young men to mass killing and bottled up the rest, those who would not volunteer, in Ireland for the duration.[13] However, the events in Ireland of the period 1913–23 are best seen as a sideshow in the general European crisis of the period, in which millions of people died. Neither Europe nor Ireland have, even yet, recovered from the great disaster of the second decade of this terrible century. No amount of Irish historicist reasoning can disguise the fact that Ireland, far from being uniquely formed by its own, admittedly catastrophic, history, is a province of Europe and behaves accordingly. Ireland shares its catastrophes with modern France, Germany, Poland, and Russia; Ireland's exceptionalism has been much exaggerated. Nowadays it accepts this cultural fate with greater equanimity and less obsessiveness in both the North and the South of the divided island.

The last reason for Irish violence was British violence. British rule in Ireland was non-democratic, unsympathetic, and absentmindedly militaristic. Irish political culture had long grown out of a polity that was authoritarian, colonial, and 'foreign'. Refusal to grant self-government and establishment favouritism towards unionism finally did the trick and provoked the Irish to a level of political violence not seen since the 1790s.

Democracy in Ireland was the child of strange parents: Anglo-American political culture and the Catholic Church. Its crucial moment came in 1922–23, when force was used to prevent it being forcibly disestablished by insurrectionist 'republicans' who mouthed democratic slogans but whose violent actions belied their words. Since the Free State victory of 1923, no alternative regime has been taken seriously in Ireland. No all-Ireland polity, were one to emerge in the future, could ever be established without the clear consent of the Northern majority. It was the democratic founders of independent Ireland who first said this openly and did so at the founding moment of the state. Now, seventy years later, the descendants of their opponents, the leaders of Fianna Fáil, have finally, after years of prevarication, openly agreed with William Cosgrave, someone whose name they have sometimes virtually forgotten or which they remember only as that of a traitor. Occasionally they secretly admired him, as in the case of Seán Lemass, Fianna Fáil Taoiseach from 1959 to 1966. The North of 1922 set a severe test for the democratic credentials of the Southerners; some of them failed that test at the time, but their successors, under the Fianna Fáil Taoiseach Albert Reynolds, passed it with flying colours in 1994. The Treaty settlement of 1921–22, much fought over at the time, is now complete, and Ireland can finally move on.

Notes

Abbreviations

AA	Army Archives, Dublin
DELG	Dáil Éireann Local Government Files
NA	National Archives, Dublin
NLI	National Library of Ireland, Dublin
UCD AD	Archives Department, University College, Dublin,

Chapter 1 (p. 1–26)

1. See, in general, Munger, *The Legitimacy of Opposition*; Schmitt, *The Irony of Irish Democracy*; Praeger, *Building Democracy in Ireland*; Garvin, *The Evolution of Irish Nationalist Politics*, passim.
2. For a portrayal, which is not too sympathetic, of the *soi-disant* republican stream in modern Irish political culture see Garvin, *Nationalist Revolutionaries in Ireland*, 139–67.
3. Until recently the standard book on these central events has been Curran, *The Birth of the Irish Free State, 1921–1923*. It has never been printed on this side of the Atlantic, which speaks volumes for Irish academic culture. It has now been supplemented by a book that has had the benefit of access to newly available primary material, Mitchell's authoritative *Revolutionary Government in Ireland*.
4. Garvin, *Evolution of Irish Nationalist Politics*, passim; Garvin, *Nationalist Revolutionaries in Ireland*, passim; Garvin, 'Democratic politics in independent Ireland' in Coakley and Gallagher (eds.), *Politics in the Republic of Ireland*, 250–61; Garvin, 'Unenthusiastic democrats' in Hill and Marsh, *Modern Irish Democracy*, 8–23.
5. See Huntington's classic *Political Order in Changing Societies*; also his *The Third Wave*, Dahl, *Democracy and its Critics*, passim.
6. Dahl, *Polyarchy*, 48–80.
7. Huntington, *Political Order in Changing Societies*, 93–139.
8. Arno Mayer provides the classic analysis in *The Persistence of the Old Regime*.

9. Pipes, *Russia under the Old Regime.*
10. See the essays in O'Connell (ed.), *Daniel O'Connell.*
11. The classic study is Bloch, *Feudal Society.*
12. On elite theory generally see Beetham, 'From socialism to fascism'; Bennett, 'The elite theory as fascist ideology'.
13. Barker, *Greek Political Theory*; Barker, *The Political Thought of Plato and Aristotle.*
14. Dahl, *Democracy and its Critics*, passim.
15. Huntington, *The Third Wave*, passim.
16. Boyce, Eccleshall, and Geoghegan, *Political Thought in Ireland since the Seventeenth Century.*
17. Desmond FitzGerald discussed the possibilities of an Irish Hohenzollern monarchy with Pearse and Joseph Plunkett in the besieged GPO in Easter week. See Lyons, *Ireland since the Famine*, 370–1.
18. De Vere White, *Kevin O'Higgins*, 225.
19. Pocock, *The Machiavellian Moment.*
20. Peter Hart, 'The Irish Republican Army and its Enemies: Violence and Community in County Cork, 1917–1923' (draft book, 1993); Garvin, *Nationalist Revolutionaries in Ireland*, 139–66.
21. Garvin, *Nationalist Revolutionaries in Ireland.*
22. Praeger, *Building Democracy in Ireland*, passim; Garvin, *Nationalist Revolutionaries in Ireland*, passim.
23. On citizenship see Kymlicka and Norman, 'Return of the citizen', 352–81.
24. Wood, *Peasant-Citizen and Slave.* On republicanism the classic work is Pocock, *The Machiavellian Moment.*
25. Wood, *Peasant-Citizen and Slave*, 126–72.
26. On blended ideologies see Dahl, *Polyarchy*, 43.
27. Kohn, *The Constitution of the Irish Free State*, 13, 53–8. Kohn comments (p. 71) that the 1921 Treaty recognised the 'integral unity of Ireland' and (p. 72) that de Valera's 'external association' formula ('document no. 2') would actually have weakened Irish independence, because it would have withdrawn the countervailing power of the dominions, led by Canada.
28. Anderson, *Imagined Communities.*
29. Gellner, *Nations and Nationalism.*

30. Donnelly, 'Propagating the cause of the United Irishmen', 5–23.
31. Ruth Dudley Edwards, *Patrick Pearse*, 261–4.
32. Johann Gottlieb Fichte, *Reden an die deutsche Nation*, in I. H. Fichte (ed.), *Fichtes Werke*, VI, 259–499; Frederick Copleston SJ, *A History of Philosophy*, VII, 84–99.
33. Lipset, *Political Man*, 45–76.
34. Michael Gallagher, *Political Parties in the Republic of Ireland*, 1985, 1–9.
35. Maurice Manning, *The Blueshirts*, passim.
36. Tom Inglis, *Moral Monopoly*, passim.
37. Malcolm Brown, *The Politics of Irish Literature*, 312–15.
38. Huntington, *The Third Wave*, passim.
39. Garvin, *Nationalist Revolutionaries in Ireland*, 1–12.
40. León Ó Broin, 'Joseph Brennan, Civil Servant Extraordinary,' 28–9.
41. Neligan, *The Spy in the Castle*, passim.
42. T.M. Healy, *Letters and Leaders of my Day*, 652–5.
43. Hopkinson, *Green versus Green*, passim.

Chapter 2 (p. 27–62)

1. This chapter incorporates a heavily revised version of arguments put forward in my 'Unenthusiastic democrats: the emergence of Irish democracy' in Hill and Marsh, *Modern Irish Democracy*, 9–23. See also my *The Evolution of Irish Nationalist Politics*, 207–70, where some of these ideas got an early airing. The standard narrative account of the birth of the Free State is Curran, *The Birth of the Irish Free State*. A creative Durkheimian interpretation of the split of 1921–22 is offered by Praeger in *Building Democracy in Ireland*. The proposition that the emergence of democracy in Ireland was a rather impressive achievement under adverse circumstances is put forward by Munger in *The Legitimacy of Opposition*. Both of these works were given honourable mention internationally and among Irish academics but were ignored by many Irish political journalists and historians. For a critique of Munger and other writers, including the present author, see Kissane, 'The not-so-amazing case of Irish democracy'. Morrisey quotation: UCD AD, Ernie O'Malley Papers, P17b/85; Mulcahy quotation: UCD AD,

Richard Mulcahy Papers, P7b/149; Hart quotation: 'The Irish Republican Army and its Enemies: Violence and Community in County Cork, 1917–1923' (draft book, 1993), 361 and passim; Blythe quotation: *Dáil Debates*, vol. 2, col. 89, 8 Dec. 1922; O'Higgins quotation: *Dáil Debates*, vol. 2, col. 68–9, 8 Dec. 1922.

2. But see Keogh, *The Vatican, the Bishops and Irish Politics*, which argues cogently that the bishops successfully held the papal authorities at arm's length, taking the view that they understood little about the dynamics of Irish popular politics.

3. References to Irish nationalist attitudes to democracy abound. The O'Rahilly articles are 'The Catholic origin of democracy' (quotation from p. 8), 'The sources of English and American democracy', and 'The sovereignty of the people' (quotation from p. 39); see also Popper, *The Open Society and its Enemies*, and Garvin, *Nationalist Revolutionaries in Ireland*, 139–66. Connolly quotations: *Socialism Made Easy* (1909), as abridged by O. D. Edwards and B. Ransome in *James Connolly: Selected Political Writings*, London: Jonathan Cape 1973, 253–84 (quotation from 280–1).

4. Edwards and Ransome, *James Connolly: Selected Political Writings*, 356.

5. Edwards and Ransome, *James Connolly: Selected Political Writings*, 357 and passim.

6. Joyce quotation: Brendan Kennelly (ed.), *Penguin Book of Irish Verse*, Harmondsworth (Middlesex): Penguin 1970, 320–4. Andrews, *Dublin Made Me*, 218. On Rory O'Connor: *Freeman's Journal*, 27 Mar. 1923. On elite mentalities see T. D. Williams, 'The origins of the Civil War, December 6, 1921–June 28, 1922', *Irish Press*, 6 Jun. 1958.

7. Peter Hart, 'The Irish Republican Army and its Enemies: Violence and Community in County Cork, 1917–1923' (draft book, 1993), 269; Miller, *Queen's Rebels*, 32–42; see also Garvin, 'Defenders, Ribbonmen and others', 133–55.

8. Andrews, *Dublin Made Me*, 207.

9. MacEntee quotation: *Dáil Debates*, 10 Jan. 1922, 394–6; UCD AD, Desmond FitzGerald Papers, P80/766, 780, 786; P80/766, 780, 786.

10. Lynch quotation: UCD AD P80/298. Cf. Garvin, *Evolution of Irish Nationalist Politics*, 114–34. For a brilliant anti-Treaty/

Fianna Fáil misrepresentation of the results of the 1922 election see Hogan, *The Four Glorious Years*, 382–4; see also Gallagher, 'The Pact General Election of 1922', 404–21. Gallagher points out that the pact heavily favoured the unpopular anti-Treaty cause; he also suggests (417–18) that the anti-Treatyites lost some seats because of poor vote management. It is undeniable that the pro-Treatyites misled the anti-Treatyites, quite understandably. However, the voters' behaviour was evidently intended to break the pact, which duly occurred. Later I will argue that Collins duped the IRA into permitting the election to take place.

11. English and O'Malley (eds.), *Prisoners*, 129; see also Garvin, *Nationalist Revolutionaries*, 139–66.
12. UCD AD, Desmond FitzGerald Papers, P/80/1360. See also UCD AD, Richard Mulcahy Papers, P7/A/23.
13. UCD AD, Ernest Blythe Papers, P24/1783, f. 127–8; *Freeman's Journal*, 7 Oct. 1921.
14. The Mellows quotations are from a memoir written by him in prison later in 1922, AA, Michael Collins Papers, A/0629. *Freeman's Journal* quotation: 12 Apr. 1922. On Liam Lynch: *Freeman's Journal*, 16 Dec. 1921. On perceptions of de Valera see MacLysaght, *Changing Times*, 125–36; UCD AD, Batt O'Connor Papers, P68, 12 Dec. 1921. Perceptions of de Valera and Collins quotation: UCD AD, Michael Hayes Papers, P53/299.
15. De Valera citation: *Freeman's Journal*, 17 Apr. 1922; Deasy citation: UCD AD, Ernie O'Malley Papers, P17b/86. For Mulcahy meeting: UCD AD, Richard Mulcahy Papers, P7/D/49, P7/A/29.
16. Andrews, *Dublin Made Me*, 205.
17. Andrews, *Dublin Made Me*, 201.
18. Lynch quotation: O'Hegarty, *The Victory of Sinn Féin*, 206–8. Some republican sources have claimed that this order is a forgery; a copy of it was, however, found on Ernie O'Malley and is in the Richard Mulcahy Papers in UCD. Hayes quotation: UCD AD, Michael Hayes Papers, P53/43; on 'saorstát' etc. see UCD AD, Hugh Kennedy Papers, P4/837.
19. UCD AD, Michael Hayes Papers, P53/318. I have been scooped on this by Tim Pat Coogan in his already classic *Michael Collins*, 244–51. See also his polite and devastating

review, disguised lightly as an introduction, of Frank Pakenham's *Peace by Ordeal*, London: Pimlico 1992. Eamon de Valera, in this incident and others, appears to have had a characteristic habit of attributing to his opponents intentions fairly attributable to his own allies or, occasionally at least, to himself. As late as 29 May 1923 he wrote to a clerical friend arguing that the Free State feared democratic elections and was essentially a dictatorship. In fact he knew, and admitted repeatedly throughout the Civil War, that the voters were hostile to his own position and that the republicans would lose an election decisively. His explanation was that the voters were afraid of the British. Actually, they appear to have been far more afraid of the IRA. To the priest he wrote: 'As I expected the weak are expected to give more and more away . . . As I had anticipated, raids etc. are being continued for the express purpose of making a free election impossible. I can see no genuine peace for the country except by understanding and agreement. There is little basis for this now but we are now in an impregnable position morally.' The sudden shift from legal-rational and democratic language to the collective self-righteousness of the Public Band is classic Devspeak; whether he actually believed what he was saying is unknowable. See Farragher, *Dev and His Alma Mater*, 143.

20. UCD AD, Michael Hayes Papers, P53/318; see also UCD AD, Richard Mulcahy Papers, P17b/127; on Stack: UCD AD, Desmond FitzGerald Papers, P80/1360; on Nolan, UCD AD, P17c/57, 1–3; de Valera quotation: Coogan, *De Valera*, 678.
21. UCD AD, Michael Hayes Papers, P53/344.
22. UCD AD, Michael Hayes Papers, P53/344.
23. UCD AD, Michael Hayes Papers, P53/344.
24. Hackett quotation: UCD AD, Desmond FitzGerald Papers, P80/1209; UCD AD, Richard Mulcahy Papers, P7a/198. Logue quotation: *Irish Times*, 12 Feb. 1923.

Chapter 3 (p. 63–91)

1. D. A. O'Hegarty, 'An outline of local government organisation' in King, *Public Administration in Ireland*, 143–60. An early, much shorter version of this chapter was published in Maurice O'Connell (ed.), *Daniel O'Connell*. I am indebted to Mary Daly, whose territory I have rudely trespassed on and

gaily tramped over but who gracefully guided me through the National Archives. Tim Pat Coogan put me right about his ancestors and gave me valuable insights in his characteristically effortless way. I have benefited also from conversations with Tom Barrington, Helen Burke, Brian Farrell, and Michael Laffan. As a boy I picked up a lot of information and misapprehensions from James Deeny, John Garvin, Michael Lawless, and Gerry Meagher. The misapprehensions are my responsibility or, alternatively, those of youth.

2. D. A. O'Hegarty, 'An outline of local government organisation' in King, *Public Administration in Ireland*, passim.
3. NA, DELG 9/18, 9 Sep. 1921.
4. See Burke, *The People and the Poor Law in Nineteenth-Century Ireland*, 125–30 and passim.
5. NA, DELG 9/18, 9 Sep. 1921.
6. NA, DELG 12/16, 22 Apr. 1921.
7. NA, DELG 22/18, 9 Feb. 1921.
8. NA, DELG 22/18, 29 Apr. 1921.
9. NA, DELG 22/18, 23 Nov. 1921.
10. NA, DELG 23/14, 7 Dec. 1921.
11. NA, DELG 25/11, 12 Oct. 1920.
12. NA, DELG 27/13, 2 Jan. 1920 (recte 1921).
13. NA, DELG 27/13, n.d. [Jan. 1921].
14. NA, DELG 31/12, 28 Oct. 1920.
15. NA, DELG 3/6, 12 Apr. 1922.
16. NA, DELG 5/18, 28 Nov. 1921.
17. NA, DELG 9/18, 4 Jan. 1922.
18. NA, DELG 7/22, 9 Dec. 1921; NA, DELG 11/23, 7 Nov. 1921.
19. NA, DELG 11/13, 11 Aug., 7 Nov. and 27 Nov. 1921.
20. NA, DELG 12/16, 12 Oct. 1921 and 3 Mar. 1922; NA, DELG 17/15, 9 Feb. 1922.
21. NA, DELG 16/19, 10 Oct. 1921.
22. NA, DELG 19/13, 10 Jan. 1921.
23. NA, DELG 21/19, passim; NA, DELG 23/14, 27 Dec. 1920.
24. NA, DELG 23/14, 30 Nov. and 15 Dec. 1920.
25. NA, DELG 24/7, 23 Sep. 1920.
26. NA, DELG 26/9, 24 Sep. 1921, 10 May and 9 Jun. 1922.
27. NA, DELG 27/30, 6 May 1922.
28. Blythe quotation: *Freeman's Journal*, 6 Dec. 1922; NA, DELG 3/6, NA, DELG 7/22, passim.

29. NA, DELG 6/44, 2 Feb. 1922.
30. NA, DELG 12/16, 21 Feb. 1921.
31. NA, DELG 12/16, n.d. [Dec. 1921].
32. NA, DELG 12/16, n.d. [Dec. 1921], and I am indebted here to a conversation with Mary Daly.
33. NA, DELG, 12 Dec. 1921 and 27 Feb. 1922.
34. NA, DELG 14/15, 6 and 8 Feb. 1922.
35. NA, DELG 16/19, 26 Aug. and 9 Sep. 1921.
36. NA, DELG 16/19, 6 Sep. 1921.
37. NA, DELG 23/14, 20 Sep. 1921.
38. NA, DELG 25/11, 22 Jun. 1922.
39. NA, DELG 26/9, 29 Sep. 1921 and 9 Jun. 1922.
40. NA, DELG 27/13, 19 Jul. 1921.
41. NA, DELG 9/18; NA, DELG 12/16, 10 Sep. and 25 Aug. 1921.
42. NA, DELG 30/11, 15 Jun. 1921.
43. NA, DELG 3/6, 8 Aug. 1922.
44. NA, DELG 16/19, 11 Nov. 1921; NA, DELG 17/15, 31 Jan. 1922.
45. NA, DELG 24/7, 19 Oct. and 15 Nov. 1921.
46. NA, DELG 12/16, 21 Feb. 1921.
47. NA, DELG, 12 Dec. 1921.
48. D. A. O'Hegarty, 'An outline of local government organisation' in King, *Public Administration in Ireland*, 152.
49. UCD AD, Ernest Blythe Papers, P24/507.
50. UCD AD, Ernest Blythe Papers, P24/1783, f. 165.
51. UCD AD, Richard Mulcahy Papers, P7a/173.
52. UCD AD, Richard Mulcahy Papers, P7a/173.
53. For an outline of the post-1920 reforms see John Garvin, 'The nature and extent of central control over local government administration' in King (ed.), *Public Administration in Ireland*, vol. 2, 162–73.

Chapter 4 (p. 92–122)
1. *Freeman's Journal*, 17 Jan. 1922. O'Higgins quotation: de Vere White, *Kevin O'Higgins*, 83–4; Hayes quotation: UCD AD, Michael Hayes Papers, P53/347.
2. UCD AD, Michael Hayes Papers, P53/344; UCD AD, Richard Mulcahy Papers, P7a/197; O'Hegarty, *The Victory of Sinn Féin*, 102–5 (quotation from p. 104).
3. UCD AD, Batt O'Connor Papers, P68, 28 Dec. 1921.

4. On women: UCD AD, Michael Hayes Papers, P53/303; *Freeman's Journal*, 21 and 23 Feb. 1922. On Sinn Féin: *Irish Independent*, 28 Jan. 1922. Woman TD (Mrs O'Callaghan) quotation: *Dáil Debates*, 20 Dec. 1921, 59. Alleged O'Higgins quotation on Collins and de Valera: as reported by Matthews in *Voices*, 400.

5. Hopkinson, *Green Against Green*, 273.

6. *Freeman's Journal*, 16 Jun. 1922; UCD AD, Hugh Kennedy Papers, P4/251. For 1995 prices, multiply by 35; for sociological relativity, multiply again by perhaps 4.

7. UCD AD, Richard Mulcahy Papers, P7b/210.

8. UCD AD, Desmond FitzGerald Papers, P80/851.

9. Dublin quotation: *Irish Times*, 7 Jul. 1922; UCD AD, Ernest Blythe Papers, P24/1783, f. 165; on reception of Free State Army: *Irish Times*, 22, 24 and 25 Jul., 1, 2 and 12 Aug. 1922.

10. *Freeman's Journal*, 21 May 1920. See Conor Brady, 'Police and Government in the Irish Free State' (MA thesis, Department of Politics, UCD, 1977), introduction, 1–2; see also his *Guardians of the Peace*.

11. Conor Brady, 'Police and Government in the Irish Free State' (MA thesis, Department of Politics, UCD, 1977), chap. 3, 3–4.

12. Conor Brady, 'Police and Government in the Irish Free State' (MA thesis, Department of Politics, UCD, 1977), chap. 3, 7–9.

13. UCD AD, Desmond FitzGerald Papers, P80/710, Report of Commission of Inquiry into the Civic Guard, 12 Jul. 1922; cf. Gregory Allen, *Irish Times*, 27 Feb. 1992.

14. UCD AD, Desmond FitzGerald Papers, P80/710.

15. UCD AD, Desmond FitzGerald Papers, P80/710.

16. UCD AD, Desmond FitzGerald Papers, P80/710.

17. UCD AD, Ernest Blythe Papers, P24/1783, f. 151–2.

18. *Irish Times*, 20 Mar. 1992, Edward O'Loughlin.

19. *Irish Times*, 20 Mar. 1992, Edward O'Loughlin.

20. UCD AD, Richard Mulcahy Papers, P7a/81.

21. UCD AD, Richard Mulcahy Papers, P7a/81.

22. UCD AD, Hugh Kennedy Papers, P4/1002.

23. See, in general, Farrell, *Arming the Protestants*. See also Bardon, *A History of Ulster*, 474–6.

24. *Freeman's Journal*, 16 Nov. 1922.

25. *Freeman's Journal*, 8 Mar. 1922.

26. *Freeman's Journal*, Apr. 28 1923.
27. Conor Brady, 'Police and Government in the Irish Free State' (MA thesis, Department of Politics, UCD, 1977), chap. 5, 26–7.
28. Coogan, *Ireland since the Rising*, 48. See also UCD AD, Richard Mulcahy Papers, P7a/202.
29. Conor Brady, 'Police and Government in the Irish Free State' (MA thesis, Department of Politics, UCD, 1977), chap. 5, 31–2.
30. *Freeman's Journal*, 1 Aug. 1923.
31. *Manchester Guardian*, 31 May 1923.
32. Hopkinson, *Green against Green*, 58–9.
33. UCD AD, Richard Mulcahy Papers, P7b/149.
34. UCD AD, Richard Mulcahy Papers, P7a/140–2; *Irish Times*, 17 Jul. 1922.
35. *Northern Whig*, 9 Jan. 1923.
36. *Manchester Guardian*, 10 Jan. 1923.
37. *Observer*, 14 and 25 Feb. 1923; *Manchester Guardian*, 19 Apr. 1923.
38. UCD AD, Richard Mulcahy Papers, P7/D/108a.
39. UCD AD, Richard Mulcahy Papers, P7a/137–8; P7a/197; *Manchester Guardian*, 10 Jan. 1923; *Observer*, 25 and 19 Feb. 1923; UCD AD, Ernest Blythe Papers, P24/221. See also Duggan, *A History of the Irish Army*, 130; *Literary Digest*, 13 Oct. 1923. UCD AD, Hugh Kennedy Papers, P4/550.
40. UCD AD, Ernest Blythe Papers, P24/221.
41. Duggan, 155–6, 139.

Chapter 5 (p. 123–155)
1. UCD AD, Ernie O'Malley Papers, P17b/86.
2. Healy, *Letters and Leaders of My Day*, 653, 654.
3. UCD AD, Ernest Blythe Papers, P24/42.
4. UCD AD, Ernest Blythe Papers, P24/42; see Curran, *The Birth of the Irish Free State*, 219–22.
5. UCD AD, Desmond FitzGerald Papers, P80/668; Richard Mulcahy Papers, P7a/145. Hayes quotation: P7b/210.
6. *Freeman's Journal*, 16 Jun. 1922; UCD AD, Ernest Blythe Papers, P24/51.
7. UCD AD, Ernie O'Malley Papers, P17b/85; Hugh Kennedy Papers, P4/283–4.

8. UCD AD, Ernest Blythe Papers, P24/1783, f. 149.

9. UCD AD, Richard Mulcahy Papers, P7a/197, 198; *Spectator*, 16 Dec. 1922.

10. UCD AD, Richard Mulcahy Papers, P7a/198, P7/D/105.

11. See Garvin, *Nationalist Revolutionaries in Ireland*, 139–66.

12. Garvin, *Nationalist Revolutionaries in Ireland*, 139–66.; UCD AD, Desmond FitzGerald Papers, P 80/743, 745.

13. UCD AD, Richard Mulcahy Papers, P7a/197.

14. UCD AD, Desmond FitzGerald Papers, P80/743.

15. On Newbridge: AA, Captured Documents, 1923–25, Dukes Collection, LOT 172. O'Hegarty quotation: *The Victory of Sinn Féin*, 245. In general, see Garvin, *Nationalist Revolutionaries in Ireland*, 139–66; UCD AD, Richard Mulcahy Papers, P7a/87a; Desmond FitzGerald Papers, P80/743.

16. UCD AD, Hugh Kennedy Papers, P4/211.

17. UCD AD, Hugh Kennedy Papers, P4/210.

18. UCD AD, Hugh Kennedy Papers, P4/308.

19. UCD AD, Hugh Kennedy Papers, P4/308, 364.

20. Praeger, *Building Democracy in Ireland*, passim.

21. UCD AD, Desmond FitzGerald Papers, P80/318, 321; see also P7/A/29.

22. Lyons, *Culture and Anarchy in Ireland, 1890–1939*.

23. Praeger, *Building Democracy in Ireland*, 233.

24. Garvin, *Nationalist Revolutionaries in Ireland*, 57–77.

25. Garvin, *Nationalist Revolutionaries in Ireland*, 57–77.

26. For an absurd example see Douglas Hyde, 'The necessity for de-Anglicising Ireland' in Charles Gavan Duffy, *The Revival of Irish Literature*, London 1894, 118–38.

27. Ignatieff, *Blood and Belonging*, 189.

28. Garvin, 'Democracy in Ireland', 42–54; see also, in particular, Ian McAllister, 'The Devil, miracles and the afterlife: the social consequences of religious commitment in Ireland' (Working Papers in Sociology), Canberra: Department of Sociology, Australian National University, 1982.

29. Emmet Larkin, 'The devotional revolution in Ireland, 1850–75', 625–52; cf. Kenneth Connell, *Irish Peasant Society*, 113–62; Thompson, *The Making of the English Working Class*, 385–440 (quotation from p. 419).

30. Kevin O'Sheil citation: *The Birth of a Republic*. Hackett quotation: UCD AD, Desmond FitzGerald Papers, P80/1219.

31. UCD AD, Desmond FitzGerald Papers, P80/785.
32. Tucker, *The Soviet Political Mind*, passim.
33. UCD AD, Desmond FitzGerald Papers, P80/1364.
34. UCD AD, Desmond FitzGerald Papers, P80/1367.
35. UCD AD, Richard Mulcahy Papers P7a/175.
36. UCD AD, Richard Mulcahy Papers P7a/175.
37. UCD AD, Richard Mulcahy Papers P7a/175.
38. UCD AD, Richard Mulcahy Papers P7a/175.
39. UCD AD, Richard Mulcahy Papers P7a/175.
40. Banfield, *The Moral Basis of a Backward Society*.
41. Garvin, 'Democracy in Ireland', passim; de Blácam, *What Sinn Féin Stands For*, 151–2. De Blácam describes these 'ideals' as being Gaelic; actually they are mainly English.
42. *Manchester Guardian*, 18 Apr. 1923.
43. Kennedy quotation: UCD AD, Hugh Kennedy Papers, P4/408; Pyne thesis: Peter Pyne, 'The third Sinn Féin party, 1923–1926', passim.

Chapter 6 (p. 156–188)
1. Foley quotation: Dermot Foley, 'A minstrel boy with a satchel of books', 204–17. On de Valera's early electoral defeatism: Curran, *The Birth of the Irish Free State*, 173–5.
2. UCD AD, Michael Hayes Papers, P53/304, on takeover of British departments.
3. UCD AD, Hugh Kennedy Papers, P4/381, 947, 948.
4. UCD AD, Hugh Kennedy Papers, P4/390.
5. UCD AD, Hugh Kennedy Papers; UCD AD, Richard Mulcahy Papers, P7b/210.
6. Cosgrave statement: NA DT/S8139. See also UCD AD, Desmond FitzGerald Papers, P80/712 (late Jul. 1922), for a similar Free State statement. On de Valera-Cosgrave exchange see UCD AD, Hugh Kennedy Papers, P4/550.
7. UCD AD, Richard Mulcahy Papers, P7/145, 12 May 1922. The anonymous writer is possibly Collins. On young IRA: *Manchester Guardian*, 19 Apr. 1923.
8. I cannot prove that there was an amnesty of this kind. Behaviour suggests it.
9. UCD AD, Richard Mulcahy Papers, P7b/210.
10. UCD AD, Richard Mulcahy Papers, P7b/12.
11. UCD AD, Richard Mulcahy Papers, P7b/56, 58.

12. UCD AD, Richard Mulcahy Papers, P7b/23, 24, 25.
13. UCD AD, Richard Mulcahy Papers, P7a/95. See also chap. 2 above.
14. See, in general, Garvin, *The Evolution of Irish Nationalist Politics.*
15. NLI, F. S. Bourke Papers, ms. 11407. On the courts see Kotsonouris, *Retreat From Revolution.* See also Mansergh, *The Irish Free State*, 292–327.
16. UCD AD, Hugh Kennedy Papers, P4/1067, 1083, 1085.
17. UCD AD, Hugh Kennedy Papers, P4/1089.
18. UCD AD, Hugh Kennedy Papers, P4/1092.
19. *Irish Times*, 13 Mar. 1926.
20. UCD AD, Richard Mulcahy Papers, P7b/59.
21. UCD AD, Hugh Kennedy Papers, P4/1149; *Freeman's Journal*, 15 Nov. 1922.
22. Curran, *The Birth of the Irish Free State*, 200.
23. See Akenson and Fallin, 'The Irish Civil War and the drafting of the Free State constitution'. On de Valera's breach with the fundamentalists see *Éire/Ireland*, no. 1 (spring 1970), 1, 10–12.
24. Akenson and Fallin, 'The Irish Civil War and the drafting of the Free State constitution', no. 1, 21.
25. Akenson and Fallin, 'The Irish Civil War and the drafting of the Free State constitution', *Éire/Ireland*, no. 4, 55–9.
26. NLI, F. S. Bourke Papers, ms. 11407.
27. UCD AD, Hugh Kennedy Papers, P4/308.
28. Chubb, *A Source Book of Irish Government*, 89–98.
29. On the evolution of the referendum in independent Ireland see Coakley and Gallagher (eds.), *Politics in the Republic of Ireland*, passim.
30. On O'Connell's international influence see Maurice O'Connell, *Daniel O'Connell*, passim; French newspaper quotation: UCD AD, Desmond FitzGerald Papers, P80/830.
31. UCD AD, Richard Mulcahy Papers, P7a/197; *Morning Post*, 18 May 1923.
32. *Dáil Debates*, vol. 2, col. 16, 6 Dec. 1922.
33. Cosgrave quotation: *Dáil Debates*, vol. 2, col. 12–18, 6 Dec. 1922; UCD AD, Hugh Kennedy Papers, P4/1092.
34. UCD AD, Hugh Kennedy Papers, P4/387, 389, 390.
35. UCD AD, Kennedy Papers, P4/389.

36. O'Hegarty, *The Victory of Sinn Féin*.
37. Coogan, *De Valera*, 426.

Chapter 7 (p. 189–207)

1. Dahl, *Democracy and its Critics*; Fukuyama, *The End of History and the Last Man*.
2. The Lipset argument is set out most completely in *Political Man*.
3. Carty, *Party and Parish Pump*; Garvin, *The Evolution of Irish Nationalist Politics*.
4. O'Leary, *The Asiatic Mode of Production*.
5. On methodological holism generally, see Popper, *The Poverty of Historicism*.
6. Popper, *The Poverty of Historicism*, passim.
7. See Cruise O'Brien, *States of Ireland*, on partition. On Kevin O'Higgins and hopes for an early North-South reconciliation: de Vere White, *Kevin O'Higgins*, 215–26.
8. Coakley, 'Independence movements and national minorities', 215–48. See also his 'National territories and cultural frontiers', 34–49.
9. Coakley, 'Independence movements and national minorities', passim.
10. See, in general, O'Halpin, 'Intelligence and security in Ireland, 1922–45', 69–71. Quotation from O'Halpin: 'Army, politics and society in independent Ireland, 1923–1945', 159.
11. Kennedy, Giblin, and McHugh, *The Economic Development of Ireland in the Twentieth Century*, 14–15.
12. Kennedy, Giblin, and McHugh, *The Economic Development of Ireland in the Twentieth Century*, 15. For an argument that parallels the viewpoint expressed here: Kissane, 'The not-so-amazing case of Irish democracy', 43–68.
13. Garvin, *The Evolution of Irish Nationalist Politics*, 110.

Select Bibliography

A. SECONDARY WORKS

Akenson, D. H., and Fallin, J. F., 'The Irish Civil War and the drafting of the Free State constitution', *Éire/Ireland*, vol. 5, no. 1 (spring 1970), 10–26, no. 2 (summer 1970), 42–93, no. 4 (winter 1970), 28–70.

Anderson, Benedict, *Imagined Communities*, London: Verso 1983.

Andrews, Christopher S., *Dublin Made Me*, Cork: Mercier 1979.

Anonymous, *The Voice of Ireland* (pamphlet), Dublin: Sinn Féin 1919.

Banfield, Robert, *The Moral Basis of a Backward Society*, New York: Free Press 1958.

Bardon, Jonathan, *A History of Ulster*, Belfast: Blackstaff 1992.

Barker, Ernest, *Greek Political Theory*, London: Methuen 1918.

Barker, Ernest, *The Political Thought of Plato and Aristotle*, New York: Dover 1959

Beetham, David, 'From socialism to fascism: the relation between theory and practice in the work of Robert Michels', *Political Studies*, vol. 25 (1977), 3–24, 161–81.

Bennett, R. J., 'The elite theory as fascist ideology: a reply to Beetham's critique of Robert Michels', *Political Studies*, vol. 26 (1978), 474–88.

Birkenhead, Lord, *F.E.*, London: Eyre and Spottiswoode 1959.

Birmingham, George A., *An Irishman Looks at his World*, London: Hodder and Stoughton 1919.

Bloch, Marc, *Feudal Society*, London: Routledge 1965.

Boyce, D. George, Eccleshall, Robert, and Geoghegan, Vincent, *Political Thought in Ireland since the Seventeenth Century*, London: Routledge 1993.

Brady, Conor, *Guardians of the Peace*, Dublin: Gill and Macmillan 1978.

Brown, Malcolm, *The Politics of Irish Literature*, London: Allen and Unwin 1972.

Burke, Helen, *The People and the Poor Law in Nineteenth-Century Ireland*, Dublin: WEB 1987.

Carty, R. K., *Party and Parish Pump*, Waterloo (Ontario): Wilfred Laurier University Press 1981.

Chubb, Basil, *A Source Book of Irish Government*, Dublin: Institute of Public Administration 1964.

Clayton, Anthony, *The British Empire as a Superpower, 1919–39*, London: Macmillan 1986.

Coakley, John, 'Independence movements and national minorities: some parallels in the European experience', *European Journal for Political Research*, vol. 8 (1980), 215–48.

Coakley, John, 'National territories and cultural frontiers: conflicts of principle in the formation of states in Europe', *West European Politics*, vol. 5. (1982), 34–49.

Coakley, John, 'National minorities and the government of divided societies: a comparative analysis of some European evidence', *European Journal of Political Research*, vol. 18 (1990), 437–56.

Coakley, John, and Gallagher, Michael (editors), *Politics in the Republic of Ireland*, Dublin: PSAI/Folens 1993.

Collins, Michael, *The Path to Freedom*, Dublin: Talbot Press 1922.

Connell, Kenneth, *Irish Peasant Society*, London: 1968.

Coogan, Tim Pat, *Ireland Since the Rising*, London: Pall Mall 1966.

Coogan, Tim Pat, *Michael Collins*, London: Arrow 1990.

Coogan, Tim Pat, *De Valera: Long Fellow, Long Shadow*, London: Hutchinson 1993.

Cruise O'Brien, Conor, *States of Ireland*, London: Hutchinson 1972.

Curran, Joseph M., *The Birth of the Irish Free State, 1921–1923*, Mobile (Alabama): Alabama University Press 1980.

Dahl, Robert, *Polyarchy*, New Haven (Connecticut): Yale University Press 1971.

Dahl, Robert, *Democracy and its Critics*, New Haven (Connecticut): Yale University Press 1989.

de Blácam, Aodh, *What Sinn Féin Stands For*, Dublin: Mellifont 1921.

de Vere White, Terence, *Kevin O'Higgins*, Tralee: Anvil 1965.

Donnelly, James, 'Propagating the cause of the United Irishmen', *Studies*, vol. 69 (1980), 5–23.

Dudley Edwards, Owen, and Ransome, B., *James Connolly: Selected Political Writings*, London: Jonathan Cape 1973.

Dudley Edwards, Ruth, *Patrick Pearse: the Triumph of Failure*, London: Faber 1979.

Duggan, John P., *A History of the Irish Army*, Dublin: Gill and Macmillan 1991.

English, Richard, and O'Malley, Cormac (editors), *Prisoners*, Dublin: Poolbeg 1993.

Farragher, Seán F., *Dev and his Alma Mater*, Dublin and London: Paraclete Press 1984.

Farrell, Michael, *Arming the Protestants*, Dingle: Brandon 1983.

Fichte, Johann Gottlieb, *Reden an die deutsche Nation*, in I. H. Fichte (ed.), *Fichtes Werke*, VII, Berlin: de Gruyter 1971, 259–499.

Foley, Dermot, 'A minstrel boy with a satchel of books', *Irish University Review*, vol. 4, no. 2 (autumn 1974), 204–17.

Fukuyama, Francis, *The End of History and the Last Man*, London: Hamish Hamilton 1992.

Gallagher, Michael, 'The Pact General Election of 1922', *Irish Historical Studies*, vol. 21 (1979), 404–21.

Gallagher, Michael, *Political Parties in the Republic of Ireland*, Dublin: Gill & Macmillan 1985.

Garvin, Tom, *The Evolution of Irish Nationalist Politics*, Dublin: Gill and Macmillan 1981.

Garvin, Tom, 'Defenders, Ribbonmen and others: underground political networks in pre-Famine Ireland', *Past and Present*, vol. 96 (1982), 133–55.

Garvin, Tom, *Nationalist Revolutionaries in Ireland*, Oxford: Clarendon Press 1987.

Garvin, Tom, 'Democracy in Ireland: collective somnambulance and public policy', *Administration*, vol. 39 (1991), 42–54.

Gellner, Ernest, *Nations and Nationalism*, Ithaca (New York): Cornell University Press 1983.

Goldring, Maurice, *Faith of Our Fathers*, Dublin: Repsol 1981.

Griffith, K., and O'Grady, T., *Curious Journey*, London: Hutchinson 1982.

Hackett, Felix, *Ireland: a Study in Nationalism*, New York: Huebsch 1920.

Healy, T. M., *Letters and Leaders of My Day*, London: Thornton Butterworth, 2 vols, n.d.

Hill, Ronald, and Marsh, Michael (editors), *Modern Irish Democracy*, Dublin: Irish Academic Press 1993.

Hogan, David [Frank Gallagher], *The Four Glorious Years*, Dublin: Talbot Press 1953.

Hopkinson, Michael, *Green Against Green*, Dublin: Gill and Macmillan 1988.

Huntington, Samuel P., *Political Order in Changing Societies*, New Haven (Connecticut): Yale University Press 1968.

Huntington, Samuel P., *The Third Wave*, Norman (Oklahoma): Oklahoma University Press 1991.

Ignatieff, Michael, *Blood and Belonging: Journeys into the New Nationalism*, London: BBC Books/Chatto and Windus 1993.

Inglis, Tom, *Moral Monopoly*, Dublin: Gill & Macmillan 1987.

Kennedy, K. A., Giblin, T., and McHugh, Deirdre, *The Economic Development of Ireland in the Twentieth Century*, London and New York: Routledge 1988.

Keogh, Dermot, *The Vatican, the Bishops and Irish Politics*, Cambridge: Cambridge University Press 1986.

King, F. C., *Public Administration in Ireland*, Dublin: Parkside Press [1944].

Kissane, Bill, 'The not-so-amazing case of Irish democracy', *Irish Political Studies*, vol. 10 (1995), 43–68.

Kohn, Leo, *The Constitution of the Irish Free State*, London: Allen and Unwin 1932.

Kotsonouris, Mary, *Retreat from Revolution: the Dáil Courts, 1920–1924*, Dublin: Irish Academic Press 1994.

Kymlicka, Will, and Norman, Wayne, 'Return of the citizen: a survey of recent work on citizenship theory', *Ethics*, vol. 104 (1994), 352–81.

Larkin, Emmet, 'The devotional revolution in Ireland, 1850–75', *American Historical Review*, vol. 77 (1972), 625–52.

Lipset, Seymour Martin, *Political Man*, London: Heinemann 1960.

Lynch, Diarmuid, *The IRB and the 1916 Rebellion*, Cork: Mercier 1957.

Lyons, F. S. L., *Ireland since the Famine*, London: Fontana 1973.

Lyons, F. S. L., *Culture and Anarchy in Ireland, 1890–1939*, London: Oxford University Press 1979.

MacCready, Neville, *Annals of an Active Life*, London: Hutchinson n.d.

Mac Eoin, Uinseann, *Survivors*, Dublin: Argenta 1981.

MacLysaght, Edward, *Changing Times*, Gerrards Cross (Buckinghamshire): Colin Smythe 1978.

Manning, Maurice, *The Blueshirts*, Dublin: Gill & Macmillan 1972.

Mansergh, Nicholas, *The Irish Free State*, London: Allen and Unwin 1934.

Mansergh, Nicholas, *The Unresolved Question*, New Haven (Connecticut) and London: Yale University Press 1991.

Matthews, James, *Voices: a Life of Frank O'Connor*, New York: Atheneum 1983.

Mayer, Arno, *The Persistence of the Old Regime*, New York: Random House 1981.

Miller, David, *Queen's Rebels*, Dublin: Gill and Macmillan 1978.

Mitchell, Arthur, *Revolutionary Government in Ireland*, Dublin: Gill and Macmillan 1993.

Munger, Frank, *The Legitimacy of Opposition: the Change of Government in Ireland in 1932*, Beverly Hills (California): Sage 1975.

Neligan, David, *The Spy in the Castle*, London: MacGibbon and Kee 1968.

Ó Broin, León, 'Joseph Brennan, civil servant extraordinary', *Studies*, vol. 66 (1977), no. 261, 25–37.

O'Connell, Maurice (editor), *Daniel O'Connell: Political Pioneer*, Dublin: Institute of Public Administration 1991.

O'Connor, Frank, *The Big Fellow*, London: Transworld 1969.

O'Halpin, Eunan, *The Decline of the Union: British Government in Ireland, 1892–1920*, Dublin: Gill and Macmillan 1987.

O'Halpin, Eunan, 'Intelligence and security in Ireland, 1922–45', *Intelligence and National Security*, vol. 5 (1990), 50–83.

O'Halpin, Eunan, 'Army, politics and society in independent Ireland, 1923–1945', in T. G. Fraser and Keith Jeffery (editors), *Historical Studies*, 18 (1993), 158–74.

O'Hegarty, P. S., *The Victory of Sinn Féin*, Dublin: Talbot Press 1924.

O'Leary, Brendan, *The Asiatic Mode of Production: Oriental Despotism, Historical Materialism and Indian History*, Oxford: Blackwell 1989.

O'Malley, Ernie, *On Another Man's Wound*, Dublin: Anvil 1979.

O'Rahilly, Aifred, 'The Catholic origin of democracy', *Studies*, vol. 8 (1919), 1–18.

O'Rahilly, Alfred, 'The sources of English and American democracy', *Studies*, vol. 8 (1919), 189–209.

O'Rahilly, Alfred, 'The sovereignty of the people', *Studies*, vol. 10 (1921), 39–56, 277–87.

O'Sheil, Kevin, *The Birth of a Republic*, Dublin: Talbot Press 1920.

Pipes, Richard, *Russia Under the Old Regime*, London: Weidenfeld and Nicholson 1974.

Pocock, J. G. A., *The Machiavellian Moment*, Princeton (New Jersey) and London: Princeton University Press 1975.

Popper, Karl, *The Open Society and its Enemies*, London: Routledge and Kegan Paul 1945.

Popper, Karl, *The Poverty of Historicism*, London: Routledge and Kegan Paul 1976 (first published 1957).

Praeger, Jeffrey, *Building Democracy in Ireland*, Cambridge: Cambridge University Press 1986.

Pyne, Peter, 'The third Sinn Féin party, 1923–1926', *Economic and Social Review*, vol. 1 (1969–70) 29–50, 229–57.

Rokkan, Stein, 'The growth and structuring of mass politics in western Europe', *Scandinavian Political Studies*, vol. 2 (1970), 65–83.

Rumpf, Erhard, and Hepburn, Anthony, *Nationalism and Socialism in Ireland*, Liverpool: Liverpool University Press 1977.

Schmitt, David, *The Irony of Irish Democracy*, Lexington (Kentucky): Lexington Books 1973.

Thompson, E. P., *The Making of the English Working Class*, Harmondsworth (Middlesex): Penguin 1968.

Townshend, Charles, *The British Campaign in Ireland, 1919–21*, Oxford: Clarendon Press 1975.

Townshend, Charles, *Political Violence in Ireland*, Oxford: Clarendon Press 1983.

Tucker, Robert, *The Soviet Political Mind*, London: Allen and Unwin 1972.

Valiulis, Maryann G., *Almost a Rebellion: the Irish Army Mutiny of 1924*, Cork: Mercier 1985.

Valiulis, Maryann G., *Portrait of a Revolutionary: General Richard Mulcahy and the Founding of the Irish Free State*, Dublin: Irish Academic Press 1992.

Winter, Ormonde, *Winter's Tale*, London: Richards 1955.

Wood, Ellen Meiksins, *Peasant-Citizen and Slave: the Foundations of Athenian Democracy*, London: Verso 1988.

B. PERIODICALS

Atlantic Monthly
Belfast News-Letter
Capuchin Annual
Catholic Bulletin
An Claidheamh Soluis
Dáil Debates
Economic and Social Review
Freeman's Journal
Hansard
Irish Bulletin
Irish Ecclesiastical Record
Irish Freedom
Irish Historical Studies

Irish Independent
Irish Political Studies
Irish Review
Irish Rosary
Irish Times
Leader
Literary Digest
Morning Post
Northern Whig
An tÓglach
Sinn Féin
Spectator
Studies

C. ARCHIVAL

Army Archives, Cathal Brugha Barracks, Dublin
    Michael Collins Papers, Dukes Collection
National Archives, Dublin
    Dáil Éireann Local Government Files, 1919–22
National Library of Ireland, Dublin
    F. S. Bourke Papers
    Frank Gallagher Papers
Public Record Office, London
    Mark Sturgis Diary
University College, Dublin, Archives
    Ernest Blythe Papers
    Desmond FitzGerald Papers
    Michael Hayes Papers
    Hugh Kennedy Papers
    Seán MacEntee Papers
    MacSwiney Family Papers
    Richard Mulcahy Papers
    Batt O'Connor Papers
    Ernest O'Malley Papers

Index